BENJAMIN KETCHERSIDE

SILICON
SORCERY

**Unlocking the
Power of AI for
Small Businesses**

First edition

ISBN: 979-8-218-51703-8 (Paperback) 979-8-218-58303-3 (eBook)

To my incredible team at Microsoft, I extend my deepest gratitude. Your exceptional talent and unwavering commitment have been the driving force behind this book.

Overwhelming appreciation goes to the small and medium business owners who inspire me daily. Your courage to embrace AI and drive innovation fuels my passion for this work.

Outstanding recognition is due to my colleagues and mentors. Your wisdom and guidance have enriched this work beyond measure.

Adoption of new technology isn't easy, but you have paved the way forward. May this book serve as a valuable guide to harnessing the power of AI in your businesses.

To my family, thank you for your unwavering support. Your encouragement has given me the strength to persevere through every challenge.

Sincere thanks to all who have contributed to this journey. Your support has been the foundation of my perseverance.

Contents

Introduction

Howdy, artificial intelligence (AI) is undoubtedly the buzzword of the moment. Companies worldwide, big and small, are investing in technology to optimize their processes and ensure they are up-to-date with it. Although we have seen the technology in use for a few decades, from spell-check on your computer to GPS and phone voice assistants, the release of OpenAI's ChatGPT in late 2022 revolutionized how people and the market generally understood the technology. While many believed that AI would lead robots to take over and dominate humanity, it has been shown this is not quite the reality.

Businesspeople are slowly understanding that AI is, in fact, much simpler than this and that it can help companies of all sizes to improve their efficiency and optimize their processes. Many who have adopted the technology are experiencing incredible boosts in productivity, sales, and benefits for time management. Incorporating AI into business has made it possible for people to become more efficient and deliver better results, regardless of their sizes and number of employees.

Granted, while many larger companies have money to invest in the technology and are wasting no time in developing it, this is not the obvious case for small and medium businesses (SMBs). Many are reluctant to invest their hard-earned dollars in something new, which still presents challenges. These SMBs want to start using AI, have plans to incorporate it into their tasks, and can even see its benefits, but challenges and preconceptions must be addressed first.

Many are attracted to the idea of using the technology and are thrilled to find qualified help with their activities. Still, these entrepreneurs have concerns that must be clarified to ensure AI adoption can take place. Some fear that AI will be costly and significantly affect their budget. Others believe that AI will be too complicated to implement and will decrease their productivity. Finally, we have those who are not as tech-savvy and fear the technical jargon and aspects of AI, believing it might be something that will hinder their progress instead of helping.

Let me be the first to tell you that the above, while certainly valid concerns for those who do not possess details about AI implementation, are not exactly precise. This is because to use AI, you do not necessarily need to know the technical jargon or how to code, or it will be costly for your business. When correctly used and armed with the necessary information, SMBs can adopt the technology according to their budget and needs. The secret is finding the best (and cost-efficient) tools, alternatives, and paths to achieving the established goals for your company.

How Will This Book Help?

This book was created to help SMBs, whether companies with employees or solopreneurs, understand how to leverage AI to their benefit. Here, you will find a straightforward and jargon-free approach to implementing the technology, becoming more efficient, and seeing an increase in all your positive indicators. Not only will you understand AI, allowing you to participate and engage in discussions on the topic, but you will also learn about all its technical aspects—from how the machine learning (ML) process works to the ethical and legal side of using AI.

With practical tips to help you optimize your operation, case studies to demonstrate successes and best uses, and prompt templates, you will have all the information you will need. By the end of this book, you will be able to implement AI in your SMB budget-friendly manner, without complication, and using the market's best practices. The best way to do all this is to do it without knowing how to code or having any prior information. All that you will see here can be performed even by those who are not as tech-savvy but want to use the power of AI.

Here, you will learn how to develop an AI strategy for your company, assess its AI readiness, establish key performance indicators (KPIs) to monitor your progress, and implement the technology throughout different areas. Whether you are a solopreneur, a small business, or even a medium company with more employees, this book offers actionable advice to guide you through understanding and adopting AI. You will be more prepared than ever to start your future operations.

Once you have completed reading the book, what seemed like a challenge will become clear to help you take your business to a new level. Read on if you are ready to start this journey and discover what AI can do for your SMB! I am sure you will find that aggregating AI to your business will only bring you benefits—simpler than you imagine. Take the next step with me into this new phase, and let's explore together!

Chapter One

Demystifying AI for Small and Medium Businesses

O ne of the most interesting and controversial topics that can be discussed today is AI. While many believe this is a new concept, you might be surprised to learn that we have been using the technology for a long time. Way before, we had intelligent machines that could talk and respond to us, like humans, scientists, and software developers who had been working on the subject matter. In fact, some claim that AI, while not with this name, has been a topic of interest since Ancient Greece. Then, some of the most influential philosophers tried to discuss "nonhuman" elements of being able to think like we do.

However, despite their efforts, they could not create robots and programs as we have today due to obvious technology limitations. As you will learn in this chapter, AI was a term coined in the mid-1950s, when technology investments became popular. With a combined effort between engineers, researchers, companies, and governments, the concept soon became a reality, reaching the heights we have today where machines can understand humans. Nonetheless, you will see that we are still far from what AI is portrayed as in popular culture: robots that will take over humanity, establish rules, and govern countries. We are actually far from this (as far as the general population is aware), and you are about to understand why.

Origins of AI

To understand where AI came from, we must go back almost 80 years to the modern understanding of ML. While there were some attempts to mimic how humans learn with the creation of the first artificial neurons and optimizing their operation between 1943 and 1949, it was in 1950 that the first paper was written on the subject. This was done by none less than Alan Turing, the British mathematician who developed the first computer for World War II to decipher German code. That year, he published a paper titled "Computer Machinery and Intelligence" that suggested that machines could be tested to show a similar intelligence behavior to humans. This was called the Turing test and was the first attempt at understanding how machines should process and learn information as humans do.

The paper written by Turing was the first of a series of events that happened in that decade, and the following events would be essential to help shape AI as we know it today. One year after its publication, in 1951, the first artificial neural network (ANN) was created; in 1952, the first machine that played checkers was created; and in 1955, what can be considered the first AI machine was developed to solve mathematical problems. While all these were significant advances in the area, they still faced three major problems that hindered the technology's development: the lack of computation memory these machines were able to retain, the access to computers, and the high cost of having a machine to train, study, and evaluate.

Finally, in 1956, the computer scientist John McCarthy hosted the Dartmouth Summer Research Project on Artificial Intelligence event that became a milestone for AI. Not only was it the first time that researchers, mathematicians, and other professionals from the area were together in the same place to discuss this technology, but it was also when the term "artificial intelligence" was coined. Although the conference was not considered the success that McCarthy imagined, there was a unanimous sentiment that AI could be achieved. It is this exact same event that propelled all the next developments in the field for the following two decades (Anyoha, 2017).

Throughout the next 20 years, until 1973, different developments and advancements in technology led to the popularization of AI study. The first was that companies were investing more in technology, and it was in this period that the first programming languages, such as COBOL and LISP, were created. At the same time, as computers became more popular and adopted by companies such as banks and airlines, technology became more accessible and cheaper, allowing more researchers to explore and use it. Programs to aid chemists were created, and natural language processing (NLP) programs were developed, leading to the creation of ELIZA, the first chatbot, and even the assembly and programming of a robot in Japan.

Companies and universities were determined to create a form of AI, and governments in the middle of the Cold War seemed eager to find new technologies that would give them advantages against their enemies. Like the British, the United States Defense Department is well known for supporting these initiatives. With their support, research continued, although not at the pace they imagined. Despite the evolution of computers and increased processing, a lack of computational power and memory needed to be addressed. Furthermore, computers were *big* and sometimes required a whole room to be set up.

While some believed that a robot that could think and interact with humans was close to being developed, this was not the reality of the time. Demotivated by the lack of breakthroughs, the programs' unreliability, the end of the Cold War, budget limitations, and investments in other areas, the U.S. government stopped supporting the research and focused elsewhere. Without money, developing the technology would be more challenging, and only those with funding would be able to continue, hindering even more the process and leading to what became known as an *AI winter*.

The AI Winter, a Brief Uprise, and a New Decline

The lack of funding severely impacted the development of AI technology, leading to almost no developments for the following two decades. There is much debate among scholars about whether it was one AI winter that lasted almost 20 years or if the period was divided into two. The main reason is brief innovations from 1980 to 1987, followed by a decline until 1993. The term "AI winter" was mentioned for the first time in 1984 and focused mainly on the fact that there were too many expectations regarding the technology.

While some companies worked on the technology during these years, few advancements occurred. One constant challenge that needed to be overcome was that related to public opinion, which debated the ethics and legality of its development. At the same time, the high cost of investing in technology and the necessary resources led a few companies to invest in it. The pioneer within the American companies to develop AI was IBM, the market leader in computation at the time, investing heavily in creating a machine that could think like humans.

Internet, Big Data, and AI Today

IBM's investments during this period paid off, and in 1997, it presented Deep Blue, a chess-playing AI program that defeated the world champion, Garry Kasparov. IBM was one of the leading research companies in the area, and it continued to prosper despite the lack of governmental investments. At the same time, the increase in access to computers and the development of modern software allowed more people to research the technology and study possibilities.

However, not only the newer and smaller size of these computers propelled AI research. There was also an increase in its processing capacity and more memory options, especially with the development of what became known as long short-term memory, which today is one of the pillars of deep learning (DL), the base of AI. Additionally, there was a significant advance in building artificial neurons and their structure to convey information. Finally, we could not leave out one of the most important parts of this process: the arrival of the internet and social media. All these steps culminated in one of the pillars for developing efficient AI machines, which you will learn more about in this chapter: data collection.

However, before we get into these details, you should understand the other developments that were made during the time that illustrate the evolution of AI. We have cleaning robots, such as Roomba, that map where the house was cleaned so it does not need to go back; there was the use of AI to recommend friends and acquaintances on social media and the increase of streaming services, the use of AI in GPS and even in spell-check in word processors. At the same time, IBM also presented its powerful AI software, Watson, that could win a Jeopardy game.

From the end of the 1990s to the beginning of the 2000s, technological advances moved at an incredible speed, with new applications constantly emerging. There was the presentation of voice-enabled assistants, AI-based recommendations, chatbots used in online services, and digital and facial recognition programs. These ran parallel to the constant developments in the industry, where researchers were getting more knowledgeable on how to program ANNs and use the computational power they had available to create more powerful machines.

As technology evolved, new machines and applications were developed, showcasing their capacities. However, despite the different approaches and research areas, many people were unaware that the technology being used was AI. As you will see at the end of this chapter, Hollywood movies that portrayed AI as something harmful that would take over control from humanity brought a certain reluctance to the general public. This all changed in late November 2022 when OpenAI, a company with funding from Microsoft, released its game-changing chatbot on the market: ChatGPT.

It was then that there was an incredible uptick in "common" individuals looking to understand the technology and that the general public finally understood that AI has been more present in our lives than previously imagined. The program's release led to a run for gold in the AI market, bringing companies and individuals to search for the best options to implement in their businesses. Google ran to develop a similar chatbot to ChatGPT, now known as Gemini, and so did many other companies.

Today, AI has become the primary research area for companies, leading to hundreds of new developments every day. Never have we seen such a fast development in something that can be compared to the impact of the Industrial Revolution from 1760 to 1830. The world is changing, and it is safe to say that we are living in the new AI era, where everyone is looking for its best applications in all aspects of their lives. With advances in the Internet of Things and other technologies, there is likely much more to see, as you will understand when we look at present AI research. But what makes AI so possible is one of the building blocks of what will feed these machines: the internet and user-generated data.

Importance of Data for AI Applications

When browsing the internet and entering a webpage, you usually receive an alert that the page has cookies. These cookies are used for different purposes, such as measuring your clicks on the page, tracking your preferences, and understanding your interests. These cookies are usually customizable, and you can decide whether you will allow the page to collect from you.

In general terms, this information is gathered by the company and used to study clients and identify how the company can improve. In this case, *data* is being collected, the backbone of AI, and what allows these machines to be as powerful as they are.

The internet has allowed massive amounts of data to be collected. When you post something on social media, you are generating data. When a researcher publishes a paper online, the published content generates data. In other words, all the information you can find online can be considered data. This data is collected by different tools and is treated to be given to AI programs that will analyze and transform this into information that the tool can use. Computers use data for the ML process when they analyze the relationship between all the elements, most common words, and other elements to identify patterns that will allow the computer to generate content similar to how humans speak.

If you are somewhat older, consider when you had to carry out research for school: You needed to go to the library and look for books and paper encyclopedias to find the information you were looking for. These were all archived in library catalog cards that you needed to manually research until you finally found the topic you were looking for. Even more demanding was to look through a book manually and find and identify the information you were looking for to help you with the paper you were writing. In the past, this was common and is how research used to be done.

Now consider a modern-day businessperson or student. When they want to find certain information, they enter their preferred search engine, type in a few words, and there is a whole list with possibilities they can read from. Not only this, but you do not even need to read the whole article since you can use the search feature on the page to find the specific term or items you are looking for. This was all made possible by computers and the internet. If you type in any random work today, you will likely find millions of results that match your desire. All of this data can be collected and used on computers.

But how was this done before? Researchers likely had to manually input all the information into the computer before it could be used. This limited the available data to teach computers. Even more restricting is the lack of enough storage space, which means that limited information could be kept on these computers. However, today, we have data servers, cloud servers, and several other storage possibilities that allow this to be efficiently kept and found when necessary.

This process has enabled AI researchers to collect more data created by the billions daily, if not hourly. This large amount of data is known as *big data,* making AI machines more powerful than we might have imagined. Big data comprises millions and billions of pieces of information that are added to the internet daily, with publications, social media posts, user navigation, and the clicks we make when web surfing. All this data is then collected, put into one place, cleaned, classified, and fed to machines, making them powerful resources. These programs can aid us in general and specific tasks, propelling contemporary AI research and transforming technology use.

Contemporary AI Research

Big tech companies' efforts to create AI applications have increased. At the same time, we have individuals who are working on creating their programs and can publish them with internet accessibility. To understand how, in theory, the process is easy to create an AI program, you only need to know how to program in Python and have access to data to train the computer. These are the two basic elements that allow new programs to be created. Anyone with access to this and certain computer power can develop their own programs.

On the other hand, those who are not as tech-savvy do not need to worry. There are plenty of applications that can be used for the most diverse purposes, which means you do not have to type not even one code line to have an AI program that suits your needs. Nonetheless, it is essential to understand the current state of AI research. However, you must first learn the different types of AI that exist. Yes, you read that right; there are *various* types of AI, each with a different purpose. Read on to learn what they are, and everything will make sense.

Understanding the Types of AI

To understand where AI research is going and what to expect in the future, it is essential to have an overview of its existing types. Today, it is commonly accepted there are seven types of AI, divided between the program's capabilities and functionalities. By dividing the technology into these different types, it is possible to see the type you are dealing with, as well as its limitations and possibilities. To better illustrate these, here is what you should know about each type and what it can do.

AI Programs Based on Capability

When discussing AI programs based on *capability*, we refer to the machine's power to perform tasks. These programs are divided into three categories, which you will explore below.

- **Narrow AI:** As the name might suggest, when dealing with narrow or weak AI, we are talking about a program with specific capabilities to work on a specific task. In this case, we could speak of a chatbot on a landing page that will answer only questions regarding the company or a voice assistant with limited knowledge. In both cases, the program cannot generate new information and will work based on the data it has and will not be able to do anything else. In this case, think about an Amazon recommendation system: It can relate what customers like based on their navigation and preferences, but it will be unable to write an essay for you since its purpose is exclusive to that webpage.

- **General AI:** General or strong AI refers to the programs that think like humans and can somewhat perform tasks like we do. If you think about our capabilities, we can learn and do things in different areas and subjects, even if it is not a specific area of knowledge. You might think this is the kind of AI in chatbots today, such as ChatGPT and Gemini, but this is untrue. This is because AI still cannot adapt past the information it has been trained for. For example, ChatGPT cannot generate images and is limited to the data that it was given. While it can perform different tasks, they are all within the same scope: text generation.

- **Super AI:** Finally, if general AI is still theoretical, then so is super AI, which is the most powerful form of AI that can exist. In this case, we are talking about programs that will work like humans, developing critical thinking, solving problems, experiencing feelings, and developing their abilities. In this case, this program will have the same, and even superior, capacity as a human. It is usually the robots that we see portrayed in movies, where they efficiently interact with us. These machines will have their own beliefs and thoughts and can learn similarly to humans, applying them to a general context and performing several tasks simultaneously.

If you think about it, it makes sense that we only have narrow AI today. Tools commonly used have a specific purpose (generating images, music, teaching, etc.), especially since creating something that would mimic a human would need incredible processing power, neurons, and structure. This translates to the need for investment, and while companies are certainly investing in this, there is also the ethical and legal debate about how these machines will be created, controlled, and monitored. However, this is just one of the possible classifications for these AI programs.

AI Programs Based on Functionality

The second category in which AI programs can be divided is their functionality. In this case, they will not be determined on what they do, but rather *how* they do it. In this category, AI programs can be divided into four types:

- **Reactive machines:** In this basic form of AI program, the machine will react to what is being asked. This is a simple form of AI and is what the first programs looked like, with little to no memory of what they were doing. Deep Blue, the chess-playing computer developed by IBM, is an example of this reactive machine since it would respond to what Kasparov would do and not analyze past or future plays. It simply reacted to the action that was taken without considering the consequences. It is possible to say that these machines will react to the present and the environment they are in.

- **Limited memory:** When we talk about limited memory chatbots, the main idea that comes to us is that they have some storage that allows the machine to remember what it was used for before, and this is precisely the case. These programs can store previously used interactions, such as what we see in self-driving cars and GPS. This is exactly the case since once you are done using the application, the program will "delete" what has been seen before. The same happens to the conversations that are kept in ChatGPT and Gemini. They will store the interactions with the tools until the history is deleted, meaning the information will be kept only for some time.

- **Theory of mind:** Next, we have the theory of mind machines, which do not yet exist. These machines can, for example, understand human beliefs and emotions. In extreme cases, they might even be able to interact similarly to humans. When this theory of mind AI is developed, it will be able to understand humans and act, for example, as a doctor listening to a patient and understanding the nuances of their feelings. This ability to understand humans is likely based on the data it stores and how the ML program processes it. For now, these programs only exist as a work in progress and on paper. Still, researchers are working to create these machines to help with presently human-dominated activities efficiently.

- **Self-aware:** Lastly, we have the self-explanatory self-aware type of AI that exists only hypothetically and is, in this case, exactly the robots we see in sci-fi movies. The machines equipped with these programs can feel, think, have needs and desires, and work almost as humans do. The difference here is that they will be *much better* than humans because they will work, think, and store information like a machine and associate it with human capabilities. This is where the main debate between specialists worldwide lies, who claim these machines can be dangerous to humanity because of the independence they can gain and their thought capacity.

As you might imagine, the next levels developers and companies are working on include the development of more advanced forms of AI. However, between its creation and use lies the general public perception and pressure, which discusses the ethical boundaries of AI and its applications today. Nonetheless, AI has been rapidly advancing and being used in different industries, as you will discover in the following section.

Potential Areas Using AI

In this book, you will explore the different areas in which AI can be used for your SMB, regardless of its industry. Today, the technology has become widespread and is used in almost all business areas. From manufacturing to music creation and medicine to education, AI is being applied and used more frequently. With the efforts made by companies to increase their participation in the AI market, research is being constantly carried out, and new achievements are being reached.

Here are some of the applications that have started to be implemented and are being optimized with AI technology:

- **Creative arts:** AI is used to create music sounds and lyrics, write books, create art, and edit videos. In many applications, it is possible to use AI to create "new" content based on existing information and generate something unique. As you will see in Chapter 14, this use has brought up significant ethical debate on copyright matters and resistance from the professionals in the area.

- **Culinary:** Another application of AI is the creation of innovative recipes based on the user's needs and dietary preferences. Using the technology, developing detailed and personalized menus for different occasions and even specific vitamin and protein intake is possible. Finally, AI can also aid professionals who develop these diets and those who cook with varying methods of preparations, ingredients, and even replacement, allowing the creation of varied options without repetition.

- **Education:** One of the industries that has seen the most significant effects of AI is the education industry. Educators are using these tools to help them create personalized learning plans and give special individualized attention to students' specific needs. Additionally, AI programs allow these teachers to optimize their administrative work by correcting tests, providing feedback, and analyzing student data to understand potential learning gaps and improvement areas.

- **Entertainment:** When you see movies with 3D images and even special effects, these are often created by AI programs. By using the technology, the TV shows and movie industry can replicate the images and voices of actors and prevent them from carrying out stunts or dangerous scenes for the content being developed without putting the actors at risk. At the same time, screenwriters and other professionals can use AI to write scripts and optimize the creation process. The fear of AI use in the industry and lack of control over its use led the Screen Actors and Screen Writers Guilds to carry out a strike that paralyzed the movie industry for almost 4 months in 2023.

- **Finance:** In the past years, AI has been a constant presence in dealing with money. The technology is used to prevent and identify fraud in financial transactions, predict stock market behavior, and understand economic changes. By studying trends and making decision-making more efficient, users can use the tool's predictive capacities and ability to establish patterns to prevent potential economic downfalls and achieve optimal financial results.

- **Manufacturing:** Companies that work with machines and in the manufacturing industry use AI to help them carry out maintenance tasks, make machine predictions, and optimize production. Using the technology, they can diagnose when a machine needs maintenance before a complete shutdown happens and forecast if it will support an increase in capacity. Businesses that have implemented AI have seen an increase in their production and a reduction in the stop times by using machines to carry out the necessary fixes and replace employees.

- **Healthcare:** The healthcare industry has shown the most game-changing results using AI. While AI programs are yet unable to replace a physician, they are being used to analyze scans and images to identify the potential onsets of diseases. This means that patients can be diagnosed before their ailment becomes advanced, such as cancer stages, and adequate treatments can be administered to ensure the diseases do not advance. At the same time, these machines can analyze patient history to find patterns and trends that might indicate a future health issue and aid doctors with possible diagnoses, decreasing healthcare costs using preventive measures.

- **Pharmaceutical:** By using AI, pharmaceutical companies can develop personalized medicine to treat patients. Researchers use vast databases to compare and find the best disease treatments, creating custom solutions with fewer side effects and more assertiveness in curing the patient. Once the necessary information is fed to the program, it is possible to simulate different scenarios in which the best solutions will be tailored to the individual's needs, once again decreasing the costs of medical treatments and potentially costly hospital treatments.

- **Security:** You are probably familiar with a few AI applications in security, which include facial and digital recognition to open applications and devices. However, the use of technology for safety purposes has started to become widespread, such as understanding crime patterns, analyzing areas, and monitoring the internet for threats. Intelligent monitoring with AI makes it possible to protect places, devices, and people and decrease the occurrence of crimes by using forecasting and trend analysis.

- **Technology:** The last and probably most likely area in which AI can be used is technology. It is used to help developers write, correct, and test code, making the process faster and more efficient. AI can also help these professionals prepare documentation and find architectural solutions to create programs and apps. At the same time, AI is largely used in cybersecurity, simulating network attacks to find vulnerabilities or prevent them from being found. In many cases, security professionals mimic how viruses work to find breach possibilities in systems and other vulnerabilities.

As you can see, AI can be adopted in almost all industries with efficiency to optimize processes. At the same time that these solutions are being implemented, they are also constantly evolving and under improvement to increase efficiency. These constant efforts allow ongoing developments in the industry to be released to the public. It is safe to say that while it is still unlikely that robots will take over any time soon, we are getting closer by the day to this reality in which we will be able to interact with machines as we do with other humans.

AI in Popular Culture

Her, The Matrix, The Terminator, Blade, Bicentennial Man, Wall-E, 2001: A Space Odyssey, and *I, Robot* are just a few of the many movies produced in which AI was the central theme. Well, it may not be exactly AI as we know it today, but AI, robots, and associated themes have long ago created a vision regarding technology in the public's mind. It goes without saying that Hollywood has been one of the drivers of how AI is perceived. From mean robots that try to take over the world to crying companions that have families and feelings to an alternate reality, these sci-fi movies are incredibly popular and have made millions, if not billions, by, in some manner, scaring the population regarding what to expect of the technology.

It should be no surprise that due to these productions, there have been several heated debates on the development of AI technology. While many fear what the future will be like once AI evolves, few know that it has been a part of our lives for a long time. Nonetheless, the images we see in movies of characters with bionic parts, others falling in love with cybernetic figures, and no option of unplugging these machines are not exactly what we have today. Can it be in the future? Perhaps. But the fact is that today, AI machines are very much controllable and depend on human supervision to work properly.

As you have seen, machines are still unable to think independently; they do not understand humans, and, as you will see later in this book, their products are usually highly identifiable due to the lack of personalization. AI still makes many mistakes; it cannot autoregulate—it must be constantly fine-tuned, adjusted, and checked for bias and inaccuracies. Therefore, while these movies, shows, books, and other entertainment materials are, well, *entertaining*, we are still far away from what they portray.

Nonetheless, they are still an incredible way to hypothesize and see what we can expect of the future and what can be created if we are not careful. Let's take it as a warning, albeit unlikely, of what to prevent, develop safeguards on, and create protection from. Will we get there at some point? Maybe. But this does not mean that we are near. Public opinion is still pushing against these developments, and we still need to see what the future holds.

What we can do, for now, is explore the best ways to use the tools that we do have and their capabilities. The current market sensations are the generative AI programs, which can create "unique" content based on the information they have been trained with. These generative AI programs are exactly where our journey of using technology in business will begin. As we move along to the next chapter, you will start to understand where and how it can be used and some of its broader applications. Are you ready to begin learning how AI can change your SMB? If so, read on!

Chapter Two

Harnessing the Power of Generative AI

A s you might imagine by now, "AI" is an umbrella term encompassing several types of technology. We can divide these into learning types (how the machine will handle the data given) and functionality (what it can do). Within this realm, several nuances can be explored, but only one we must understand for SMB application purposes: their functionality. For example, consider the Amazon recommendation system: It is excellent for forecasting and predicting what a user will like but is inadequate for generating images.

Nonetheless, these are still too different types of AI, just as spell-check on the computer cannot recommend products, the GPS cannot select music, and a chatbot trained in limited data cannot talk about different subjects. In this case, it is important to understand that all AI tools have a specific purpose, usually divided into forecasting, classification, and generation. When using AI for business purposes, tools with all these capabilities are likely implemented into your processes.

While forecasting and classification programs are easy to understand, mainly due to their self-explanatory names, understanding generative AI is somewhat more complicated. You can probably infer from the name that *generative* means that the machine does "generate" new things, but there are specific rules for this generation to take place. As you have seen in the previous chapter, AI follows the rules and the process it has been given during the learning process, which will determine the type of information it will create.

In this chapter, you will learn about generative AI, some areas in which it can be applied in your business, how to implement it, and precautions to take. Yes, generative AI is incredible and can provide many resources and alternatives. Still, there are downsides to them that you should be aware of to avoid reputational, production, and even cost issues. Read on for a general overview of these incredible programs and some specific characteristics you should know about. These will include different business applications, further explored in the following chapters.

Introduction to Generative AI

In general terms, AI is the capability of a machine to think and process information like a human. This information will depend on the type of data it has been exposed to, allowing it to "learn." Machines can learn different things, such as creating images in programs such as Dall·E, text as in Google Gemini, music with Beatoven.ai, and so on. Usually, these AI programs will have a specific use since they require incredible processing power to do more than one task.

To illustrate the need for these amounts of data, let's use ChatGPT, one (if not the most) popular AI program presently. ChatGPT is a generative AI tool created by OpenAI that generates text-related content in diverse areas. To do this, the program is trained on millions of data points sourced from the internet. A program will "scrape" online information and bundle these into datasets that will be used to train the machine. When this happens, the ML process will teach the computer to predict what needs to be generated based on the word association it identifies in the database.

This word association will help the machine relate the most commonly used words and create sentences and content. The trick, however, is that these sentences will only be possible to create if the *data is contained in the training set*. If the machine has never seen this information, it will be unable to generate the content, no matter how many data points it has. This means that, in some way, it is *copying* the information from somewhere else, in either structure, content, or idea. Although the information generated is "new," it was obtained elsewhere.

Think about this as being similar to a teacher–student relationship. Suppose the teacher is giving you a class on human evolution and, at the end of class, they ask you to write an essay describing what you learned using your own words. They will give you five keywords to use in the content while developing your idea. While you create this content, it will be original because you are writing it, but it will be a "copy" of what the teacher has taught you. In the case of ChatGPT, it is as if they are writing this essay using sources from many different websites, books, and articles and structuring them in a way that will answer your question.

When the issue is images, this is even easier to imagine due to the characteristics of the type of information. Let's say you go to a museum and photograph all the exposed paintings. You then feed all these images to a machine and characterize each with a painter's name: Cezanne, Picasso, and Van Gogh. You will also feed the machine different real-life pictures, such as apples, buildings, and home appliances. Once the machine learns, it will have examples of each of these, so you can ask it to create the painting of an apple using Van Gogh style or a microwave using Cezanne. However, it will not be able to draw a garden resembling Picasso's style since you did not "train" it with landscape images.

This means that generative AI is handy as long as the developer knows what information to add to it to make it so. Suppose you are creating a chatbot for your company. In that case, you will need technical information about its products or services *together with* general language training so the computer can understand what the human is asking. After all, computers do not understand our language, and we do not understand theirs; it is through AI programs and a specific technique called NLP that this communication is possible.

Understanding the Similarities and Differences Between AI Programs

Here are a few descriptions to help you recognize generative AI programs from those with other capabilities. Each type of AI program will have some examples to illustrate its work. Remember that some can be convergent, with the same capabilities and functionalities.

- **Generative AI:** Systems that can create new content (images, videos, text, or audio) that mimics human creation.

  - *Examples:* Dall·E, ChatGPT, DeepBrain, Pictory, Microsoft Copilot, and Beatoven.ai.

- **NLP systems:** Can understand, interpret, and generate human language based on text or speech input.

  - *Examples:* Google Translate, spell-check, plagiarism scanners, ChatGPT, Alexa, and Siri.

- **Recommendation systems:** Provide personalized suggestions to users based on previous customer behavior and identified preferences.

- *Examples:* Netflix, Amazon, Hulu, Spotify, social media, and different ecommerce platforms.

- **Prediction systems:** Use historical data to forecast future events by applying statistical models and probability.

  - *Examples:* Weather forecasting, GPS, stock market prediction, word prediction in cell phone editors, and sales forecasting.

- **Classification systems:** Categorize data into classes and groups based on specific features and characteristics.

  - *Examples:* Spam detection, medical diagnosis programs, and Google Photos.

- **Computer vision systems:** Gives the computer "eyes" to interpret and make decisions based on visual data and situations that require visual information.

  - Examples: Facial recognition, Instagram filters, autonomous vehicles, and medical imaging analysis programs.

As you can see, AI programs can be used for diverse reasons, and indeed, more than one tool will be able to help you with your SMB. At the same time, generative AI tools currently show the most promising results, especially when the subject at hand is reducing human tasks, such as automating email and review responses and customizing products. In the following chapter, you will learn how to choose the best AI tool (or tools) for your business. But in the meantime, let's explore what generative tools can do for you. In the following section, you will find a few of its applications, and guess what? This is just the beginning; there is still much more to see!

Applications of Generative AI in SMBs

Since the arrival of ChatGPT, businesses have been working to find the best ways to implement AI and be more productive and efficient. This is likely also the reason that led you to this book: learning how to use and leverage AI to make your business more profitable, like the large companies in the industry. Market giants are currently investing millions, and sometimes billions, to implement the technology and stand out from their competitors. You can stand out, too; best of all, doing so does not mean you need a large cash flow to invest in AI.

As you will see in this section and the following chapters, there is more than one way to adapt the existing tools without making hefty investments or having coding knowledge. It is all about finding the correct method and the adequate tools. By doing so, you will be able to optimize tasks and improve the services or products offered by your company. The general example of ChatGPT will be used for this section since it is the most widely known tool, but others will be explored in more detail as we continue exploring AI applications and use. Read on to find some of its uses and examples of how AI can help your business.

Generating Content

One of the most popular applications of generative AI is for content generation. It is common for users to log into tools such as ChatGPT and ask questions, create texts, or even get aid in research matters. While general uses include writing, finding specific information, and sometimes even recipes, businesses can use these tools to help them in different, and sometimes the same, areas. For example, a businessperson with a blog on their webpage can use the tool to brainstorm subjects to write about, create an outline for this content, and even discover the best search engine optimization (SEO) keywords to use and increase their reach.

However, reducing AI to only these tasks is a simplification of what it can really do. Other applications include data analysis to help understand clientele's general feelings about the company, finding the adequate response to a negative review, responding to customer complaints, writing product descriptions, and much more. These can all be achieved by adequately prompting the tool to provide the best answers.

Finally, we cannot forget that generative AI can create text for you in addition to all these peripheral tasks. Although you will learn at the end of this chapter that using AI-generated content without editing might not be the best solution for your company, you can prompt the tool to create texts you can use. These include but are not limited to marketing and campaign ads, video scripts, social media posts, technical articles, and even code!

Automating Repetitive Tasks

Another area where generative AI has proven to be efficient is in automating repetitive tasks. Imagine you have an email address that receives customer service inquiries, but a person is responsible for analyzing and elaborating on a greeting for each of them. In this case, you can use AI to create automated and personalized confirmation responses and classify each subject by priority level. When you do this, it will be possible for the customer service agent (or yourself) to focus on the most important messages and answer these emails instead of spending time writing greetings and classifying them.

Suppose your business involves managing large amounts of data. In that case, you can use generative AI to analyze reports, perform data entry and classification, and generate the necessary reports with its analytical abilities. Creating easy-to-read, relatable, and tone-adjusted reports that you only need to edit will optimize your productivity. You can also edit and create images for campaigns, social media, personalized jingles, and catchphrases with the selected theme.

Creating compelling presentations based on reports, images, and other data can also be a productive way to employ generative AI. Once you upload the necessary content, it will take a few prompts to generate a slideshow you can use for clients and prospects, investors, and suppliers. What is even better is that because of its incredible capability, it will be possible to customize presentations to different audiences using the same data. This means that instead of spending time finding solutions on how to create an attractive presentation for each group, you will be able to do this in a few minutes with the help of these tools.

Customizing Products

If you are starting your SMB or are looking to bring a different product to the market, AI can also be the solution to help you achieve this. Since generative AI tools can access millions of data, they can analyze your product and compare it to others in the market you might not even imagine exist. By feeding the tool with the details on your product and the target audience, you might obtain relevant insights to improve or customize them to reach more people and generate better results.

Restaurant owners can use the tool to improve their recipes, developers can ask for comment improvement, web designers can optimize the pages they create, and marketers can enhance their campaigns. Businesspeople can use AI for almost any product they need help with, regardless of whether it is customization, finding the best target audience, writing a product description, or drafting attractive content that will attract more interested people. Imagine these tools as a specialist in the area you are working on with years of experience and recognition; this is the type of help you usually get without any cost.

Enhancing Services

Similar to enhancing products, the same can be said for the services provided by your SMB. By using generative AI, you can identify the best solutions to deal with different audiences, as well as learn what attracts them when looking for service providers. You can use AI tools to carry out market analysis and identify the strengths and gaps in existing services and what are the differentials the public is looking for. Additionally, it is possible to create tailor-made solutions by comparing what is offered in the market and benchmark best practices to assemble a list of what you will cater to.

When AI is used to identify specific niches, understand market needs, and tailor solutions, it increases the likelihood of making assertive decisions and thriving in your business. Another advantage is brainstorming out-of-the-box solutions and supporting the critical thinking process by supplying the pros and cons of each solution you consider. Lastly, you can use AI to conduct A/B testing to analyze potential reactions to the services you provide (or will provide) and research case studies to forecast effectiveness, leading to customer loyalty and retention.

Data Generation and Augmentation

If you are an SMB and still lack the necessary data to carry out analysis, you should not worry. Generative AI can use your data to create a synthetic dataset that will enhance and argue what you have based on the information you provide. By associating your data with other events in the database, it will be possible to extrapolate the information and obtain forecasts regarding your business according to the parameters you establish.

Whether you want to identify whether the number of clients or sales will increase, whether an environmental event will impact your business, or whether a marketing campaign will be more efficient, using AI tools makes this possible. You can train ML models to cater to your business's specific needs by feeding your data to the program. The best way to illustrate this example is one we have seen before: Using ChatGPT capabilities, you can upload your business data and use the tool's database to create conversation-like chatbots for customer service on your landing page.

Preparing to Implement Generative AI

Using AI and implementing it into your business requires planning and effort. Although several tools can be used online, the most significant advantage comes from integrating with your existing systems or adapting them so this can be done. You will need to develop a strategy to identify the areas in which AI can be efficiently applied, the tools that offer you the best cost–benefit to apply, the time you will need to dedicate to learn how to use the tool, and the computer processing you have for the tools' installation. Your AI plan will be the first and most crucial part of the process, and it will come with the need to conduct a few business assessments.

There is no need to worry if you are unsure how to carry out this plan. In Chapter 11, you will find a complete roadmap for successful AI implementation, from assessing business needs to scaling and overcoming challenges. In the meantime, there is another element that we must explore: ensuring you have adequate training to use these tools. In this case, this crucial element is prompting, which is key to having generative AI tools answer your needs as you expect.

Prompt Importance

In a simplified explanation, prompts are the instructions you will give the AI tool so it can give you back the information you need. They are the means to achieving optimal results and information from AI tools, making it an essential technique to master. Knowing how to write prompts correctly will show that the program's output will provide more assertive and directed answers. Here are five tips you should keep in mind when you are creating prompts for the best outcomes:

- **Be objective but detailed:** You must use instructions without fluff when using an AI tool. However, this does not mean you should leave out essential details. Objectivity does not equal simplicity, and this must be clear in your mind. Offer the tool with all the relevant information necessary in a simple manner, without using jargon and complicated or overly technical words.

- **Define a purpose:** To achieve the best outcomes from AI, you must define a purpose. Answer the questions: *Why am I creating this prompt? What do I expect to achieve?* Only when you have clarity on why you are prompting the tool will it bring you the best results. Summarize what you want it to do in one sentence.

- **Assign a role:** Since the AI tool is the specialist, you want to ensure that the correct point of view is used for the query. Therefore, you must include information about the role it should assume within the prompt when giving you the answer for greater accuracy and refinement.

- **Avoid negatives:** Despite its incredible capabilities, AI is still a machine, and, as such, it tends to get confused with instructions and words. Therefore, you should use affirmative commands with what you *want* it to do instead of what it *should not do*. Using negative words with these tools might confuse them, leading the programs to misunderstand the command and bring you incorrect information.

- **Specify the audience:** Another issue you must be specific about is the intended audience you want to reach. The results for a query that targets university students will have a different approach for executives who work in the pharmaceutical industry, for example.

Here are a few prompt examples to understand how these should be written:

- *Act like an expert marketing specialist and devise two marketing strategy options for a company that works with high-end electronics. The campaign should be tailored to attract readers of the major American newspapers with high purchasing power.*

- *You are an SEO specialist creating a strategy to increase the search engine results of a webpage dedicated to selling used books. Provide me with a list of keywords that can be used for this purpose, an example of their use in a text, and how the strategy should be implemented.*

- *I have a women's shoe company and want to create a social media marketing strategy to attract more users to my webpage. Act as an experienced online marketing professional and create three strategies I can use for this purpose, including suggestions for text to be added to the post and image examples I can use to attract more attention.*

- *You are a chef specializing in Italian cuisine who has trained under the best professionals in the area and has been in the market for over 20 years. I want to modify my menu to attract more middle-class clients between 25 and 35 during lunch hours, usually with the fewest clients. How would you suggest I change the menu or recipes to make the food options more affordable, and what options could I use for this purpose?*

As you can see, you do not necessarily need to add all the details within a prompt. The important part is that you have a direction for obtaining the first results. After this, you can iterate and ask follow-up questions for content refinement and more details. At the same time, prompts are only part of the skill set you will need to work with AI efficiently. You must consider other elements when considering its implementation in your SMB.

From tool limitations to budget restrictions, there are several issues you must look out for before you start. The last section of this chapter will focus on some difficulties you might face when working with AI in your business to help you understand how to overcome these challenges with simple solutions. Shall we check them out?

Overcoming Implementation Challenges

It would be a lie to say that implementing AI is a swift process that presents no challenges or that there is no learning curve. More often than not, especially those who are not as tech-savvy might have difficulty using these tools. It makes it even more complicated when new AI tools are being released and updated regularly in an industry that is evolving faster than ever.

Although we will explore the challenges regarding each specific topic as they are discussed chapter-by-chapter, here are some common setbacks users face when implementing AI for the first time in their SMBs.

- **Hardware limitation:** Although AI tools usually use their own servers to process the information you request, you will need a certain computational power to use them, especially if you are installing and integrating them into your own systems. This means you will need a computer that has good processing power and can handle the requests. At the same time, you will need a good broadband internet connection since these AI tools are usually online. To solve these issues, you should check if your current devices and connections support using free online AI tools such as Google Gemini, Microsoft Copilot, and ChatGPT. Nonetheless, you will likely know if your internet and computer(s) need to be updated if you are a constant user.

- **Cost:** Many people believe that AI programs are costly. The reality is that many programs range from free versions to premium options. Additionally, you will have the costs for data collection, hardware, internet, training, and other unforeseen requirements that might come up. To ensure that you are not spending too much on a solution that might not bring immediate results, you should prioritize the tools and areas you want to implement AI into first, evaluate the different options, and establish a budget you should stick to to avoid excessive spending.

- **Technical expertise:** Those who are not tech-savvy and have difficulty dealing with computers and technology might struggle to implement AI solutions on their own. However, the good news is that most AI applications today are user-friendly and pose no difficulty when installed. At the same time, if you are still unsure and would instead like to obtain help, you can hire an IT consultant to help you with the installation or use the customer support features these tools present to help you throughout the process.

- **Data limitations:** These might be among the most challenging aspects of using AI for a company, especially when the company is not used to making data-driven decisions. Businesses without data will need to start a data-oriented strategy, which might take some time to achieve significant results. This might also mean an extra effort to canvas old reports, files, and other documents to gather the necessary information for the program. If you remember what was mentioned earlier, data is the backbone of AI, and it is only with relevant data from your business that you can effectively use it. Therefore, there is no way out: If you do not have the necessary data to work with, you will need to start collecting it for optimal implementation.

- **Scalation possibilities:** When you start a business, you want it to prosper and grow—at least, that is what many SMB owners expect. Therefore, when choosing your ideal AI solution, you must think about the future and that your company will be successful. If you select the incorrect tool, you might have more trouble and challenges if escalation is needed. This is one of the main reasons why you need to monitor the plan you have created continuously: If the results are promising, you already need to start to think about scaling solutions that will be the right fit for the size of your business. Choosing a tool that is not scalable and cannot support your company in the future might be an issue when you need to transfer the systems and all the information it contains.

- **Privacy and security:** Another of the greatest challenges individuals have with using AI tools is the lack of privacy and confidentiality of the data being used. In many cases, platforms will use the information you feed the tool to train the machine, which means that your data, even if it is sensitive, will become public. This will be critical in specific industries, especially when dealing with customer and proprietary data. To overcome these issues, you should always read the privacy and security statements of the tools you use and understand when your data will be used. You can also ask the provider questions about data use and confidentiality to ensure no problems during implementation. As a general rule, specialists do not recommend uploading sensitive information to these tools and, if necessary, that it is uncharacterized so that it cannot be identified by others.

- **Cutoff and update dates:** Some presently popular AI tools have training data cutoff limitations. This means they are only trained with data up to a certain date or of a specific subject, which might not be adequate for all purposes. Suppose your SMB needs updated market information that can usually be found online. In that case, you should opt for tools connected to the internet to obtain information from online sources in real time. Especially for market research purposes, this update will be crucial to provide you with accurate and reliable information.

- **AI hallucinations and reliability:** Although reliability was mentioned in the previous item, generative AI users should be aware that not everything that not all AI outputs are reliable. There is a term in the market known as *AI hallucinations*, which refers to when the program starts to deliver information that is made up, untrue, or inaccurate. This means that when dealing with generative AI tools, you should always verify the output with traditional research to ensure you will have it all correct. When individuals use AI output without verification, they expose themselves to issues that might affect their reliability.

- **Robotic tone:** The last issue regarding generative AI, specifically the tools that deal with NLP and text generation, is the robotic tone they demonstrate in the outputs. Today, with the tools' current limitations, it is possible to identify that a text was written by AI due to the lack of emotion, personalization, and repetition these tools offer. Therefore, if you are using a generative AI tool in your business, you should once again always review the tone and the nuances of the output. Although these tools can efficiently help set the tone for the message you intend on sending, a "human touch" is always welcome to make the message more personalized.

Generative AI tools are certainly here to stay due to all the positive aspects they offer businesses. Despite all the challenges they currently offer, improvements will likely be made shortly, and new difficulties will arise. Those who have already started implementing them in their business and understand their strengths and challenges will be one step ahead of the rest when new versions come out. After all, it should be no surprise that every day, some tools available on the market are updated or have a new release.

Yes, there will certainly be issues, and the process might not be as easy to implement as many make it seem; this is especially true for SMBs with budget limitations and do not usually have a tech team to support them and consult when there are doubts or issues. However, implementing generative AI into your business might be the only thing missing that will take you to the next level. Imagine being able to reduce your tasks considerably by automating processes. Or creating a marketing campaign that will go viral. These can be the push you need to grow and develop.

At the same time, to be able to do this, it is essential to understand what types of tools are available on the market, how they can be used, and how to identify if they are a suitable match for your company. In fact, this is so important that it is exactly what we will explore as we move on to the following chapter. As you continue to read, you will be introduced to the world of AI tools, how to evaluate and test them, and how to decide if they are a good option for your SMB. By using the information you are about to learn, you will be able to make informed decisions when the time comes and identify the best solution for your business. If you are ready to start diving deeper into AI, read on! There is still plenty to see and learn.

Chapter Three

Choosing the Right Tools

I f you are new to the AI world, you may feel that ChatGPT is the best way to go. After all, it is the tool everyone is talking about and has become the go-to for many businesses. However, if you stop reading for a moment, go to your browser, and type in *AI tools for businesses*, you will find hundreds, if not millions, of results. Many of these will be titled, "The Best AI Tools for Your Business or [number] Tools for Your Business." Yes, there is a world beyond ChatGPT, and this is exactly what you will explore.

To understand this, let's go back to November 2022, when the OpenAI tool was released to the public. Reaching more than 1 million users in just 5 days, ChatGPT became the benchmark of what AI tools should be like. This led to a gold rush, with companies implementing AI into their systems or developing AI tools. Many of these tools, such as Microsoft Copilot, are powered by ChatGPT, but they have features specific to a particular market.

In less than six months, hundreds of AI tools appeared on the market, either with proprietary development or by using ChatGPT to power them. Similarly, there was a waiting list with OpenAI to use the software to develop plugins that would work with it and enhance the services provided. However, not only were most of these plugins available under a subscription fee, but you also needed to have a ChatGPT Plus subscription to install them. This was a problem until it wasn't, and companies started developing solutions to put on the market.

At the same time, you must be asking yourself, *But then, how do I determine the best AI tool for me? Isn't ChatGPT able to do it all?* This is a good question and one that should be explored in detail. As you know, ChatGPT is a general-purpose chatbot, which means that it *might* have specific information to carry out specific tasks, but it also cannot. You can use different tools in the market for distinct business purposes, including client relationship management, accounting, and analyzing and monitoring KPIs. These tools are more suitable and will perform better.

This chapter centers on the different aspects of how AI tools will fit your business. You will soon understand that the tool should adjust as much as possible to the service or product provided, not that you should make incredible maneuvers to use it. Solutions currently offered on the market show a vast diversity, meaning you are not limited only to ChatGPT. As you read, you will understand how to make this decision, and it is even possible that you find more than one tool that suits you, each for a different purpose.

As you read, you will find the elements you must look out for when selecting the AI tool (or tools) that will be implemented. You will learn about the different criteria that will help you during the decision-making process, and some tools will even allow you to test them before hiring the service. Yes, vendors are doing whatever they can to stand out on the market and, as a businessperson looking for an AI solution for your SMB, you can take advantage of this. If you are ready to dive into the world of available AI tools, read on! You will undoubtedly be amazed by everything you are about to learn.

Understanding Types of AI Tools for Businesses

The first thing you must do to understand the power of AI tools is to learn their different capabilities. As you are about to discover, there is an AI application for almost anything, making it easier to manage business tasks regardless of your industry. Depending on your chosen plan, these tools can be free, paid, or freemium. For a more general view of the different functionalities and capabilities of these tools, here is a small summary of AI tool types:

- **Audio** – AI audio applications will aid the business in creating sounds and songs, transcribing audio, and editing podcasts. (AI Music, Soundtype, Beatoven)

- **Chatbots** – Chatbots are commonplace in AI. You "speak" to the machine, and it provides you with answers on a topic. (Microsoft Copilot, Gemini, Claude, ChatGPT)

- **Code** – AI-powered code platforms help individuals enhance and improve their code, fix bugs, and comment on what the code is doing. (GitHub CoPilot, Code Snippets, Codeium)

- **Document interaction** – These AI tools can be used to summarize and analyze documents, create slides, read spreadsheets, and identify forms. (ChatDOC, Slides AI, Free Chat with PDF)

- **Customer management** – These AI-powered tools will help manage client relationships, evaluate reviews, monitor satisfaction, and understand behavior. (User Evaluation, June, Zeda.io)

- **Design** – With these AI-powered tools, art for social media posts, webpages, and other types of design can be created. (Canva, PageGPT, Autodesigner)

- **Finance** – Financial management is easier with these financial tools, which work as ledgers and carry out earning and yield analysis. (LedgerBox, FinChat, PrometAI)

- **Images** – With these tools, editing and creating custom AI images is just a prompt away. They use several styles and formats. (Dall·E, Midjourney, PlaygroundAI)

- **No-code** – It is ideal for those who want to use a data analysis feature but do not want to develop a ML application. (Watermelon, Softr, LazyAI)

- **Operations** – These AI tools are specific for areas such as legal document analysis and logistics monitoring. (Reclaim, Legaliser, AdCopy)

- **Productivity** – With these AI-powered tools, the team can monitor all KPIs and productivity measurements in one place. (Notta, BoodleBox, Zentask)

- **Sales** – These allow easy sales monitoring sales and product development, including trend analysis.(SalesCred Pro, Ditto.ai, Loman AI)

- **Social media** – These are for those interested in enhancing their social media presence and who want to create ads and marketing campaigns effortlessly. (Clickable, Supergrow, Viff)

- **Video** – When these AI-powered tools are used, creating videos from scratch or editing and enhancing the ones you already have is possible. (Descript, Synthesia, Vizard)

- **Writing** – Writing tools are the most popular in the market, and they offer different capabilities, such as translating, grammar checking, and content creation. (DeepL, Elephas, Grammarly)

With these many options, you might already start to feel overwhelmed. After all, how is it possible to decide with so many possibilities? Although this might seem like an impossible task, it is not as challenging as you might imagine. This is because there is a structure you need to follow to ensure the tools you are purchasing match the needs and priorities you have for your SMB.

To help you make this decision, in the next section, you will learn all the parameters that must be analyzed for optimal decision-making and to help you achieve the best cost–benefit. Once you are done reading it, you will see that it is easier than you imagine, and adding these criteria to the roadmap you create will give you a clear view of needs and objectives. Read on to learn more about how to do this and each feature you should understand to make the best decision.

Matching Business Needs and Objectives

In the previous chapter, you learned that it is necessary to create a roadmap where you establish the business needs and priorities. This list will allow you to identify where to use AI and what tools to focus on during your research. For some, this might be software that will help create social media ads. For others, it might produce content and articles to post on a webpage. Even new businesses will use AI to build their complete structure, which is also possible.

Once your priorities are identified, it is time to see what tools best suit this need. In this case, you will need to conduct a comparative analysis and study each feature to determine whether it is adequate. You should now worry if you do not immediately find the tool you seek with all the necessary features or desired cost. There will be time to explore and even test these tools before you commit to one of them.

Although this section is divided into six, when you compare them, the recommendation is to create a table in which each column is a feature, and each row is a tool. In this document, you will write down all the features in a summarized manner, allowing you to have an overview and make the comparison process more manageable. For each area of potential AI use, you should create a different table so that the tools it contains are relevant only to that business area.

Finally, before we start, as you research these tools, you may find a solution for a need that is not established as a priority but offered at no cost. If this is the case, you should not miss the opportunity to note the name and the web address so you can return to it later. Later, when you are writing the roadmap, you will be able to determine whether this tool can be added to the implementation plan.

This being said, let's explore the six criteria you should consider when analyzing the best AI tool for your business. From understanding the technical requirements to analyzing how much its implementation will cost, there are different aspects to consider before deciding. If you have a pen and paper next to you, or even your computer, prepare to take notes on all you are about to learn.

Assessing Technical Requirements

The first thing you must take into account when looking for an AI tool is its technical capacity to implement it. This means understanding whether your internet connection is fast enough, whether your computer or other device has the processing capability, and whether the operating system (OS) can run this. All these structural and hardware characteristics will be the first element you should look at. To understand more of these technical capabilities, let's break them down into parts to see what you should consider for each element.

The first thing you must consider is the internet connection. Your connection should be broadband with a significant speed since most AI tools will run on the cloud and return the result based on online processing. You must have a constant and reliable connection to ensure you have no delays and that the program operates efficiently. This will also be essential if your systems constantly connect and manage the information online, such as chatbots on a webpage that convey the information to the sales team. Although the chatbot will operate on the cloud, you should be able to count on the internet connection to have the necessary information delivered once it is obtained.

Next, we have processing capability, which your hardware will directly influence. While most AI applications will run online, and you will not need the computational power, this is not true for the programs you download. Many apps today are processed online, but you might have specific applications that you will install and operate locally. If this is the case, you will still need an internet connection, but you will also need the device you are using to support the tasks you are asking it to carry out. Also, remember that slow apps can impact your client response time and even solve problems. So, the best idea is to check if your devices meet the minimum requirements for the software to operate.

Finally, we have the matter of the OS you are using. In this case, it is essential to know that some programs might only run on a specific OS, such as Linux, Windows, or Apple. While this is not a problem for the apps you will be operating online, it does mean that you will need to verify compatibility if you are downloading it. In some cases, apps will have different versions according to the OS, which means you must know the version of the OS you are using to ensure that the app runs appropriately.

Once you have worked out the details regarding these technical matters, you can look deeper into each tool's technical elements. Ideally, you should have a list of the available capacity (broadband connection speed and hardware characteristics) to narrow down the options. If you cannot invest more into updating these elements right now, understanding what you have will make it easier to narrow down the tools and not feel frustrated because the ones you selected are incompatible.

Evaluating Features and Capabilities

Now that you have looked at your technical capacity, it is time to consider what you need. While it may seem obvious, you should not choose a chatbot as a tool for which you will need to generate images. At the same time, if you need a tool that generates videos, you should not be limited to one that will only create pictures. These are basic features you must understand, and most tools will come with a great variety of them, but possibly not exactly what you will need.

In this case, ChatGPT offers an advantage for Plus subscribers, which costs around $20 per month. The tool has over 100 plugins you can add to the tool (some with an additional cost) that will increase the capacity of what it can do. This means you will not only use the chatbot to generate text but also integrate with Dall·E for images, Zapier for client management, and much more. In this aspect, ChatGPT can be one of the most affordable tools on the market, even if you are paying to subscribe to the paid version and adding plugins.

At the same time, depending on what you need the tool to do, ChatGPT Plus will not be enough. This will happen when the tool offers specific characteristics integrated into one, such as customer relationships and metric monitoring. In this case, if you do not need all the additional features provided by general chatbots, you can invest more money in a specific tool that will bring you more results. Doing so will help you target a determined feature that will be more efficient and have additional capabilities.

Choosing an adequate tool with the proper features and characteristics can determine the success of AI implementation. It is not uncommon to see entrepreneurs investing money and effort in learning how to use a tool only to discover that it is not comprehensive enough to cater for all the business's needs. Therefore, studying all the different possibilities and speaking to the tool vendor (sometimes, even requesting a demo) will help you make the right decisions and clear any doubts.

To compare different features, you must clearly establish what you will need in your roadmap. Only by determining the characteristics you want the tool to have will you understand if it is appropriate for you. The recommendation for this comparison is to make three lists: one of what the tool *must have*, one of what it is *good to have*, and another one with the *optional capabilities*. As you read and study each tool feature, you should write down where each feature fits in and compare it with the same you list have created for the requirements.

Vendor Assessment

In addition to the information you will receive for the tool, you must consider the support the tool's vendor will provide. If you have any issues with the program, you should have an easy way to speak to customer support. Whether this is an online chat, a 24/7 phone service, or an email, you must have an accessible and reliable way to contact the vendor. Especially in the case when you are not tech-savvy or are just starting out, the vendor should be able to help you when you need it within a reasonable timeframe.

Another element you must consider when considering the vendor is their transparency with the provided information. In this case, they should be able to explain how your data will be treated, the privacy and security information about what you will enter, and if your input will be used to train the machine. Data privacy and confidentiality are essential to many businesses, and being able to trust what the vendor will do with your input is essential.

The last element that must be mentioned, closely related to the previous elements, is the credibility of the company providing the services. As you already know, dozens, if not hundreds, of vendors currently offer AI-powered services, so you should look for established companies with good ratings of their online communication. Looking at the different opinions on the tool and the customer service should give you a good idea of what to expect, and it is even more reliable if you get a recommendation from a current user.

Having someone who uses the tool is not critical to selecting it, but having someone you know who trusts and uses it will make you feel safer. At the same time, this person can help you understand the tool better, including its advantages and deficiencies. Therefore, whenever possible, you should look for recommendations from similar businesses and other entrepreneurs to understand how they use AI, what they recommend, and even their previous experiences with different tools.

Ease of Integration and Implementation

There is ease of integration and implementation in a more straightforward approach that is directly connected to your technical capacity. As a business, you might have good existing systems that cater to your needs. Ideally, the AI tool you will select should be easily integrated with these tools so that a replacement that will cost you more does not need to be carried out. At the same time, if you can find a program that offers AI functionality added to the other features your current system has, this might be an option that will also help you save money.

Nonetheless, if this is the case, you will need to account for another aspect of this implementation: the cost and ease of transferring all the information from the existing system into the new one. While some tools will carry out this process automatically, others will require a laborious process that includes downloading, uploading, and even manually inserting data into the new tool. If you do not have the time or the resources to carry this out within a reasonable time frame that will not impact your business, then this AI tool might not be good for you.

On the other hand, if possible, you should find an AI tool to enable you to carry out the same process if you need to change programs. After all, when implementing an app, you ideally plan to stick with it, but certain challenges can appear throughout this use that might lead you to want to change. If this is the case, you should ensure that carrying out this process once again will be as efficient and effortless as possible to avoid extra labor, cost, and time spent in the process.

User Experience Training Needs

Many SMBs will sometimes have one or more employees within the company. When implementing AI, it is important to think about these users and how they will be trained to use these tools. As an employer or entrepreneur, you will likely have people assigned to different tasks, so they might need to train them on the tool's features. Therefore, you should understand if the vendor offers training sessions for its use and if there is support to help in the case of newly released features.

In other cases, the AI tool you might be looking to implement will need to be used by customers. If this is your use, you will need to ensure that it is possible for users to easily learn how to use them. It is not uncommon for business owners to implement a tool and then have issues with their clients because they do not know how to use it. This might mean that instead of optimizing the operation for these individuals, you will *lose* them due to them struggling to use the tool.

Whether the technology users will be employees, customers, or even yourself, you should consider that they might not be as tech-savvy as the

tool requires. When you are selecting a tool, it must have a friendly interface and be intuitive, allowing individuals to discover on their own how
to use it and even troubleshoot if necessary. By taking these precautions,
you will be able to ensure a higher implementation success rate and overall
satisfaction with the changes being carried out.

Cost Considerations and Budgeting

Although all the previously mentioned requirements are essential, the cost
of implementing these tools is likely the most relevant. In this case, you
should consider not only the hardware and structure elements you must
invest in but also how much you will spend by implementing the tool. All
costs associated with this implementation should be considered, including
others apart from the ones you have seen in the previous sections. In some
cases, the price of the AI tool is not relevant for that specific moment, but
it might be for a future opportunity.

To start, you must establish a budget to identify your investment capacity. In this case, consider all the associated costs included in the AI
implementation. However, these costs should be what you can see as the
embedded costs. *What does that mean?* you might ask. In this case, it could
be the cost of your time dedicated to learning how to manage the new
software. Perhaps it is the overtime you will need to pay employees so they
can start after work to learn how to use it. Maybe even the initial data
collecting and other work you might need to carry out does not have a
visible cost but will have a financial impact.

Ultimately, you should add all the costs and identify which fits the
budget you have established best for this implementation. Regarding the
budget, you must establish one that is not so narrow that it will not allow
you to have spare cash for possible emergencies but also offer you the
option to implement these changes. Just as you budget for the elements
in your company, implementing an AI tool should be considered in the

overall budget. If the cost of the tool is higher than the budget you have available, you might need to leave it for later once your business starts to have more income.

As you might imagine, these costs will be essential in determining the tool and critical to the decision-making process. However, they should not be analyzed independently of the other features. After all, a tool that offers more than one capability might have a better cost–benefit ratio than one that offers both together since you will save time with training, implementation, and data collection. This analysis must analyze the tool's overall benefits. In other words, you should identify the *added value* this tool will bring. Sometimes, a more expensive tool will increase your earnings, compensating for its implementation. Therefore, you should avoid deciding based only on the cost since it might become a problem in the future.

The Bottom Line

As you can see, many elements must be considered before deciding what AI tool to implement. All the elements you have seen are part of this crucial process, but this does not mean that other aspects cannot be considered. These should all be part of the roadmap you will establish, allowing you to have a broader view of all uses and applications of the new tool.

Throughout this section, you have seen different tables, and you might find that these will be a useful tool to analyze potential resources. You can choose to implement them one at a time and individually analyze them, or you can create all the tables in one big spreadsheet and study the different concepts together. This individual preference will depend on your organization and what is easier for you to work with. Nonetheless, it is good practice to implement them during this phase of the process, as it will give you a broader view of what you are looking at.

Lastly, as you are carrying out this process, one recommendation might also prove to be useful: Discard the tools you are not interested in. You can make this selection in two steps, which are independent of each other but will streamline your options. To carry out this process, as you research, take note of the tools you are interested in and list the ones that do not interest you. This will help you eliminate the unwanted ones faster just by looking at the name rather than having to analyze them all over again. If you want to make this process even better, making a small note of *why* this tool is discarded is also good practice as a way to remember.

After selecting the tools that will be considered and those that will not, you will fill in the table. As you conduct the analysis, you can cross off or color-code the ones you want to make them more visible. You can then narrow the selection until you have made your final choice based on the roadmap and your business's needs and requirements. Ideally, you should have three or four different tools to move on to the next phase of the process, which we will explore and will be a critical point when deciding the tool.

Testing and Piloting AI Tools

When selecting and filtering the tools you will implement into your SMB, you mustn't consider only what you can see on paper. Some tools might present an incredible performance in theory, but when you put them to use, they are not as efficient as promised. For this reason, you should always *test* these tools before deciding to sign up for one. Vendors often offer demos and free trials for those interested in signing up for their tools. You should use this opportunity to "take them for a ride" and ensure they perform according to your expectations.

But what do I need to look out for? This is an excellent question since many people will test the tools and decide what happens during the test phase. However, when the time comes to use them in the business, they do not correspond to expectations, and performance will be far from what was promised. To ensure you have the most relevant experience while testing these tools, here is a small checklist you should consider for the trial phase:

- **Test performance during peak hours:** Testing the AI tool during the business's busiest hours will help you understand if it can support the demand and needs. You should look at two aspects of performance in this sense: how it impacts the employees' use of the tool and how the tool responds to an increased processing demand.

- **Use data similar to real-life situations:** You want to ensure that the tool will be useful for the data you will input. Therefore, you should use fictional and uncharacterized data to simulate the type of information you would input to ensure what the output will be.

- **Test the emergency and support services:** Many vendors might promise they will support you immediately if you have difficulties, but this might not be true. Therefore, as you use the tool, test customer services to see if what was promised is true.

- **Test the backup capability:** One of the most challenging matters a business can face is losing its information. If you are using one of these AI tools to store customer information and metrics, ask the company to provide you with backups and understand how this process takes place to help you decide if they have the necessary tools to support this demand.

By taking these steps, you will be ready to decide what is best for your business. If the tool you selected performs well during these tests, it will likely perform well in real life, helping you have a smoother implementation and use during your daily operations. If they present any issues, you should try to see how they can be solved with the vendor the possible steps to fixing them. Sometimes, it is just a matter of discovering the right process to ensure optimal use, so communication is essential.

However, none of these AI tools will be useful if you do not have the data to feed and train it. This means you must have at least a reasonable database to help ensure you have optimal results. If you are unsure of how to do this, do not worry! As we move on to the next chapter, you will understand the data collection process, the type of information needed, and other actions to ensure what you will give the machine (and what you have) will be useful. Shall we take a look?

Chapter Four

Data Gathering and Preparation

N ow that you have chosen the tools you want to use, a critical part of the process comes. As you know, AI tools are fueled with data, and if you want to personalize them for your purposes and obtain accurate and reliable results, you must use your business's data. Granted, the required data might be more general for tools such as ChatGPT and generating text, offering a broader sense of what needs to be written about. In this case, you can create and generate text by providing a few keywords and a general context.

While this makes the tool more straightforward to use, it also will provide you with information that any other person would be able to find. At the same time, tools like ChatGPT will use stored data to train the machine, which means the input you give it will later be used in the ML process, making the information public to others. This use means two things: The first is that others might later use confidential information. The second is that you might (and probably are) be violating user and client privacy by exposing their information to others.

For the previously mentioned reasons, it is *essential* to understand the data privacy agreements and terms for the tool you will use. To still mention ChatGPT, it is possible to turn off its data-saving features, but this also means you will lose all the conversations you have with the tool, leading them to be deleted and, therefore, defeating the purpose of having a program to help you manage your business. There are better tools you can use to ensure this safety and bring you better results.

Nonetheless, before we get ahead of ourselves and start looking at some of these tools, it is essential to know the required data for optimal business use. In this chapter, you will gain a comprehensive understanding of adequate data sources, how to manage them once collected, the importance of evaluating and documenting this data, and finally, how it will be implemented into your AI tool. While this last element will largely depend on the tool you will use, here we will look at a different approach, precisely, how to use this data when dealing with tools that protect data confidentiality versus those that do not.

I can only imagine you are curious about these applications. After all, the most frequently asked question is, *What is relevant data for my business?* followed by, *How do I ensure my data has quality?* These are both excellent questions; you will find the answers as you read this chapter. If you are anxious to learn this specific and essential part of AI implementation in your business, waste no more time! Read on and discover how to associate the information you have (or will have) and transform it into business profitability and production machines.

Understanding Data Sources

Let's start by addressing the first question: *What is relevant data for my business?* The answer will depend on your business area. While some information will be useful for all types of SMBs, others will be specific to your niche. For example, restaurants will have specific data that must be collected, which differs from that of a marketing agency. In turn, these will vary from a T-shirt customization business to a babysitting agency, requiring specific details only relevant to that industry.

But what are these data sources, and how can I know what is relevant? The answer to this question will refer to your established roadmap, where you will determine what you want to achieve. Depending on the metrics you want to analyze, the process you want to enhance with AI, and the tool you will use a different dataset will be needed. Here are some of the general metrics that will be useful to all businesses:

- revenue

- yield

- cost

- leads generated

- new clients

- customer satisfaction

- customer retention

- reviews on products or services

- frequently combined products/services

- marketing campaign results

- frequently asked questions

Whatever the industry you work with, these metrics will usually be relevant for the business. They are not area-specific but refer to the most commonly measured business KPIs. While these are important, it does not mean they are the *only* ones that should be examined. There are many more you can use related to the product or service of your business, and this will depend on what you are willing to explore. Here are examples of five specific metrics for specific industries:

Restaurants

- dishes returned

- most ordered dishes

- number of visitors per party

- busiest days and times

- amount of perished products

Babysitting agency

- number of children per job

- most common neighborhoods

- age of children per job

- guardian tardiness frequency

- periods with the most demand for service

Software development company

- bugs reported

- customer service activation

- crash frequency

- reason for crashes

- response time

As you can see, these businesses all require specific metrics, usually tailored to their offerings. If you think this data is difficult to find, rest assured that most of them will only demand that you have a good documentation and registration system. If you are diligent with your record keeping and have a good tracking system to identify your KPIs, it is possible to create a file with all this data easily (nonetheless time-consuming). If you do not, you must start building a recording system to allow you to have somewhere to source it from. This specific information will be sourced from the channels you adopt and the registers you make. Even for SMBs, having these records will help you analyze the business's overall situation.

Similarly, data can also be sourced from other places despite not being specific to your business. These include direct *scraping* from the internet, online repositories with general-purpose databases, third-party vendors specialized in compiling and selling this information, and the available data from the organizations that generated them. These are all valid and (mostly) reliable sources you can use and obtain data from. However, they will be relevant to understanding a market situation or trend, or for competitor analysis, which might be helpful but not specific to your business.

The best and most reliable data you will obtain come from your company's records and numbers. Internet and repository data is easy to obtain but unreliable since it may be outdated and inaccurate. Third-party data is usually reliable, but you will need to pay for this information, and this cost can be expensive for the data you are looking for. Finally, we have organizational data, which companies generate and publish themselves, but these are usually large companies that might not be relevant to your industry.

The most relevant data you will use are those generated by your business. They can be sourced from invoice systems, online customer reviews, polls and surveys carried out on customers, logs with daily movement, and much more. Knowing that this data cannot come in any format is crucial. It will frequently need to be adjusted to the tool you will use and, if possible, preprocessed and analyzed before input. In some cases, depending on the software you will use, it might be necessary to *uncharacterize* this data so the information is kept private. Let's explore these requirements and what must be done to ensure optimal results.

Defining Data Requirements

Now, for the second question: *How do I ensure the quality of my data?* There are a few steps you must follow. This does not mean you must be a data master or need all the details—quite the contrary. Most of the time, AI tools analyze the primary information or keywords to identify the essential elements required for an analysis. Nonetheless, the more information you have, the better the results will be.

As you have seen, this data can be collected from several sources, and the ones you will use will depend on you. For example, if you are collecting online reviews, there are ways (free and paid) to obtain reliable information from sites such as Google and Yelp. You can conduct polls and surveys to read their opinions if you want more customer insight.

These processes are usually carried out by adding data to spreadsheets, which are easy to manage and can sometimes be used to add information to business intelligence (BI) tools. In fact, several BI tools can be used to carry out these analyses, prepare forecasts, and understand trends; this will also be explored later in the book. However, for now, we must focus on collecting the best-quality data with your available tools.

Remember, this step will depend very much on what you have recorded. Usually, businesses must create these documents or enhance those they already have. The more information the spreadsheet has, the more complete the AI tool processing will be and the better results you will obtain. To help you achieve these optimal results, dive into the following sections to understand the fundamental processes to carry out.

Data Collection Strategies

Data collection is demanding, but it is not hard. As mentioned earlier, if you have good records, this will be easy to tabulate in a spreadsheet and create a powerful document to feed to the AI tool. You can use different strategies to collect this data, and what you will collect will depend on the established objectives. The first step will be to assess what you need, what you have, and what you need to put together.

Fear not if you are alarmed by all the "must create" data. While it may seem that this information will be difficult to find, it might not be the case. In today's modern and connected world, most of this information is available on public platforms, which you can export with the appropriate tools, such as Google Maps or Yelp, and this will be a huge headway start for many. With the reviews you find on these channels, you can have at least four of the five "must create." The frequently combined products and services, just like the FAQs, can be obtained from experienced and general client-facing employees. The remaining two, marketing results and leads generated, will depend on the commercial staff and the forms you can create for them to fill in.

Questions during the process are normal, but to help you identify all the potential sources for the data, here is a comprehensive (but not exhaustive) list of the places and the actions you can conduct to obtain them:

- Carry out polls and surveys with employees.

- Conduct polls with employees and staff from each relevant area.

- Use social media metrics to monitor campaigns and engagement.

- Export data from Google Maps, Yelp, TrustPilot, and others (apps might be required for this).

- Customer complaint files.

- Emails and messages from clients on the company webpage or email.

- Review purchase invoices and sales receipts for a period.

- Measure contact frequency in communication channels.

- Monitor webpage analytics.

- Create a client log with information collected during contact.

Many more could be added to this list, especially considering the specific business you work with. As it would be impossible to list them all comprehensively, you can use the examples we saw for industry-specific KPIs to create questions to ask and identify the sources where you can find this information. Use the examples you have seen with the KPIs above to understand the possibilities. Here, you must use your creativity to find the best options and create business-specific solutions.

Data Preprocessing

Once you have collected all the necessary data, it is time to add them to tables and spreadsheets. This is likely the most time-consuming part of the process, especially if you do not have the necessary workforce, time, or enough information to add. For the first two issues, you might consider hiring a temp or an intern to help you with the data entry. For the latter, you should not worry, as we will explore how to augment this data in the following section.

However, you should know that data preprocessing is much more than simply entering the data in a spreadsheet. This is actually only the first part of the process. For the data to be adequate and ready to use, you will need to make the necessary adjustments to it, which usually involves six different steps, known as *data cleaning*:

1. **Remove duplicates:** Duplicate information can confuse the tool and directly impact the results. For example, if you add the same invoice twice, you will be modifying the real results of the business's income. The same can happen to a rating if you duplicate a negative review. Therefore, you should remove all the duplicates so the data is as unique and accurate as possible.

2. **Identify outliers:** After the duplicates have been removed, the next step is to analyze whether there are any outliers within this data. An outlier could mean a client who spent an unusual amount of money on a service or product for more or less. This is a typical outlier but should not be confused with a lower or busier business period. These are important to identify trends and should not be deleted.

3. **Handle missing data:** Sometimes, we have missing data. In this case, it can be a customer who left a review item blank or a piece of information you do not have. In this case, you can delete this review or use a standard value that will not impact the overall result. This could represent taking an average of the other data points with similar characteristics and filling in this number for the empty data point.

4. **Transform:** Now that there are no outliers or missing data, you must transform the collected data. Doing so will make it relevant for the analysis, such as removing the irrelevant data point columns or creating new data points based on your collected data. One example is if you do not have the yield but have the income and the cost, you create an additional column to calculate the yield.

5. **Reduce:** The data is now almost ready. Although it is uncommon for many SMBs to have excessive data due to time and personnel constraints, if this is your case, you must determine the relevant points to be kept and those you will discard. This can mean putting together similar data points or deleting those you believe are irrelevant for that specific purpose or the relationship you want to establish.

6. **Standardize:** The last step in preparing the data points is standardizing them. This means establishing the same format and measurement units for each category. If you are dealing with money, transform all numbers into dollars; if it is temperature, transform all the data into Fahrenheit, and so on.

Your data is now ready to be used and fed to the machine if you consider there is relevant and sufficient data for such. However, in many SMBs, this is not the reality. Data is usually missing or insufficient, so you must augment it with synthetic data to help the AI tool process the information. The good part is that it will not require as much effort; the spreadsheet you have just prepared will be just enough to help you create these additional data points. Move on to the following section to find out how.

Data Augmentation

One of the many advantages of generative AI is the ability to create synthetic data to complement your existing set. When this is done, you will be able to prompt the tool to create fictional data points to help you forecast trends and aid you with the decision-making process. While it is possible to have these datasets created from scratch, which is ideal for companies just starting and wanting to understand the market, when you have your data, the AI tool can build upon what you have.

AI tools will enable this process seamlessly by inputting your information for situations like this. Some tools that allow you to do this are Greter.ai, Mostly.ai, and Augmentmlg. These are all-purpose tools that can generate textual and other types of data. At the same time, you have other more targeted tools to use to create specific content, including images, sound, and others.

Once again, to decide the best tool for your business, you must conduct the analysis you read about in the previous study and see the best applications. You should remember that ideally speaking, its use will be temporary, decreasing in need as you build your databases. Therefore, depending on how fast this proprietary information will be compiled and created, you will need a one-time use for the tool. As your database grows, the synthetic data will become more irrelevant as you start working with real and real-time information.

On the other hand, if you are planning an expansion or are facing market uncertainty, this synthetic data will be useful to aid you in providing the data to make forecasts and understand potential outcomes. In this case, you will ask the AI tool to generate the data based on a specific scenario, with which you will merge your data and see the results it will bring. This resource is commonly applied in scientific and financial research to understand the outcome possibilities of an event.

If you will use AI for this, the ideal approach is to start with a hypothesis you will prove or disprove as the analysis is being carried out. By doing so, it is possible to reduce the amplitude of the data and work within the relevant scenarios for your purpose. If an initial idea is not formed, the data will be pointless since you will not know what to extract, and even worse, you won't know what to ask. Remember that AI tools work based on prompts; if these are unclear, the output will likely be as well.

Data Privacy and Security

The last element you must explore when dealing with data is how this information is used. Today, many governments are working on protecting citizens' data and the information provided, as shown by the need to authorize cookies when surfing online. While this is still being discussed in the US, in Europe, for example, the General Data Protection Regulation (GDPR) was established to protect user privacy. For SMBs working with clients abroad, this is an essential regulation to be aware of.

When collecting data, there are cases in which some data will need to be characterized and others will not. In the anonymous category, polls and surveys can be used as such, only with the answers being registered. The same applies to general information such as reviews and frequently asked questions. These will help you gain a general understanding of the audience while also enabling you to categorize them into groups such as frequency, income ranges, and age.

Conversely, when dealing with specific situations or wanting to understand a client's behavior, you must use their unique data. This is where the risk lies, especially when using free and unmonitored tools, since this information may be made public to other individuals. When this happens, it can expose confidential and sensitive data, presenting a risk to all parties.

For these reasons, when collecting identified data from clients, you must have signed consent that will allow you to use this information. Usually, this consent will inform how the data will be used, protected, and stored. It should be clear to the user, and the limitations should be respected for legal compliance. If the user does not authorize or has limitations on how the data will be used, this must be noted, and the business should proceed accordingly.

One of the ways to use sensitive information without exposing your company is to disguise the information. When you uncharacterize it, you will remove the specific sensitive details of what the data says and replace it with a cipher only you understand. For instance, if you use a public tool without revealing your income, you can separate the different ranges and classify them with a letter. This way, you can say that clients from the X area have an A-range spending habit and from area Y a B-range. This way, you won't provide the tool with information but still offer the necessary data for relevant results.

Data privacy and safety rules are becoming stricter as AI evolves, and having consent for both the clients' and the businesses' data is essential. It is usual to hear people say data is "gold," and, in many cases, this is true. The better your data and insights you can gain from it, the more likely you will receive better results. For these reasons, you should remember the data should be stored in a safe place (both from hackers and from system failures), with a backup, and that it is accessible when needed.

Versioning and Documentation

Data is always changing, and while it is good practice to look at past information to try and understand what will happen in the future, we must also look at present data to identify present trends and market signs. This means you need to have a good backup for the registered data and constantly update what you use. Ideally speaking, you will have different versions of the data, and the AI tool you select to implement should be able to support this feature.

By creating different versions of the data, you can track what happened to client behavior and the business over time, giving you an accurate snapshot of that moment. At the same time, you can see how the changes happened and identify possible drivers for these. By understanding how the business changed and the impact of these factors, you can make more accurate decisions.

Versioning, however, also refers to the different ways this data will be stored and used. In this case, the AI tool should have a comprehensive relationship analysis among the factors. In an extrapolation, you should be able to identify how the local festivities and the weather impacted your sales. By having these different versions of how the data is entered, kept, and compared, it will be possible to create different scenarios to enhance decision-making.

Meanwhile, keeping different versions of the same data will also require documentation on how this data was kept. This documentation should be stored for reference and traced if necessary. Suppose you have a meeting and take notes of an interview with a client. In this case, the date and the time should be accurately registered to document this specific moment. This will enable you to create a timeline of customer interaction and business progress and give you insight into services or product performance.

To ensure data reliability, you should verify that all information is registered. Some examples include registering poll and survey results in a spreadsheet before inputting them, keeping electronic copies of reviews stored in the cloud, and not only using the AI tool. If you would rather input this information in the tool and not create duplicates, ensure that the content you add is downloadable as many updates as necessary.

Once you have a safe copy of the data, store it in the cloud or another safe device following good market practices for document storage. Safeguarding electronic documentation includes using strong passwords, storing them in different places, keeping the information updated, and encrypting confidential and sensitive data. Furthermore, ensure that only those needing and using this data for business purposes can access it to prevent incorrect use and theft.

Exploratory Data Analysis

After you have collected the data, a crucial step must be carried out, which many individuals do not do. Known as the data exploration phase, it is not complicated to carry out and should be done by all SMB owners. The process is so simple it might surprise you: Download the information (if in an AI tool), open the spreadsheet, and look at what you have. In other words, do not rely only on the AI tool to analyze and make relationships between the data points, but look with your own eyes and manipulate this data to see what you can find.

This does not need to be lengthy or demanding; rather, it is a review of what you have to see if anything stands out. Those who are more used to spreadsheets can even "play" with the information and see what they can find. You might want to create a dynamic table to see what might pop up or put this information in spreadsheet graphs to see if anything catches your eye. This is not a complex process but something you should do to understand your business better.

If you are not tech-savvy or do not know how to create these tables or charts, you can use other simpler options for this exploration. You can use filters to see the most frequent information that appears or classify the data in a specific order. You can also color-code data points to see what stands out and add numbers. When dealing with spreadsheets, the possibilities are nearly endless, and you only need to take some time to take a deep dive.

Finally, some are more experienced with technology and will use BI tools to help them. The most popular and well known in the market is Power-BI, which can be downloaded online at no cost. If you are a Microsoft subscriber, you will have access to some additional features. All you will need to do is upload the spreadsheet you are working on and move the different categories and classifications. When using these tools, it will be possible to manage and explore the data, including finding mistakes and inconsistencies, using user-friendly and mostly intuitive software.

As you can see, exploring your collected data is not hard to do! It is actually a fun task to carry out once you understand how it works, and it comes with the added benefit of gaining more insight into your business. It is a win-win situation where you will be able to understand company numbers better and find insights that can lead you to new products or services. Therefore, if you have not yet carried out this study for your business information, start doing so little by little. You will see there is much to gain!

Data Integration and Fusion

Suppose you have collected all the data and necessary information related to the business objectives. You have them all in different spreadsheets and documents. You have explored the data sets and established a hypothesis. If this input was not implemented using an AI-powered tool, it is time to add it to the program. This is the "moment of truth" when you will finally understand if the data is enough and suitable for the intended purposes.

You should ensure the tool supports the document format you use to upload this information. You must also verify whether any previous filtering and classification are needed or if additional manipulation must be made. This is a crucial part of the process since this data will fuel the tool that will guide your decision-making for the foreseeable future. Therefore, incorrect data integration can lead to imprecise decisions, risking your SMB.

When you integrate this data, you should first have the result checked, rechecked, and triple-checked. Remember the previously carried out exploratory analysis? This is when it will come in handy. Because of your business knowledge and the previous data exploration, you will already *know* the general information that should be generated. This means that by reviewing the AI tool's results critically, you can determine what the results look like. At the same time, remember that you have separate files with the information. You can go back to it, compare the different information, and check what the input looks like.

The Data Revelation

As you can now see, all your steps will culminate in how the AI tool will understand and establish relationships from the data. The data will now be applicable for customizing chatbots, customer relationship programs, service and product development, forecasts, and decision-making AI tools. The more varied and comprehensive this data is, the better your AI tool will generate results. The more correct and precise it is, the more reliable the output will be.

Yes, it is a demanding and time-consuming process that sometimes requires additional investment. Think about it as the kickoff that will be done once since you will continue to update and follow the format as new information is obtained. It will be added to the tool as you obtain it, leading the software to learn more and generate optimal results. It is a process with tangible outcomes that will impact your work and business. Rest assured: There is no downside to working with data.

The best part is that now that all the information is available and you have added it to the AI tool, you can start exploring how these tools work. Yes, you read that right! Starting in the next chapter, we will see the different implementations of AI tools within business areas and how they can be leveraged to achieve the best results. Perhaps not all situations will apply to you or fit your objectives.

Still, the idea here is to give you an overall view of how AI can improve productivity, efficiency, accuracy, and profits. If you are excited to continue this journey and start considering the different applications, read on! You are about to see how AI can forever change how you do business—from customer relationships to sales and financial management.

Chapter Five

Revolutionizing Customer Service and Support

C ustomer services have been using AI for longer than you might imagine. Suppose you are on the phone with a call center and are asked to briefly mention the reason for your call; this is usually AI. When you are automatically routed to the department you want to speak to among a series of options, this is also usually AI. Those on a landing page talking to the chat box for support and to answer questions are certainly using AI. The same can be said about automatic messages with *unmissable* offers *just for you*, sale opportunities, and even "happy birthday" discounts.

All the previous examples are AI. They might not have the same functionality or application but are nonetheless the technology in action. On the phone, this is AI speech recognition. In the chatbot, it is generative AI. When selecting the department, it is predictive AI; for the offers, it is recommendation systems. These are all systems and formats we have mentioned in previous chapters, and that, as you can see, are the technology in action.

You might wonder if these are expensive or difficult to implement. The short answer is *not at all*. The main reason is that they are especially validated and long-used tools that can be implemented while maintaining a budget. In this chapter, you will explore all the potential for using AI tools to enhance and personalize your customer service. As you will see, it is not all about generative AI but also about a wide variety of tools that will make processes more productive and efficient.

AI-Powered Customer Service

Depending on your business, dealing with clients can take the whole day, distracting you from other work matters. Items such as responding to emails and client inquiries and offering support are everyday activities that must be carried out. After all, the customers are paying, and you want them to return and continue using your product or service. Employing AI to carry out these tasks can benefit mainly due to their aggregated benefits.

Although you might think that AI, and more specifically generative AI with chatbots such as ChatGPT, Gemini, Claude, and Microsoft Copilot, will greatly help you, there are other tools you can use and implement in different areas. Chatbot NLP features will be useful for responding to draft messages and creating content; you can also use AI for sentiment analysis, forecasts, predictions, recommendations, and assistance.

Recent surveys have shown that 80% of SMB owners claim that neglecting AI could lead to missing a competitive edge, while 87% of those adopting the technology say it has helped them meet business objectives (*Report Reveals How AI Will Transform the SMB*, 2024). At the same time, 49% of SMB entrepreneurs claim that they have difficulty keeping up with the pace of AI development. Nonetheless, 96% of them are willing to invest in these tools and expand their AI implementation within the next two years due to the promising results that it has shown: 53% more efficiency in adjusting to market trends, 51% decrease in operational costs, and 41% on reaching new clients.

Many customers see the advantage of having a 24/7 system they can use in emergencies, and sales increase when recommendations are offered based on previous purchases. Companies such as Lufthansa, KLM, and even Domino's are using AI to help answer customers' frequent questions and help them navigate websites. Not only does this significantly decrease the necessary resources for a call center, for example, but those that do reach out through a human-guided service will be for more specific issues that the machine cannot solve.

In the case of your SMB, this might mean answering fewer unnecessary phone calls, emails, and even instant messages, leaving you time to focus on other business tasks. You will also save money by not needing to hire specific personnel for these tasks, allowing you to keep within the budget. Several tools can be effortlessly used to automate these processes and streamline communications for those who are not as tech-savvy, and sometimes at a lower cost than you might imagine. You will learn about some of these customer-oriented tools throughout this chapter.

Additionally, for entrepreneurs, it is a fine line between being good at what they do and being able to cater to all these customer needs. You may be an excellent web designer with no skills to deal with the public. AI tools can help you draft emails and find a communication channel with them. They can also help you understand the intended tone the client wants to convey and offer solutions to their requests. Even if there is a complaint, you can use these AI tools to help structure a message that will be direct according to the company's policies.

This is not to say that AI use in customer service is without its challenges—not at all. These must be considered and thought about before any implementation. This will also be explored, and you will see the attention points to look out for. Read on to explore five implementation possibilities for your SMB, tools to cater to these needs, and cases in which the AI adoption was so successful that business results were significantly impacted.

AI-Powered Chatbots

If you are a frequent internet navigator, always looking at websites for different companies, you might have noticed an increase in the number of "virtual assistants" available on these pages. Usually, these are AI-powered chatbots that will answer questions and provide information regarding a service or product a company uses. These assistants have different characteristics; finding the ideal one for you will be key to the tool's success.

Generally speaking, these chatbots are powered by limited information on the company. This means they are trained with specific business-related data and can only provide the information on issues it has learned. These chatbots can be more or less limited, depending on your available budget for investing in the tool. The two most common situations are tools with reactive or generative capacity. Here is an overview of both:

- **Reactive capacity:** These tools are usually limited to restricted information. In this case, these tools will provide you with options. You will select a number or a keyword from the provided list, and it will offer you general information on the topic. In this case, the tool will be unable to generate or understand queries different from these limitations, which are usually the most frequently asked questions customers ask.

In more advanced features of these tools, you will ask a question, and the system will identify the keywords, once again providing you with a list. These chatbots can be frustrating for customers with specific issues who will later be directed to a phone number or email because the issue cannot be solved. On the other hand, they can efficiently solve simple problems related to your offering, especially if these do not require much discussion or have options.

- **Generative capacity:** Chatbots with generative capacity are more robust and can converse with users. In this case, it will also be limited to the business information it was trained in, but it will have a more significant explanation and interaction capacity. These tools will generate complex answers to unstandardized queries, allowing the user to have a "conversation" with the bot.

They can offer solutions to different problems from varying points of view and in several forms, allowing you to reach a larger audience. Using generative AI with the chatbots for your page will reduce the number of users directed to human-led customer service and solve problems more efficiently. The downside of using these tools is the cost, as they require more investment than those with restricted and preprogrammed answers.

Several tools on the market are available to create and implement these bots. For generative AI programs, you can use ChatGPT's application programming interface (API) to embed your data and train it specifically for your business, for example. While this will give your company incredible AI power, it also translates to a higher cost due to the tool's features and potential data privacy obstacles. You will also need some coding and development knowledge or hire a professional with these capacities to implement the tool into your website.

On the other hand, tools on the market offer chatbots as an additional part of their service package, such as Zendesk, Freddy AI, and HappyFox Assist. The main advantage of using these programs is that they are often exclusively used for these purposes, meaning that you will also have personalized support for implementation and troubleshooting. Usually, these tools are low-cost and contain features such as routing and triage, a native AI knowledge base, and even sentiment detection.

Enhancing Customer Interactions With Virtual Assistants

In our fast-paced communication world, customer requirements are becoming increasingly demanding. One of the main issues businesses have to deal with is responding to inquiries "now," with no delay, and in a 24/7 fashion. Companies that do not have this are losing to competitors with a prompt customer service channel that allows them to troubleshoot issues and solve minor problems with just a few keystrokes. It is no wonder that we have seen an increase in the number of landing pages with chatbots that will enhance customer interactions with the company.

The Scandinavian bank DNB needed to release its customer support staff to address more complex issues and increase customer service phone availability. Implementing a 24/7 AI system into its landing page rerouted 20% of the customer traffic to its website in six months, decreasing the volume of calls received by the support center (*How DNB Automated 20% of AI Customer Service*, 2024). After implementation and customer training, the bank was able to automate almost 60% of all the inquiries made by clients across all channels, bringing the company a result of 68% in customer satisfaction rates.

Although DNB is one of the largest companies in the region, this does not mean that implementation is restricted to corporations with a significant presence in the market. The only difference is the reach of the chatbot tool since numbers will be proportional to the number of clients you have. By implementing these virtual assistants, it is possible to create a "chat-first" approach, decreasing the need for support staff and the dedicated time SMBs will allocate to simple queries. In an overall view, this means that the process will have cost efficiency and scalability, allowing more clients to be handled simultaneously.

Bringing this AI-powered possibility to the business is crucial to optimize customer service. The process will undoubtedly demand fine-tuning and adjustments, but it is possible to create customer polls and surveys to understand the main issues they need help with. To understand the reach these virtual assistants can have for your business, here are five SMB applications you might be interested in learning about:

- **Restaurants** – You can create a virtual assistant on the restaurant's landing page to answer frequently asked questions, such as dishes suitable for dietary restrictions and delivery possibilities. The virtual assistant can also help make reservations without calling the establishment.

- **Retail** – SMBs in the retail business can integrate their chatbots with inventory systems and aid clients in identifying a product's availability. The tool can also implement general information such as estimated delivery time, order tracking, and so on.

- **Technology** – If your SMB works with technology, chatbots can help customers troubleshoot issues, obtain program alternatives, and find the best solution that fits their needs. Implementing this system will allow you to provide 24/7 service without logging in.

- **General services** – Those providing a specific service will find virtual assistants helpful in incident reporting and scheduling meetings. By integrating the virtual assistant with your agenda, you can schedule meetings, visits, and other client-related tasks.

- **Hospitality** – SMBs providing hospitality services, such as B&Bs, can use chatbots to make reservations and determine date availability. Other features include specific service requests and activity opportunities nearby for those visiting the region and wanting to explore.

As you can see, developing a chatbot for your SMB can be an excellent way to increase efficiency and enhance customer experiences. By decreasing the need to pick up the phone and call or write an email, these clients find immediate support, allowing queries to be solved independently without impacting how the business operates. Some of the features will depend on integrating with other systems; this can be an advantage to your business's operation.

Although we will discuss personalizing experiences further in the chapter, it is important to understand the potential chatbots have for this purpose. The more features and systems you can connect to streamline tasks, the more efficient and productive you will be. At the same time, AI can help predict what these customers will request based on their behavior and habits. Let's see how ML can be used to increase efficiency and predictive analysis to optimize customer satisfaction.

Predictive Analytics for Anticipatory Support

Suppose your business has a product that is a sales hit and constantly needs replacement. If you do not have an alert to notify you of low stock, this may lead to customer dissatisfaction if there isn't enough stock. However, it is possible to integrate ML and customer behavior into the equation to automate the notification process when you need to order more. By teaching the machine when and how frequently your sales happen, it is possible to estimate habits and anticipate demands.

The same situation can apply to those who provide services. If you have a system crash and what you provide becomes unavailable, instead of waiting for all your clients to contact you and inform them individually of what happened, you can create an automated message to automatically inform them. In both cases, in inventory management and customer communication, by providing anticipatory support, you will have optimal efficiency and solve problems in the operation before they happen.

When companies implement these predictive analysis solutions into their information flow, it is possible to optimize how the operation is being carried out. Businesses can use AI data analysis capabilities to understand the driving factors to increased sales, allowing them to prepare inventory for this period better. At the same time, by using a data-driven approach, you can forecast and anticipate behaviors that can lead you to prevent problems or even develop new products and processes.

In the medical industry, predictive analysis is used in patient data to identify when they will need healthcare assistance, preventing health complications. Companies like Northumbria Healthcare NHS Foundation Trust use ML predictive analytics to evaluate patients and turn data into medical insights. By converting the medical data of over 400,000 patients into statistics, it was possible to classify them into risk groups and understand the common points between identified infirmities (*Northumbria Healthcare NHS Foundation Trust Adopts the Responsible AI*, 2022).

In an SMB application, if a doctor's practice implements AI and inputs its patient's information into the system, it could help offer a predictive analysis for when additional exams and follow-ups need to be made. By constantly updating the information in the database, it is possible to monitor patient development and suggest medical evaluation when required. This could be optimized by patients receiving automated polls to fill in for regular well-being checks and exam requests to update their health condition. When all this information is compiled, the system will provide an analysis, and the medical professionals can monitor these patients, allowing anticipated intervention and less potential for health complications.

Personalized Customer Experiences

One of the greatest advantages of integrating AI into customer service tools is perhaps the possibility of increasing customers' personalized experience with your business. Today, it is not uncommon for businesses to try to identify customer preferences and associate them with personalized experiences. We see it in online clothing stores, supermarkets, and the service industry. For a practical application of this feature, consider services provided by Amazon and Netflix.

In the first case, it is possible to cross-sell and upsell, finding products related to the customer's choice while navigating. By finding products associated with what is in the cart, the business can provide information on other products the user hadn't even considered, enhancing their experience and allowing the possibility of more products being sold. On the other hand, when Netflix offers clients similar content to what users like to watch, it can increase customer satisfaction by providing items tailored to their tastes and preferences. Both are opportunities to increase client retention and satisfaction.

Consider your SMB and what it offers clients. By offering out-of-the-box and personalized solutions to their requests, it is possible to increase sales and, consequently, income with a one-stop shop for all needed solutions. Small travel agencies, for example, can use AI to create a traveler profile and provide them with the best options for their trip. This means tailoring their experience according to the travel purpose, the age of those joining them, and the location where they will stay. While larger companies such as TripAdvisor provide similar services, this information is not as specific as it could be.

At the same time, we could talk about independent developers who are setting up their businesses. While a client can reach out for a specific service, by using AI, it is possible to understand different needs and applications for the program that will be used. This means they can integrate different solutions into the same tool and increase the value charged for the service. This will optimize their time, as they will develop one solution for all the needs and offer a cost-efficient solution, showing the client their capability and capacity.

Larger companies, such as Coca-Cola, Nike, and LEGO, have created AI-based systems to help increase customer engagement by receiving product suggestions. When clients can personalize their experience, suggest new product development, and tailor the experience to their needs, it leads to greater engagement. Smaller businesses will see increased customer retention and satisfaction statistics when they apply this strategy. In both the cases of Nike and LEGO, it was possible to identify an increase in customer loyalty due to the personalization of the shopping experience. Allowing these led the companies not only to create a stronger client base but also to use the collective creativity to develop and implement new products and services (Hicks, 2024).

Omnichannel Support and Integration

Although we have discussed system integration with AI tools, it is essential to understand how powerful this resource can be. In many cases, businesses disregard the need for this integration, which is essential for a seamless flow. To help illustrate this matter, let's consider the example of integrating a chatbot into a restaurant reservation system. Suppose your SMB operates in the food industry, and you have decided to implement a chatbot onto your webpage to allow customers to ask questions and make reservations.

Information might be missed if this chatbot is not integrated with other systems, leading to customer dissatisfaction. Consider the following situation: A customer enters the chatbot to ask about gluten-free options in your establishment. After the chatbot responds, the customer proceeds to make a reservation for dinner near a window table. Once they arrive at the restaurant, the hostess, who does not have access to the chatbot information, asks if they have a reservation and has no prior information regarding their dietary restrictions. When seated, the customer is offered a menu without these options, and, to make matters worse, there is no window seating available. They will then need to request it, repeating information previously given to the chatbot and not provided. This repetition of excessive details can lead to complaints, and the client may never return.

Now, suppose that you have an integrated system where all the information is kept, and the necessary employees have access to it. One hour before they arrive at the restaurant, they receive a reminder of their reservation and are prompted to confirm that it still stands. At the same time, they can be given information about available parking nearby or valet services. When they arrive, they provide their name, are immediately led to a window seat, and are offered a gluten-free menu. This level of personalization will likely lead to increased customer satisfaction since all the information they have provided before will be readily available.

Hence, using omnichannels to integrate systems and provide information through different channels will give this customer a better experience. Those with a good experience will likely return, spend more, and become loyal to the business. While this example uses simple integration to demonstrate the efficiency of these channels, you can use as many channels as necessary to allow seamless communication. This includes integrating elements such as

- social media

- phone calls

- emails

- text messages

- chatbots

- landing pages

Currently, the market offers tools with different levels of complexity and prices for these integrations, such as Salesforce and Meta (with Facebook, Instagram, and WhatsApp), Zendesk, Customer IQ, and Replicant. At the same time, it is also possible to integrate and develop personalized existing systems to create optimal communication between channels. You can tailor each solution based on the size and industry in which your business operates.

All these integrations and the AI-powered solutions you have seen so far will culminate in an effortless process to only activate human support when necessary. The agent must deliver optimal performance that aligns with the company's strategy when needed. Therefore, in the final section of AI customer service tools implementation, we will explore how these tools will enable SMBs to improve agent performance, regardless of whether this agent is you or the hired support staff.

Improving Agent Performance With AI

No matter how much we try to automate business, there are times when it will be necessary for a human to come in and solve the problem. All the necessary information must be available, whether this person will be you if you are a solopreneur or hired staff. By keeping information updated and organized, it is possible to offer optimal service and inquiry resolution. Additionally, by having an AI tool that centralizes all the necessary information, you can optimize the time needed to search for files, find answers, and identify customer information.

When agents are provided with all the necessary and relevant information in one place, they can create better customer relationship management, especially if all the information is duly registered. In some cases, as you will see in Chapter 8, this will help you make informed and data-driven decisions that can be crucial for the business. Another advantage of having AI-assisted human agent customer service is the decreased time to provide relevant information and even develop solutions to the client's problems.

AI-assisted agents will be able to use these tools to focus on what *really* matters. This means reducing the time spent finding elementary answers or solutions and focusing on complex matters and sentiment analysis to avoid client loss. The time to answer queries will be reduced, and problem resolution will be faster. The agent can focus on what is bothering or making the client uneasy to increase satisfaction and loyalty. By offering AI support to agents, SMBs will find consistency in the offered service. This means the same information will be provided across all channels, regardless of whom they speak to.

Finally, mentioning the cost–benefit advantage of implementing these tools in your business is essential. They can be used to train new employees or recycle knowledge when necessary. By creating a robust database with company information, they can prompt these tools and have them act as teachers in solving common problems or offering advice during client interactions. This training capacity will allow the necessary knowledge to be available at all times in an updated and consistent manner, standardizing how the team is trained and how information is conveyed.

As you can see from all the information up to now, there are more than a few advantages to implementing AI into customer service for your business. Nonetheless, this does not mean that implementation does not come with challenges. As it tends to happen with novelty, SMBs must prepare for the pitfalls they might face during the process. Even if this is the case, you should not worry. As you will see in the following section, there are steps to successfully overcome these. Read on to find out what they are and the best course of action.

Overcoming Challenges and Pitfalls

Any new technology or novelty in a business will create advantages and challenges. The same can be said of AI applications in SMBs. The difference between overcoming these in an SMB and a large corporation is how fast you can implement the solutions that will make the systems more reliable. For this reason, it is essential to keep a constant feedback loop and evaluation services to ensure that all is going according to plan.

When these new adaptations occur, it will be commonplace to face obstacles, and being prepared to overcome them will be the difference between a satisfied and dissatisfied customer. Although all chapters (starting with this one) will have a client-based approach to AI implementation and improving business problems, predicting those directly impacting the user experience is essential for optimal service. Here are the most common issues you can face and potential solutions to resolving them:

- **Budgetary restrictions** – Conducting the necessary research can solve one of the most common restrictions on AI implementation in SMBs. Today's market offers numerous solutions at different prices, feature implementations, and performance levels. To ensure you find the best solution that balances cost and benefits, remember to refer to your AI implementation roadmap and determine your business's priorities.

- **Lack of training (staff)** – If you have staff who will use these tools, you should ensure that the service you are hiring offers the necessary training to guide them through the process. Even if you are the only one being trained, the software or product you are implementing should provide a user-friendly interface and robust documentation to help train personnel on its use.

- **Lack of training (customer)** – Customer training is a more sensitive topic since each will differ. Ideally, you should constantly communicate the new procedure to clients when implementing an AI tool. If necessary, the necessary documentation with a step-by-step approach should be made available to help them navigate the new process. Remember that if the client cannot use these features, they will be pointless, thus making it essential they have an optimal use and experience with the tools.

- **Technology limitations** – As you have seen in previous chapters, ensure that the hardware and software you are using can support the tools you will implement. While this might mean an initial unforeseen investment, it will be possible to revert these costs into income in the long run. Ensure that the technology you invest in is scalable and will support future demands to avoid needing to update systems and hardware again with new applications.

- **User resistance** — This is a more delicate issue, especially since controlling and predicting user behavior is impossible. The key to ensuring that customers and users adopt these new implementations is consistently demonstrating how they will optimize your company's customer service operations. By maintaining constant communication, illustrating benefits, and helping clients understand how this will make their journey easier, a more significant buy-in to AI use will be possible.

- **Escalation** — When adopting an AI tool, remember that it must be adequate for your future plans. This means that within your research, you should predict its scalability and adaptability for the operation's growth and new user needs. It is essential that during this process, you select a tool that will adjust and grow according to business needs.

- **Support and troubleshooting** — The final issue you should be aware of is the lack of support from the tool vendor. To prevent troubles or lack of support, you should ensure they have the tools to help you troubleshoot and resolve problems when necessary. Whether they are a large company or an SMB, they should be able to adjust to your needs and demands by providing just-in-time resolutions to any issues you must have. To ensure this is the case, look for recommendations and reputation evaluations during the research phase.

The Future of Customer Experience

It is safe to say that as technology expands the reach of AI tools, they will be more embedded than ever in customer service and experience. Ensuring that your business has a head start on its implementation will help you adapt for the future and be better prepared for new developments. If you identify this in the created roadmap as where your SMB could benefit the most, do not hesitate to look for adequate solutions.

Whether these are voice-activated or virtual assistants, chatbots, or any other options you have seen in this chapter, dedicate time to educating and communicating with customers regarding the changes. As users become more demanding of personalized solutions to their needs in a world of customized services, there are only benefits to obtain from this implementation. You can enhance sales and marketing techniques by providing these services to ensure your client base continuously increases.

In fact, this is exactly what we will explore in the next chapter. While maintaining the clients you already have is essential, you must also know how to leverage AI to increase this number and, consequently, sales. From helping you find the ideal audience and potential customers to developing tailored marketing campaigns, AI can do it all. Let's move forward to understand how to do this and obtain the best advantages from implementing AI into these processes.

Chapter Six

Supercharging Your Sales and Marketing

The first objective all businesspeople have, regardless of their industry, is to make more money. It does not matter if you have a restaurant, a web-designing company, an office supply store, or an online clothes store. Whatever your SMB does, you likely created it to help you increase your income, which means the more money it makes, the better off you will be. Businesses with positive results will give you options such as expanding, franchising, and even early retirement. All these are benefits to enjoy when your sales are going well.

At the same time, sales usually go hand-in-hand with two elements: customer satisfaction and marketing. If the client is unhappy, as you have seen in the previous chapter, they will likely not return or recommend your business to others. Similarly, if your business is not seen or heard about, it will be difficult for customers to know it exists. Therefore, to ensure steady sales, you must invest in these two areas, and the revenue will be the natural result.

However, many SMB owners have the same problem: They do not know how to be "commercial" about their business or feel they lack the creativity to create campaigns that will attract more customers. They are great at what they do, real experts, but they have difficulty showcasing their abilities and the optimal services or products that can be provided because they do not have adequate tools. If this is your case, know you are not alone.

It is common for professionals to struggle in these areas, especially if communication is not their strong point. This might be your case, and if it is, know that AI tools can help you overcome these barriers. On the other hand, it might be the case that you *are* good with sales and communication but have difficulty creating advertisements to convey your vision. It is not that you cannot communicate with clients personally, but rather that you don't know how to create marketing campaigns to attract those you do *not* talk to, generating leads.

Finally, we have the case of those who are excellent at what they do, great at communicating, and creative when generating campaigns but simply do not have the time and energy to focus on this. This is the case for another great portion of SMBs: The budget is limited, they are low on staff, and those who work there are overloaded with work to tend to needs from areas that are low or have no staff. On these occasions, you, the owner, will need to take time to create these if your agenda allows it.

All these are common situations with SMBs, even more frequent than most people imagine. This does not mean there is no solution; far from it! You will find that AI tools are great allies to help you supercharge company sales and create incredible marketing campaigns. From customer segmentation to lead identification and content creation for your communication channels, all this can be delegated to these tools. In this chapter, you will discover how to do this, saving time and energy and optimizing the tasks at which you excel. Are you ready to see how?

The Role of AI in Sales and Marketing

AI has a significant role in sales and marketing, helping SBA business owners to increase their reach and identify the target audience. The marketing and sales processes work together, with marketing helping to fuel sales, and sales showing the public toward whom the ads should be directed. In many cases, entrepreneurs may find it difficult to penetrate or identify the intended niche, especially if starting or looking to reach new clients. AI can help you do this and find adequate paths to achieve your objective.

Another significant role AI tools will play in business is to analyze business-related data. In this case, you can explore your audience and the areas in which you can improve your numbers. These include when your peak sales happen, the channels by which potential clients are reached, the products individuals are the most interested in, and even the best pricing opportunity for your products. AI's analytic capabilities can, in all cases, be leveraged to obtain insights on information relevant to your company.

This application of AI in business is not new. Companies such as Uber and Airbnb have been known to apply dynamic pricing to their operations to increase their yield when there is a high demand for a particular service or product. At the same time, other businesses use AI to forecast when they will have the most demand, allowing them to prepare for significant sales seasons and understand if their inventory must be stocked. These are all excellent opportunities to use these tools and make data-based decisions.

Finally, it is essential to recognize that AI has a creative power that will help you power communications and content creation. You can generate relevant articles for your website, blog, and marketing campaigns with the correct prompts and information. In the case of generative AI chatbots, they can generate multichannel cross-content campaigns. In a nutshell, this means conveying the same or similar content in different ways according to the channel you will use for communication, whether they are technology-based or not. From flier campaigns, location marketing, and sporadic promotions to social media and video campaigns, there are AI tools that will help expedite and optimize its creation and implementation.

Can AI be used to personalize these campaigns and reach different audiences by slightly modifying the content? Yes! It certainly can! As you have seen in the previous chapter, AI plays a significant role when creating tailor-made solutions for customer service personalization, and the same can be said for marketing campaigns and sales techniques. By offering the AI tool with the characteristics and intended result for the campaign you will create, it is possible to develop custom approaches depending on the target's characteristics.

Personalization to Increase Engagement

As you have seen in the previous chapter, customer engagement is essential for your business to grow. However, to ensure you have the best results, you must be able to attract the target groups that will bring you the largest sales volumes, and this can be a challenging task when you have limited time and budget. AI tools will help you increase efficiency and potentialize the marketing's reach. Leveraging the technology will enable you to find the preferences among customers of each group and tailor your message to attract them even more.

When you can make the customers identify themselves with what you have created, there is a bigger chance they will engage with your brand, ultimately leading to more purchases. Especially when dealing with online channels, it is essential to remember that there are diverse users on each platform, each with their own preferences, likes, and values. Therefore, the more you can personalize your communication to tend to their needs, the more likely they will engage with you.

Today, it has become the norm for customers to expect their experience to be tailored to their needs. Recent research has discovered that "81% of customers prefer companies that offer a personalized experience, and

70% say a personalized experience in which the employee knows who they are and their history with the company (past purchases, buying patterns, support calls, etc.) is important" (Hyken, 2024). This means that focusing on the right platforms and segmentation will make an incredible difference to your strategy.

This is the first of the process explored in this chapter: how AI tools can help you with sales and marketing. As you explore the potential of these tools for your business, you will see that they can make a difference in your results. Ultimately, "customers want convenience, and part of that is being able to connect with a brand the way they want to connect" (Hyken, 2024). Let's explore how it is possible to achieve this with AI and the impact its use can have on your business operations.

Customer Segmentation and Marketing

Large companies usually have a marketing department with specialists to identify customer profiles and determine the best action to take to increase sales. Many times, the process of identifying customers includes detailed research and a vast amount of data. These include polls, surveys, website data collection, and behavioral patterns gathering. As you might imagine, all this requires specialized professionals and a significant budget to optimize the operation.

At the same time, with the arrival of AI tools, especially those that work with NLP, it is possible to use them for all companies to perform the same analysis at a near-zero cost. What is even better is that the more time goes by, the more advanced and specialized these tools become, generating more accurate and precise results. To illustrate, let's look at an application of how the free version of GPT-4o would work.

The newly released version of the tool offers users who do not pay subscriptions the opportunity to use the tool with internet access. In addition, you can also use GPTs, which are programs created by third parties, and use the tool's capabilities for a specific purpose. In this case, this combination makes it possible to explore the tool's powerful database and obtain real-time information by accessing the internet and using specialized GPTs. With a quick search by clicking on "Explore GPT," you will find the options for

- carrying out specific customer segmentation analysis

- analyzing customer demographics

- separating customers per interest groups

- identifying customer preferences

- personalizing customer communication

While all this is possible with ChatGPT, remember that several other tools can help you do this, which are easily found on the internet. Ultimately, the main benefit these tools will bring is the ability to analyze large amounts of data and identify insights where they are not obvious. This means you might be able to establish relationships and gain knowledge of elements that will help you strategize and take action to improve your business performance.

By focusing on customer segmentation and targeting your marketing to their needs and demands, you will be able to diversify strategies and create different forms of communication for each group. This will ensure you have a larger reach, potentially increasing brand engagement and resulting in more revenue. Understanding what a target audience or customer group prefers will help you tailor products and services, adjust the strategy, and find alternatives to expand your business.

AI is an excellent tool for doing this and will seamlessly act as an assistant to perform these tasks. Use its capabilities to conduct customer behavioral and psychological analysis to create effective strategies that produce results.

Doing so will strengthen your customer base and increase sales potential. We will look at attention harnessing next: using AI tools to help you optimize lead generation and increase the client base.

Optimizing Lead Generation

Lead generation is possibly one of the most important tasks your business must carry out. This process means you attract potential customers to your communication channels to make potential sales. For example, when you post an ad on social media for a product or service, the idea is to have clicks so that interested parties go to your webpage or channel and purchase. Although lead generation is not the sales process, it is a significant part of helping you make your selling more attractive.

Lead generation is usually composed of four parts (Aggarwal, 2024):

- **Lead capture:** This identifies information that can lead you to customers. This could mean collecting phone numbers, email addresses, social media handles, and other communication methods. These leads will allow you to reach the customer, offer solutions, and promote your business. When doing so, you should ascertain that you capture the necessary information from them so you can send messages to remind them of your business offerings. This is especially relevant considering the number of businesses in the market today.

- **Lead magnets:** Social media is undeniably a good channel with the best resources to capture potential user interest. However, there is a large gap between the customer looking at a social media ad and clicking on it to enter your website to make a purchase. One of the best ways to capture leads is to ask customers to click to receive a benefit associated with your business, such as a discount, information, or even a free product. Doing so will prompt them to insert their information and provide you with details voluntarily.

- **Lead qualification:** When you obtain leads, you must qualify them to analyze whether they will likely make a purchase. This means classifying them based on their interests and seeing their potential to become customers. In these individuals, you should focus and further segment them according to their characteristics.

- **Lead segmentation:** Segmenting your leads into specific groups will help you better understand their interests and which one you should send each type of communication to. To some, you will direct email messages; to others, you might use push notifications. You will be able to choose the most relevant criteria for the business to determine when and where to send each message. One example of how to do this is to separate loyal customers from those who only make seasonal purchases, sending more messages to the latter during the holiday season.

This process can be overwhelming, especially when you do not have the knowledge or experience to carry out the task. Luckily, AI can help you with the process and provide you with the necessary tools to do it. Think about social media platforms such as Facebook and Instagram. When you prepare an ad for this audience, you must describe who your target is and all relevant details. Based on this information, it is possible to direct the ads to each group for the algorithm distributions. At the same time, these tools will not determine *who* you should choose; rather, you should use your choices to determine the other users to whom information should be reached.

For optimal use, the business owner must provide the parameters, which is when the segmentation will prove to be useful. Here are the steps one must take to optimize AI during this process and ensure optimal reach:

1. Capture leads with lead magnets.

2. Qualify leads based on business interest criteria.

3. Segment leads into groups.

4. Design the campaign directed toward each group.

5. Upload the camping and select the targeted profiles.

In this simple step-by-step process, AI can be used in all phases, although perhaps the first one should be done by you. The main reason is that it will be the most crucial in the process, as it will gather the raw data used in the process. Nonetheless, you can use AI tools to categorize, clean, and organize the database that will be analyzed. Once all the necessary data has been gathered, it is possible to leverage AI to do almost any other task, such as creating buyer profiles, finding different target customers, diversifying strategy, and personalizing messages. Doing so will give you a competitive advantage over other businesses.

When you have the necessary information, go back to the social media example and determine the interests, age group, gender, and location of the target audience. These will be provided by the AI tool, which will help you find suitable candidates and optimize how you will spend your budget. At the same time, while it will be possible to target a group of *usual* customers and increase their purchasing potential, you can also use it to find other groups to target, especially if you want to diversify your customer base. If this is the case, you must remember each group will be attracted to a distinct message and tone; which leads us to the next step of the process: campaign creation and content enhancement.

Campaign Creation and Content Enhancement

SMBs are usually composed of people who excel in an area and have decided to work for themselves. In this case, they will be responsible for most of the business operations and managing the day-to-day operations. In many cases, this can be overwhelming and challenging, especially if there is no prior knowledge of the peripheral tasks that must be carried out. One of these areas is marketing and attracting more customers to your business.

You have seen that AI can help you segment the customer base, but what are the best ways to reach them and ensure the message is well received and resonates with them? This is a common question since what we think is a good approach might not always sound the same to others. In this case, you must find the best alternatives to provide this audience with the content they expect to receive and a campaign to attract their interest.

For many companies, this means hiring a specialized marketing team or outsourcing the task, but this might not always be possible or feasible. This means you might need help creating marketing campaigns, which can be difficult when you do not have the necessary knowledge to create enticing content that will bring results. It is not uncommon for SMBs to face these challenges, which is one of the main reasons why AI tools have become so popular with owners in these industries. Luckily, AI can often help with marketing campaigns from end to end and help you achieve the ideal ad.

AI tools allow anyone to use "normal" conversation and minimum knowledge to create incredible campaigns. These can have poetic texts and beautiful images that will captivate the audience. It is essential to create quality content that will resonate with the target and spark their interest in knowing more about your business. Whether you want to create a video, a jingle, an inspiring text, or a full-blown campaign for different challenges, AI can help you.

AI can help with everything from understanding what the audience wants to translating it into effective content and leading them to take action. Think about it: After segmenting the customer base and identifying the leads to attract, you must efficiently prompt the tool and ask it to tailor the content to each. This will be especially useful when creating, for example, cross-platform campaigns. Let's look at two examples of how this can be applied in a social media context.

Suppose you have a business that customizes cups for specific events. They can be used at weddings, christenings, birthdays, and company events. This means you have a vast public you can reach, demanding that you create specific campaigns for each of these. In this context, you could use AI in the following manner to streamline your production, enhance content, and create campaigns:

- **Increasing cross-platform reach:** Cross-platform marketing means you will use the same campaign across different channels. In this case, you will use the same topic and different approaches to target the same audience. In this case, you will need to create different text, for example, to reach brides who see the ad on Instagram and those who see it on Facebook. Nonetheless, you are still reaching brides but do not want the content to be repetitive. Instead, you will bring a different approach and elements, thus enhancing the content to ensure they are attracted to your brand.

- **Diversifying the same message to different audiences:** Conversely to the previous item, you may want to reach different audiences, and they will each need a distinct approach. What attracts brides might not necessarily be the same as what will attract parents for christenings, adult birthdays, and even children's birthdays. In this case, you must create similar ads with a different focus based on each customer you want to reach. You can enhance different product features to ensure they are attracted to what you are offering.

In both cases, you can use AI to diversify the approach and create different campaigns. Using these tools, you can craft one ad that will be modified based on the target and the channel without having to rethink the strategy and approach. By using a prompt asking the tool to adjust the content to the different audiences, situations, or platforms, it will be possible to enhance the content with just a few keystrokes. This approach will save you time and ensure a more targeted approach with the intended audience, converting more sales with an optimized strategy.

Dynamic Pricing and Offer Optimization

Another advantage of using AI is identifying the pricing options and offer optimization. If you have used ride-sharing apps, such as Uber, you have probably noticed that the price is higher during certain periods when the demand is larger. An AI algorithm determines this by leveraging the increased interest in a product or service to make it more expensive and generate a larger yield based on need and demand.

If you have an SMB, it is possible to use these algorithms to determine the products most in demand and the best time to optimize the price. Consider an airline company to see how this works in a large business. The prices will be higher or lower depending on the seat demand based on the time of the year. Prices might be higher during the summer or school vacations but lower during the winter, depending on where you are going, such as beach destinations. On the other hand, when it is winter, you might see these prices rise for popular skiing destinations.

At the same time, this might not necessarily affect the prices and how much you are selling, but it creates a sense of urgency in those buying a certain product. Still using the same airline example, suppose you want a ticket to go skiing at a certain destination and enter a website to look for a ticket. It is common to see the information on the website: *last 2 tickets available.* This can happen for two reasons: The first is that these are really the last tickets available, and the business is pushing to sell them at a higher price, or that they are *not* selling enough tickets for the destination and want to increase its sales.

In both situations you have seen above, AI is used to help companies make more sales and optimize their prices to earn more. In this case, while implementing the algorithm might not be as budget-friendly as you wish, leveraging it optimally may benefit your company. These include associating them to understand market trends and customer behavior, possibly making your profits rise. In this case, the value of implementing a more costly solution would be an advantage to your SMB since, in the long run, the results would be identifiable.

Here are a few ways you could use these AI algorithms in SMB examples to help you understand the potential:

- optimizing prices in ecommerce, higher for those that sell more and lower for those that sell less

- finding dishes that sell less in a restaurant and offering them for a lower price on certain days, such as a dish of the day

- promoting a new product for users to try and obtain customer loyalty

- associating a market trend to an offered service or product to leverage its price and availability

- optimizing sales for products you want to release from inventory without reducing the cost

As you can see, leveraging AI into these possibilities can enhance your sales process and even your marketing strategy, allowing you to gain more interest from potential and existing customers. This will be an opportunity to showcase what you offer without decreasing the price significantly or offering high discounts, allowing you to maintain a relevant income. Associated with this algorithm and bringing it even more significant power are those associated with price optimizations and have sales forecasting and insight features. Let's take a look at how these can be used to help your SMB prosper in the currently competitive market.

Sales Forecasting and Insights

Sales forecasting is a crucial business aspect that is usually part of the business plan that will help you understand how you will perform. By carrying out this process properly, you can understand your sales, especially when you analyze the customer segment you are targeting and obtain insights into their behavior. This is a significant and ongoing process for all businesses that will eventually help you make projections regarding investments and strategy.

In the previous section, you saw how AI can help you optimize prices and sales. However, this will be much less effective if you do not know who you will target, how, and their behavior. A sales forecast will help you establish the metrics you want to achieve. Usually, businesses will determine their KPIs and understand their performance based on the results. Forecasting sales and achieving the desired results means your business is going well, and you have the right strategy. Not reaching it means you might need to make adjustments.

With the help of AI, it is possible to obtain insights into all these KPIs and see what and where you need to improve. Here are a few metrics and examples of how this can be used:

- Customer time on the website – AI tools can track and trace customer behavior on the website, the areas they are most attracted to, where they click, and prompt feedback to understand why the purchase was not made. By using AI to leverage this cookie collection, which is common to most websites, it will be possible to understand what needs to be improved and what is working well.

- Number of clicks and conversions – AI can help you understand how your customers are attracted to your marketing efforts and how often this leads to a conversion. When it is applied, you can identify how many customers can go to the webpage based on an ad or another affiliated channel and how often this leads to a purchase, helping you identify the ads that have the greatest impact and the best channels.

- Most and less popular products – Using AI, SMBs can analyze their performance and see the most popular and less popular products, not only based on sales. This means the tool will analyze the clicks, how often people access certain pages, and their interactions, such as saving to a list. It is also possible to see what products are frequently bought together.

- Average spending per customer type – Another popular use of AI is understanding what kinds of customers purchase what products and their average spending per these. By leveraging this use, it will be possible to segment the customer base according to their habits and preferences, allowing you to target them in marketing campaigns.

- Number of products in the cart – When you leverage AI, you can use its analytical capacity to see how many people leave their carts with products, how long they take to purchase, and even if they do purchase. This will give you more precise forecasting and insights into their behavior and the drivers of what leads them to buy.

As you can see, AI can bring significant advantages to businesses that want to have a deep analytical sense of your performance, how customers interact with their pages and advertisements, and purchase patterns. This will let you analyze the data and have insights into each of these areas, giving you a better idea of how your business performs and what drives customers to buy or not, allowing you to optimize your strategy. The gathered data will give you a chance to make decisions based on what is happening with facts; a data-driven decision-making process to support critical analysis.

Data-Driven Decision-Making

Decisions you make usually determine if your business will make or break. Business owners usually need an overview of the business operations and specific data to analyze problematic or overperforming areas. By analyzing these specific metrics, you can understand what your business is doing well, what needs to improve, and where expectations are being met. This could mean that you can think of other solutions to associate with well-performing products or services and rethink the strategy or design of those that are not.

Data-driven decisions are an essential part of the business process, but it is important to consider that it should not be the only part of the process. While the data can be used for analysis and an important aid in supporting your decisions, you must use it wisely. Therefore, you should always use this as an additional tool for your critical thinking process. As a business owner, critical thinking will be essential to make the best decisions, and you will need to exercise it to determine the steps you will take.

AI can, for example, tell you that a product is overperforming with a certain group in a specific channel. This means you will need to determine what *other* groups you want to focus on or if you want to reach more customers within this group. This will be a decision you must make and the budget allocated. At the same time, if you have a product or service that is not performing as you wish according to the data, you will need to use critical thinking to understand if this is because of the marketing channels, groups, or budget allocated to campaigns. It can, perhaps, even be something that is not interesting to others.

The AI tool can give you the data and the necessary analysis, but it will be up to you to make the final decision and understand the following steps. Ultimately, it will be a matter of understanding what drives clients and promotes sales, allowing your business to make an income and generate money. As you have seen, AI can be an incredibly powerful tool, and focusing on the tools that will give you access to this is essential. In many cases, you will find there are tools for specific purposes and others that will aggregate them all—you will have to decide based on budget and application to determine what is best for you.

However, it is not only on the *outside* or what customers see that AI can help you with. As we move on to the next chapter, you will see how these tools can help you optimize your business process, automate tasks, and make operations more efficient. From optimizing the logistic chain to making document management easier, you will see its different implementations and how this can help you in the most varied areas. Let's keep moving forward and exploring!

Chapter Seven

Streamlining Operations With AI–Driven Business Process Automation

As an SMB owner, you likely do not have the time or resources to manage all processes independently. This is normal, and usually, budgetary constraints prevent you from hiring all the personnel you might need. At the same time, you have limited hours in the day to manage all the necessary tasks, and inevitably, some of them are left behind, especially when not a priority. When this happens, it can lead to stoppages in the processes or delays when addressing important matters.

While many believe that process automation (BPA) focuses more on machinery and large production plants, this is not necessarily true. BPA can refer to the automation in any part of your process, from document management to sending emails to clients and potential leads. As you might imagine, AI is a great facilitator for this process, as it will be able to understand your demands and instructions to make your tasks more seamless and efficient.

Leveraging AI to carry out BPA will help you have more time for matters that require your personalized attention and aid you in carrying out repetitive tasks. In this chapter, you will explore how AI can be used to streamline your operations with BPA and make your processes more efficient. Learn how to use AI as an assistant to improve time management and automate operations that do not require significant intervention. If you are curious about how AI can help you optimize your workflow, read on and discover its power for BPA.

Fundamentals of BPA

Business processes are any activities or tasks that must be carried out to achieve a result or outcome. Since it is related to the keyword *business,* these directly relate to our company and any process you must carry out. These processes can include, but are not limited to

- payroll

- lead generation

- customer interaction

- sales orders

- data collection

- IT support

- invoicing

- software and system backup

All these activities require repetitive tasks and do not necessarily need human oversight to be adequately carried out. When you use BPA, managing a high volume of tasks, such as customer calls or inquiries, solving issues with a time-sensitive nature (like system backup), and optimizing resources (such as using a program to input and generate invoices) is possible. When businesses implement this automation within their processes, it can streamline activities and produce faster results. Additionally, by leveraging technology, you can obtain relevant insights from processes and analysis you can use for the decision-making process.

It is not uncommon for many SMBs to believe that they will be unable to implement BPA into their businesses, either because they do not meet the necessary criteria or think it is costly. In both instances, this assertion is incorrect since all companies can benefit from BPA, and there are software options that are not as costly as you might imagine. For example, you can use an AI-powered accounting program to help you separate your invoices and receipts per category and help you during tax season. This BPA costs anywhere from $49.99 a month to $399.99 a year.

The basic idea of BPA is to help you optimize resources, allocate money, and apply the process to the business areas that require it the most. For example, $399.99 might seem like a lot of money to spend on a yearly plan for accounting software. However, consider how much time you will save when preparing for tax season and the hourly rate you will not need to pay an accountant to review the information. In fact, this software will perhaps help you avoid them altogether if you have the necessary skills.

According to Chiu et al. (2015), "work that occupies 45% of employee time could be automated by adapting currently available or demonstrated technology." Although this does not mean that all jobs could be fully automated, only 5% of the currently existing positions would allow this, it does mean that 30% or more of current work activities in the US can be automated. AI has significantly impacted the process, allowing companies to adapt and adjust their activities so employees can focus on more relevant areas and not on constant repetition.

Therefore, the question that remains is where these opportunities can be implemented in your SMB. Different businesses will have distinct needs for automation. A customized T-shirt printing company will not have the same needs as a restaurant, and it will not have the same needs as a software development business. *So, how do I identify this?* That is an excellent question you are about to explore next.

Identifying Opportunities for BPA

It is common to feel overwhelmed when managing your SMB, especially due to the tasks that need to be carried out with limited resources. However, it is important that, as an owner, you take some time to identify the processes that can be automated and that will facilitate your daily activities. This means understanding time-consuming and repetitive tasks that do not need additional insight. By taking the time to do this, you will find it easier to increase your efficiency and productivity.

Five elements you should consider for this identification are:

1. **Identify your objective:** When deciding to carry out a BPA, identify the objective you aim to achieve. These can include responding to clients faster, automating invoices, or any other process that demands unnecessary hours and can be automated. The objective should be clear and significantly improve what you are doing today.

2. **Identify automatable tasks:** Take some time to identify within your SMB the tasks that can be automated. Consider the repetitive tasks you carry out manually. Within the established objective, identify all the associated activities that can be automated to offer a more streamlined, optimized process to save time. When thinking about these tasks, consider that "frequently repeated tasks are good candidates and more expensive than performing a task

manually once or even a few times" (Luther, 2023).

3. **Analyze cost–benefit:** Once you have tasks that can be automated, you will need to carry out an analysis to help you identify the ones that represent an excellent cost–benefit opportunity. If these tasks allow you to save resources and time, then they are a good opportunity. In many cases, you will need to understand the cost of the solution you want to implement and compare it to the price of carrying it out manually. If this offers a saving opportunity, you should establish it as an option. If not, then consider its implications for the overall business operation. By understanding this, it will be possible to determine the tasks you will start with.

4. **Prioritize:** Prioritizing the tasks you will automate first is essential. You will soon see that you must complete one automation at a time until you are sure it fully functions. Therefore, once you identify the objective, you should prioritize making your work more efficient. According to Luther (2023), business owners should consider focusing "on automating a single type of process across the company, rather than to switch between very different processes continually. Rollouts of automation may be faster, cheaper, and high quality if you don't try to implement too many different types of changes."

5. **Establish a plan:** Now that you clearly understand all the areas where you can implement BPA, it is time to establish a plan and prepare for its implementation. Once again, it is essential to remember you should not try to automate more than one process at a time, nor move on to the next one until you are sure the first task is automated correctly and works well. By defining a plan and a strategy, you will be able to determine the timeline

for implementation, the deadline for its completion, and KPIs to establish if it is efficient. The plan should guide you through all the steps and be the roadmap to optimize solutions.

Author's note: Consider the solution's scalability when identifying potential business areas for BPA implementation. This means the solution you select must support increased demand, making it easier for your business to grow. In this sense, looking for programs that will serve your business needs at the moment is always advisable but can also take over more demand if necessary.

To help you identify areas for automation, here is a short list of areas to consider:

- HR processes include onboarding, job description creation, resume filtering, and onboarding processes.

- Financial tasks such as invoice generation, receipt filing and identification, and accounting processes that will facilitate tax filing.

- Marketing activities include brainstorming, creating campaigns, finding leads, identifying target audience preferences, and multichannel communication.

- Customer relationship interactions include automatic responses, chatbot implementation, and review analysis.

- Logistic processes include inventory management, purchase responses, order management, and transportation updates.

With these areas in mind, it is time to start considering the implementation process. As you can see, BPA implementation is key to the process, regardless of whether you are working independently or have employees. The software you select should have certain characteristics that allow significant buy-in and ease of use. Let's take a closer look in the next section.

Implementing BPA Solutions

BPA solutions will undoubtedly make your life easier—as long as you can ascertain a seamless process and involve all the relevant stakeholders. This means that, for example, if you are implementing a chatbot to help with customer interactions, they are knowledgeable of the change and that their needs are tended to by the application. If there is no buy-in from the relevant stakeholders in the process, your implementation will likely fail, causing distress as well as time and financial loss.

Although the process is different for each SMB, it involves having user-friendly systems that can be integrated with other software, giving you more freedom and facilitating its use. During this process, a few key elements you should consider evaluating, and that should be provided by AI software supplier, include

- available documentation for support

- training relevant key users

- support channels in case of a system crash

- accuracy and reliability

- backup capability

Even so, with all the necessary support, you may need technical assistance and guidance when implementing BPA solutions. This is especially true if you are integrating them with other existing systems. When doing so, you must ensure that all the existing information is backed up during integration. The success of BPA solutions depends on the seamless integration of these tools with existing business processes and software.

It is important to choose AI tools that are compatible with your current systems and scalable to accommodate future growth. When selecting a BPA solution, you should consider the software's flexibility, ease of integration, and the availability of APIs, which allow for smooth data exchange between platforms. This level of interoperability ensures that the BPA tools enhance, rather than disrupt, daily operations.

Another critical aspect during implementation is ensuring data security and compliance, especially given the increased regulatory pressures on businesses to protect customer and operational data. When implementing a BPA solution, you should prioritize systems that offer robust encryption, regular security updates, and compliance with industry standards. It is also essential to ensure that the system you are integrating into your existing programs does not threaten any information you already have.

These precautions will protect the business from potential breaches and build trust with customers and partners. Additionally, implementing role-based access controls within these systems can help manage who has access to sensitive information, further safeguarding your business. Ensure compliance documentation and an AI policy for when the tasks can be automated and when the AI is used. There should be clear guidance on the rules employees must follow and adhere to.

Although the technical side is essential for the business, you should remember that successful BPA implementation requires a structured approach that accounts for the unique challenges faced by SMBs. Beyond simply integrating new technologies and informing those who work with you that the changes will be made and they will be trained on them, it is essential to create a culture of adaptability and openness to change. After all, it is not all about technology; it is also about the people who use it.

One of the ways to achieve this is to involve all relevant stakeholders early in the process, ensuring they understand the benefits and functionalities of the new system. When you provide comprehensive training and continuous support, you can address concerns beforehand and ease the transition.

You should also consider establishing a feedback system that can measure the effectiveness of the implementation and take action if any adjustments are necessary. These steps will help you support the BPA implementation and help employees feel more confident about their actions.

During the implementation process, keep change management into account within a controlled environment and ensure that each step of the process is monitored. This management should happen when the new AI program is implemented, during employee training sessions, and daily use. It might take some time to get the whole team used to the new system, but eventually, they will be able to identify the benefits it will bring. You should ensure that all the relevant stakeholders are informed and trained on the process for optimal results.

After the implementation, it is time to explore more areas where BPA can help your SMB. One of the main areas of struggle for these companies is the complexities of document management. Whether managing financial documentation, employee records, or corporate documents, AI can transform this process. Businesses can automate the organization, retrieval, and analysis of their documents by leveraging AI-powered document management systems. These systems can intelligently categorize documents, extract key information, and even detect patterns that might go unnoticed. As you will see in the next section, this will help streamline your operations and significantly reduce the time and resources spent on managing paperwork.

Optimizing Document Management

Consider your daily operations. Have you ever noticed how much paperwork you have to deal with? There are different types of documents for every business area, and depending on your industry, these can have an incredible volume that is hard to manage. AI-powered document management systems are revolutionizing how SMBs handle their documents, making the process smoother and more efficient regardless of their knowledge of technology. These systems use advanced features to automatically process, classify, and retrieve documents, saving time and reducing the number of errors that can happen when they are human-managed.

Imagine no longer having to spend countless hours sorting through paperwork or countless digital files to find what you need. This is certainly not a good use of your time. The matter is even more essential when dealing with regulatory issues or when tax season comes. Not having your company's documentation organized can even get you fined. The good news is that AI can organize all this and find documents for you in seconds. This will help speed up your workflow and ensure you can make faster and more informed decisions based on accurate and immediately available information.

One of the most significant benefits of AI-powered document management systems is their ability to automate document classification. Traditional methods often require manual sorting, which is time-consuming and susceptible to mistakes. With AI, you can implement a system that automatically categorizes your documents by recognizing patterns, keywords, and context. These are invoices, contracts, and customer records, among others, which can all be sorted without manual intervention. This automated classification reduces the risk of misfiling and makes it easier to retrieve documents when needed.

Depending on the program you are using, it is possible to store these documents within its *secure* database, which will help you search for what you need. Instead of filtering through folders and files, you just need to type in a keyword, and the AI will locate the document you need. This is particularly useful for SMBs that may not have the luxury of having dedicated employees or an IT department to manage their digital files. The AI can even learn from your search habits, improving accuracy and speed. This means you will spend less time searching for information and more time focusing on your core activities.

Next comes the matter of compliance with regulatory requirements. AI can be an essential tool to help you manage these, especially those with strict document storage, access, and retention regulations. These programs can be adjusted to automatically ensure your documents meet these requirements, such as flagging documents with missing essential information, ensuring sensitive files are securely stored, and automating retention and archive tasks under legal guidelines. This will reduce noncompliance risk, which can lead to costly fines and other legal issues.

At the same time, once again, you must remember that when choosing automated document management software, you must read its privacy and security policies. Sensitive documents like contracts, client information, and financial records must be stored safely and cannot be used by programs that do not protect the data. Due to this, you must always read the terms and conditions of the software you plan on implementing to ensure it meets the requirements. ChatGPT, for example, would be an example of what not to use since it uses inputs and outputs to train the machine, which might make your data vulnerable.

Still on the compliance issue, you should know there are AI compliance management tools you can use that will continuously monitor changes in regulations and adjustments in document management practices. When you have a program that takes this proactive approach, your business will always be prepared for audits or regulatory reviews without needing to track every update manually. The AI system can also generate reports demonstrating your compliance efforts, providing peace of mind and freeing up resources that would otherwise be spent on these tasks.

If you are a nontech-savvy business owner, implementing these programs might seem challenging and even risky. It is impossible to say it is not, especially because these systems need human monitoring and oversight to ensure efficiency. At the same time, most of these tools are designed to be user-friendly, offering intuitive interfaces and easy-to-use features that do not require technical knowledge. Many vendors will also provide the necessary training and support so you get the best outcome, which is essential.

If your option is to use an AI system to organize these documents, be sure to ask all the necessary questions relevant to your industry when speaking to a vendor. It will help you streamline your operations without needing to be a tech expert, but you will need to supervise the whole process. When you can implement automation in these tasks, you can increase your focus on the business and save increasingly more time supervising the program as you learn how it works.

Streamlining Supply Chain Operations

Depending on the SMB you run, it might be essential to implement BPA to streamline your supply chain operations. In this case, AI can optimize key processes such as demand forecasting, inventory management, order processing, and logistics coordination. These advancements lead to improved efficiency, reduced operational costs, and enhanced competitiveness in an increasingly complex market. For SMBs, which often operate with limited resources, integrating AI into the supply chain can significantly change how they operate, especially regarding market demands.

One of BPA's biggest impacts on supply chain operations is leveraging its ability to predict demand accurately. Traditional forecasting methods rely on historical data but often cannot adjust to real-time market changes. At the same time, when you add AI into the mix, it can analyze incredible amounts of data from different sources, including market trends, consumer behavior, and even weather patterns, to accurately predict demand. When this happens, you can anticipate customer and market needs, reducing the risk of overstocking or understocking as well as aligning your production and purchasing strategy with a realistic market demand.

Inventory management is another critical area where AI-driven BPA can significantly improve efficiency. By automating inventory tracking and analysis, AI can provide real-time insights into stock levels, identify slow-moving or obsolete items, and suggest optimal reorder points. This will help you avoid the costs associated with excess inventory and ensure popular items are always in stock, leading to higher customer satisfaction.

A restaurant, for example, can use these AI tools to analyze the dishes that are ordered the most and always have a supply of ingredients to make them and fewer of those for the dishes that are ordered less. If you have a product delivery service, you can use AI to optimize your operation by suggesting the most efficient storage locations and picking routes, helping you with stock management. The possibilities are endless, and all you must do is understand where the process can be automated and where AI can hel p.

If you consider order processing, for example, implementing AI BPA can significantly reduce the time and effort required to manage customer orders. The program can automatically validate order details, check inventory availability, and suggest alternative products if an item is out of stock. It can also streamline the invoicing process by automatically generating and sending invoices to customers, reducing the risk of error and speeding up payments. This translates into faster order fulfillment, improved cash flow, and an effective customer experience, contributing to greater busines s efficiency.

Logistics is another area to look into when dealing with an AI-powered BPA supply chain. This is one of the most complex areas to make changes, but it can be greatly enhanced when AI is leveraged correctly. Using its power, you can optimize routing and delivery schedules by analyzing traffic conditions, fuel costs, and delivery time windows. This will ensure that shipments are delivered on time and at the lowest cost possible. You will see in Chapter 15 that logistics companies, such as UPS, are already implementing this strategy. For SMBs, which may lack the extensive logistics networks of larger companies, this BPA can level the playing field by making operations more efficient and cost-effective.

Finally, AI-driven BPA can help SMBs improve supplier relationships and negotiation outcomes. AI can identify trends and potential issues by analyzing supplier performance data, such as late deliveries or quality concerns. Since the information will be readily available, you can address these problems promptly and proactively. It can also help you negotiate better terms with suppliers and provide data-driven insights into market prices and demand forecasts. All these actions will help you secure better deals and ensure a more reliable supply chain, reducing the risk of disruptions.

While these solutions may sound incredibly complex, remember that most applications are user-friendly and designed to integrate with your existing systems. This means that your business, even with limited technical expertise, can already start benefiting from an AI-driven supply chain without a steep learning curve. You should always consider the previously mentioned elements when deciding, especially the support you will receive from the vendor and the potential scalability over time.

But how do I decide if my AI-powered BPA is being successful and bringing me advantages? That is an excellent question, which will be addressed in the following section. After all, AI BPA implementation might sound beautiful as you read it here, but at the back of your head, you wonder, *How much will it cost?* This is a valid concern, especially if you do not start to see the immediate results. Let's move on to the following section and see how you can effectively measure the results of this implementation and, even then, when AI can help you with the process.

Measuring Success and Return on Investment

Measuring the success and return on investment (ROI) of AI-driven BPA initiatives is essential to determine whether their implementation delivers benefits. This can be done by implementing metrics and KPIs that can be used to track progress, make informed decisions, and further optimize operations. The key here is to focus on actionable insights that align with the business's specific goals and to choose the metrics that truly reflect the BPA implementation results.

One of the most important metrics is the process cycle time. This metric measures the time it takes to complete a specific business process from the beginning to the end. Since reducing process cycle time is the main objective of implementing BPA solutions, you should measure how the operational efficiency is affected. For instance, if the order processing time decreases by 40% after AI implementation, this indicates a significant efficiency gain. Regularly monitoring this metric will help you identify the bottleneck in your SMB and further refine the process.

At the same time, you might be implementing SBA to reduce errors in manually performed tasks. In this case, this will be another critical metric to observe and measure to validate the effectiveness of BPA implementation. Manual processes are prone to human error, leading to costly mistakes and rework. When you automate these processes, the incidence of errors will be reduced, and you will be able to track the results before and after the AI tool is implemented. Metrics such as output quality, number of disruptions, and reduction in general error rates will help increase customer satisfaction.

Another reason why you might be implementing AI-driven BPA solutions is to reduce your operational costs. In this case, the metric will be directly related to the ROI, and you should calculate the total costs of implementing and operating the tool. These will include hardware and software, training, maintenance, and other necessary materials. Once you have the sum of these costs, you will need to measure them against the financial benefits gained from efficiency, reduced error rates, and lower labor costs.

Suppose an AI system allows your business to reduce your workforce by 10% while maintaining or improving productivity. This means that the cost savings this will represent can be substantial. You should also factor in the long-term savings from avoiding errors and rework, which can add up significantly over time.

Several alternatives exist to help you monitor these KPIs, such as a scorecard approach, which will provide a comprehensive view of financial and operational performance. This method includes traditional financial metrics like cost savings associated with process metrics. This system is mainly efficient due to its holistic understanding of how the newly implemented BPA affects the business. It will ensure that the focus is not only on cost but also on improving overall business performance.

Based on your insights, developing an action plan and establishing benchmarks to evaluate performance is possible. You must regularly review these baseline metrics before the implementation and then set a target for each KPI. To reduce the process cycle time by 30% or cut errors by 50% by the first 6 months of implementation, you must accurately determine how these metrics perform today. Once you have done so and implemented the AI tool, you will be able to monitor these metrics better and establish the impact they had on the business.

In addition to manually tracking each metric, you can use AI tools to help analyze and monitor these metrics. By doing so, you will leverage the tool's data analysis capacity to generate actionable insights and monitor what is happening in the business in real time. Many AI-driven BPA solutions present today come with built-in analytics capabilities that automatically track performance metrics and generate reports. These tools can identify trends, flag areas needing attention, and even suggest optimization strategies. For those owners who may not have the necessary time or expertise to evaluate the data manually, these can be beneficial and another process automation.

Leveraging the power of AI can improve processes and maximize ROI, allowing you to invest in other areas of the business. However, despite all these benefits, AI-powered BPA implementation is not easy or comes without its challenges. As you will see in this chapter's last section, this can happen in different business areas. Let's explore these and the potential solutions to solving them without creating too many disruptions.

Overcoming Implementation Challenges

As it will generally happen with any change, it is important to consider possible unforeseen circumstances, resistance, and setbacks when implementing AI-driven BPA. These can result from several challenges, including concerns about data quality and quantity, the complexities of integrating new business processes and programs into existing ones, employee and customer resistance, and lack of the necessary support, to name a few. Proactively addressing these challenges is key to ensuring that you have a smooth and successful implementation, maximizing benefits, and minimizing obstacles.

Here are the four elements that were previously mentioned and that offer the most significant challenges for SMBs implementing BPA systems:

- **Data quality issues:** As you know, AI solutions depend highly on data to produce accurate output, and this is also the case for BPA processes. Poor data quality (e.g., incomplete or inadequate) can lead to underperformance of the AI system, resulting in incorrect analysis or providing misinformation for decision-making. These significant challenges will undermine your efforts to implement an AI solution and lead to wasted money and time.

  Solution: To overcome this challenge, SMBs should prioritize data gathering, cleaning, preparation, and validation before implementing AI solutions. This includes verifying the data-gathering process and auditing existing information to identify and correct errors and ensure the new data complies with established standards. AI tools that include data preprocessing features can automate some of these tasks, improving overall data quality and the reliability of the BPA system.

- **Resistance to change:** This challenge can result from several different elements and, due to this, can appear in different ways. These include all the skepticism about AI's benefits to the business and the fear of job displacement. Employees might be concerned about how AI-driven solutions such as BPA will impact their roles or may feel overwhelmed by learning new technologies.

  Solution: SMB owners should focus on change management strategies emphasizing communication, education, and inclusion. Start by clearly communicating the benefits of AI-driven BPA to the team, highlighting how it will reduce mundane tasks and allow them to focus on more meaningful work. When you can provide hands-on training and ongoing support, you will see that employees will feel more confident and capable of using these new tools. Finally, remember to engage your team in the process and decision-making to reduce resistance, as they will feel they are a part of the plan.

- **Integration difficulty:** When you have existing software and programs in your SMB, integrating them with new tools might be a challenge you must overcome. This is because many of these companies operate with a patchwork of systems and manual work, which might not immediately be possible to integrate with an AI system. The main risk is that the implementation process can become costly and time-consuming if the AI tool has to be extensively customized to adjust to your needs.

  Solution: To mitigate these issues, it is essential to thoroughly assess the current systems and processes before selecting your solution. You should prefer to contract tools designed to interoperate with others, which can be easily integrated with existing systems. Another option is to carry out the integration in phases, so the process is done step-by-step, and you can target specific areas at a time. This will allow you to troubleshoot more assertively and refine your issues without risking major disruptions to your operation.

- **Lack of vendor/ technical support:** The last item that should be mentioned is the essential presence of vendor support when purchasing an AI-driven BPA system. Especially for the SMB that does not have a dedicated IT team or tech-savvy employees, you must consider the importance of third-party support whenever necessary, especially during and after the implementation.

  Solution: You should select a vendor that offers a full support system with technical assistance, training options, customization, updates, and vendors with a track record of successful implementations by requesting referrals and other partners' experience.

In this chapter, you have learned about successful BPA implementation in your SMB, including the best strategies to ensure a more successful process and other details you should keep in mind. As we move on and continue exploring AI's capabilities to help your business and the best ways to implement it within your operation, it is time to understand the power of leveraging AI's data analysis capacity to help you in different business areas. In the following chapter, you will learn how data can help you throughout the decision-making process, regardless of the type of analysis you will carry out or the decisions that need to be made.

Chapter Eight

Unlocking the Power of AI–Driven Analytics for Informed Decision–Making

C onsider your business's market today. How fast do industry trends change? It is likely that, regardless of your business area, it is fast-paced, at the same speed that information on social media travels online. In a time when a video can go viral and "make or break" a product, it is essential to keep up with what customers want and how to adapt to these changes. Therefore, anticipating future trends and making informed decisions is critical for success.

When the issues at hand are forecasting and using data, SMBs face unique challenges due to the limited resources to keep up with the market's conditions. In addition, they often do not have the necessary data to work with, and when they do, it might not be as organized as necessary to perform analysis. To help you understand why your company should change into being data-driven and shift its efforts in organizing this information, this chapter will explore how advanced analytics can extract valuable insights from large and complex datasets.

As you read, you will understand how to transform your SMB data into actionable intelligence. This will enable you to make more accurate predictions, optimize your operations and decision-making processes, and effectively leverage this capacity to drive your business forward.

Analytics for SMBs

Ai-driven technologies are transforming the way SMBs operate. One of the areas in which these tools have excelled is in allowing these businesses to analyze data and extract actionable insights, which enable them to compete more effectively. By applying the technology, these companies can enhance their capabilities, which previously were only available to large companies with heftier resources. Among the most impactful AI-driven analytics are ML algorithms, predictive analysis, NLP, and data visualization tools, enabling companies to make more assertive decisions. Each plays a crucial role in different industries and business functions, helping SMBs optimize their operations.

To help you better understand each of these, as an extension of what you have seen in Chapter 4, here are the main elements you should consider:

- **ML algorithms:** These are the heart of AI that allows AI programs to perform advanced analytics, enabling systems to learn from data and improve their accuracy over time. These algorithms can be applied in SMBs to perform customer segmentation, demand forecasting, and recommendation systems. For example, a retail business can use ML algorithms to analyze customer purchasing patterns, segment its audience more effectively, and tailor marketing campaigns. This is also an example of Amazon's powerful recommendation system, which uses ML to identify the purchases made by customers to suggest related products. ML can predict equipment failures by analyzing historical data in manufacturing, enabling proactive maintenance and reducing downtime.

- **Predictive analysis:** This process is usually supported by ML algorithms and takes a step further into data analysis by forecasting future outcomes based on historical data. You can use this in your company to anticipate customer behavior, forecast market trends, and evaluate potential risks. In the finance industry, for example, it can be used to assess credit risk by analyzing borrower data, which is something that large banks use these tools for. In the supply chain sector, predictive analysis will help forecast demand more accurately, ensuring optimal inventory levels.

- **NLP:** This technology is one of the most popular among the general population in applications such as Gemini, ChatGPT, and Claude. This is because it enables machines to understand human language, thus making it ideal for customer service functions, including chatbots and other automated response systems. A business in the hospitality industry can use these chatbots to handle customer inquiries and free human agents to handle more complex tasks. Another great advantage of these tools is the ability to analyze and evaluate customer feedback to understand the overall sentiment, allowing you to make data-driven decisions to improve their satisfaction.

- **Data visualization tools:** Many data visualization tools are enhanced by AI, one of the most popular being PowerBI, a program created by Microsoft. These are essential for turning complex datasets into easily interpretable visual formats. These tools will allow you to visually assess trends, patterns, and outliers at a glance, making it easier to understand the data. Using these tools makes it possible to identify the working strategies and those that are not, creating a clear comparison to communicate to stakeholders. In logistics, for example, visualization tools can map out supply chain operations, highlighting inefficiencies and areas for improvement, enabling more efficient resource allocation.

While many other tools could be named, these are just a few examples of AI-driven analytics technologies with applications across different industries. To successfully use these tools, you understand their potential and how they can best suit your business. It is essential to start by identifying the business functions that could benefit the most from it, regardless of the area. Once these are identified, you can explore the available technologies and choose the solutions that align with your budget, technical capabilities, and business goals.

The first step, however, is ensuring you have the appropriate data to feed these tools. As you know, AI is fueled by data, and the quality of what you input will determine the output you will receive. In the following section, we will explore best practices regarding data management and how you can implement them in your business.

Data Collection and Preparation

The data you upload to the AI program and its quality will directly impact the quality of the information you receive. Collection and preparation are fundamental steps in analytics, especially when leveraging AI-driven technologies. For SMBs, the effectiveness of the analytical process will depend on proper data collection and preparation, including cleaning, integration, and transformation. These are essential to ensure accurate, consistent, and reliable data, enabling meaningful and actionable insights. Continuing the discussions from Chapter 4, this section will explore the importance of these processes and offer strategies for you to ensure high data quality.

To recap what we have seen before, effective collection is the starting point for any analytical process. You must gather data from several sources, including but not limited to customer interactions, sales transactions, supply chain activities, and social media. While this may seem easy, the challenge lies in ensuring the collected data is comprehensive and relevant to the business's objectives. For example, a retail business might collect data from in-store sales, online purchases, and customer feedback forms. Each source will provide valuable insights into customer behavior, but they need to be collected systematically and consistently for use in analytics. Furthermore, this data must be standardized to ensure what you are providing the machine with is reliable, complete, and comparable.

After the data is collected, the next step is cleaning, which involves identifying and correcting inconsistencies. This process is crucial because inaccurate or incomplete data may lead to misleading analytics results, ultimately impacting business decisions. The good side is that you can easily perform this cleaning process by using everyday tools such as Excel or Google Sheets and applying filters to identify incorrect information. Suppose your customer database contains duplicate records or incorrect contact information. In this case, any analysis performed on this data would generate unreliable results. When you perform data cleaning, some of the steps you will need to carry out include

- removing duplicates

- correcting typos

- standardizing formats

- filling in missing values

- removing unnecessary data

After you have carried out the cleaning process, it is now time to prepare the data to be processed. If you are collecting this data from different sources, they must be combined to provide a comprehensive view of the business. While you might not have all the insights you need just by looking at customer information, the machine might find insights you overlooked when this is associated with sales and their region. An SMB can have customer data, for example, located on different platforms, and you will need to integrate their information to have a more holistic and insightful analysis. Since this integration can be complex, you should look for AI-powered data integration tools or platforms to help you seamlessly perform the task.

The main thing to remember as you carry out these processes is that the data quality and reliability are fundamental. Poor-quality data can lead to incorrect conclusions and misguided business strategies, negatively impacting your company. To ensure you have established the best data collection and processing procedures, here are a few tips to consider:

1. Implement data governance policies and data management strategies.

2. Verify data accuracy and reliability before entering it into the system.

3. Establish regular data audits to check the information you have.

4. Periodically review datasets and store irrelevant or unnecessary information in a safe place.

5. Keep your data uploaded to the cloud or a safe filing system to ensure it is protected.

6. Adopt standardized data collection procedures.

7. Manually review the available information before inputting; your

eyes are an important ally!

Following these steps will help you input and work with high-quality data and ensure that the information you obtain from AI tools is more reliable and efficient in decision-making. *But what are these decisions, and what can AI tools do for my business?* Those questions will be explored in the following sections of this chapter. Let's explore how AI-powered data analytics can become an essential asset to your business!

Understanding the Past: Descriptive Analysis

Sometimes, businesses want to understand how they have performed in the past, the events that have led to their current situation, and a more comprehensive understanding of their historical data. For an SMB, this analysis can be particularly valuable as it will prepare the business for more advanced analytics, which you will read about soon. When you use descriptive analysis, you answer the question: *What happened?* With it, it is possible to understand business trend patterns and key performance metrics that will help with decision-making in the future. Understanding the past will give you insight into the future and allow you to plan more confidently.

The descriptive analysis usually follows a three-step process: data aggregation, summarization, and visualization. To help you better understand each of these, here is a breakdown of each stage:

1. **Data aggregation:** The first step involves collecting and compiling data from various sources to create a unified dataset representing a business's activity over a certain period. This step allows the data to be analyzed to identify patterns guiding strategic planning and resource allocation.

2. **Data summarization:** The second step will condense the large

datasets into key metrics and statistics that are easier to interpret, thus reducing the complexity of the data. These summaries provide a snapshot of the performance, making it easier to identify trends or anomalies to investigate.

3. **Data visualization:** The final step is to transform all the data and insights into charts and graphs that will help you visualize and understand what the machine has analyzed. With them, it is possible to highlight patterns and outliers that might be missed in a simple spreadsheet, which will give you more insight into performance.

Descriptive analysis will help your business understand historical trends and use these insights to build predictive models forecasting future outcomes. Suppose your business notices a consistent increase in sales during certain months of the year. It can use this historical data to predict future sales peaks and help you organize your inventory accordingly. By leveraging this data, you will be better equipped to anticipate and respond to changes and trends.

At the same time, this descriptive analysis can help you benchmark performance evaluation. Analyzing historical data makes it possible to establish performance baselines for future projections and KPI establishment. This can allow you to, for example, set more realistic sales targets or increase customer satisfaction. By using this historical data, you can monitor and measure progress over time, focusing on improving areas that need attention and enhancing those that are excelling.

Explaining the Why: Diagnostic Analytics

If the descriptive analysis answers, *What happened?* then the diagnostic analysis is the next step to answer, *Why did it happen?* Answering this question is essential to understand the reasons for trends and inconsistencies in the output provided. It will help you make decisions to avoid the same mistakes or enhance existing processes. Contrary to what you saw in the previous section, this is not about following steps but identifying the possibilities for these anomalies through educated guesses, uncovering factors that influence outcomes, and identifying areas for improvement. Three suggested techniques are

- **Root cause analysis:** This is the most common technique used in diagnostic analysis. It involves investigating an issue and asking, *Why?* until the underlying cause is identified. When the root cause is identified, you can directly address the problem, implementing a targeted strategy to mitigate the impact and prevent future similar events.

- **Correlation analysis:** When you carry out a correlation analysis, you establish the relationships between different variables within your data. In this case, you will analyze how the change in one variable will impact the others. Although correlation does not imply causation, it can provide insights into factors influencing business outcomes. Identifying the variables that create the most impact will allow you to optimize your strategy for better outcomes.

- **Hypothesis testing:** The last method to discuss is hypothesis testing, in which you test specific assumptions about your data and then carry out the analysis to identify whether what you assume is true. Implementing this technique will prevent you from taking action based on intuition and allow you to work based on data for decision-making. By validating or disproving this hypothesis, you will ensure your decisions are made on evidence and not "gut feeling."

For SMBs, detecting and understanding anomalies is essential for managing risks and capitalizing on opportunities. For example, suppose a retailer notices an unexpected spike in product returns. In that case, diagnostic analysis can help uncover the reasons behind this anomaly, such as a defect or a mismatch between expectations and descriptions. Understanding this will allow you to promptly rectify issues, improve customer satisfaction, and protect their reputation.

The insights you will obtain from this analysis will allow you to not only react to outcomes but also understand the factors that drive success or contribute to challenges. This means you can anticipate potential issues and address them before they escalate. Forecasting these outcomes can be essential to determining strategy, and it is exactly the predictive power of AI tools that we will explore next.

Anticipating the Future: Predictive Analytics

When you conduct a predictive analysis, you answer the question, *What should I expect?* To do this, you must understand future trends and outcomes originating from your historical data. By using predictive analysis techniques, you can obtain insights into the future from what happened in the past. SMBs that know what to expect from the future can make more informed decisions, optimize operations, prepare for challenges, and explore opportunities.

To transform raw data into actionable insights for the future, three recommended strategies are

- **Regression analysis:** This analysis will help you understand the relationships between variables and how changing them affects future outcomes. When the data is correctly added to the model, future trends can be established based on anticipated changes in these factors. This can, for instance, allow you to set accurate sales targets, forecast demand, and allocate resources more assertively to prepare for market conditions.

- **Time-series forecasting:** While regression analysis will help you understand the variables, time-series forecasting is useful for SMBs looking to predict trends over time. This method will collect data points recorded at specific intervals to identify patterns and projections and inform future trends. Understanding these patterns makes it possible to prepare more effectively for high-demand periods or hold back when sales are low.

- **ML models:** Although ML is a general term for how machines understand the data, it can also mean an AI program that will learn and forecast based on past trends and actions to provide recommendations for the future. These algorithms will learn the data, understand behavior, identify patterns, and allow the business to take action promptly.

Prediction analysis is a broad field that can be applied to everything from customer behavior to machine breakdown forecasting and financial planning. In finance, you can use predictive models to identify potential financial risks and make more informed investment decisions. This will allow you to make smarter and more targeted investments and allocations to ensure forecast cash flow, for example.

The key advantage of applying predictive analysis to your SMB is the competitive advantage it will give you in dynamic markets. Doing so will allow you to stay ahead of the competition, respond quickly to market changes, and make strategic and data-driven decisions. By adjusting your business strategy to incorporate these predictions, you can mitigate risks before they happen and seize opportunities before competitors identify them.

Recommending Action: Prescriptive Analytics

The final and next logical step to your data analysis will be to answer, *What should I do?* This is when you will implement the prescriptive analysis, guiding you to take the best possible actions to achieve your goals. When you leverage AI models to carry out prescriptive analysis, you will be able to explore the impacts of your decisions, considering different variables and applications in the business. With a prescriptive analysis suggesting recommendations on what you should do based on past trends, you will have an assertive strategy to make more informed decisions that maximiz e efficiency, minimize costs, and drive growth.

Prescriptive analysis can be achieved using three powerful models you can leverage based on your resources and needs. They are:

- **Optimization models:** This core component of prescriptive analysis allows you to identify the most efficient way to allocate resources or configure processes. By finding the optimal balance, you can reduce waste, avoid stockouts, and improve cash flow. You can also leverage AI to carry out more specific tasks, such as optimizing employee schedules and programming actions during slower periods.

- **Simulation:** The simulation technique is exactly what the name suggests: You will test different scenarios and assess their potential outcomes before making decisions. By running these simulations, you can identify potential bottlenecks in the business, plan for optimal outcomes, and evaluate trade-offs between investing in one area or the other. Simulating different events will give you more security during the decision-making process since you know what outcome to expect.

- **Decision trees:** This analysis method is more intuitive and accessible, making it easier for those not used to data analysis to make accurate forecasts. A decision tree is a graphical representation of possible decision paths and their associated outcomes, helping you to weigh the benefits and the risks of different options. By breaking down complex decisions into a series of manageable steps, it will be easier to understand the implications of each choice and select the best course of action.

When an SMB implements prescriptive analysis into its processes, it will be able to understand the trade-offs and variations each decision it makes will have in its operation. By providing a framework for evaluating different options and their outcomes, it is possible to develop strategies to respond to new information, unexpected events, and changes in trends. For example, if the market conditions suddenly change, you can use prescriptive analysis to reassess your pricing strategy, marketing campaigns, and supply chain arrangements.

Another advantage of implementing prescriptive analysis is that it enables your business to be more flexible and adaptable when facing changing conditions. Creating the possible outcomes for different scenarios leaves you prepared for any situation that might happen, allowing you to quickly adjust your strategy and have an "emergency plan" for different events. This resilience and adaptability are essential for long-term success in a dynamic business environment.

The Power of Images: Data Visualization

Data visualization is essential to AI-driven analytics, especially for SMBs looking to leverage data to drive decision-making. The volume and complexity of the information your tool will generate can be overwhelming, making it difficult to understand or obtain insights without the right tools. When you add data visualization tools into the mix, this gap is closed since the raw data will be transformed into visual formats such as charts, graphs, and dashboards that will make it easy for all stakeholders to analyze and understand.

- **Dashboards:** This is a very powerful tool that consolidates different data points into a single interface that can be monitored in real time. The interactive nature of these tools allows users to drill down into specific datasets, customize views, and explore different scenarios with just a few clicks.

- **Charts and graphs:** Although these are more traditional ways of visualizing data, they are still useful and important when the matter at hand is having visual aids. These include pie, bar, line, and even comparison charts. Their straightforward design will allow all the necessary parties to understand the information faster, allowing for more informed decision-making.

Effective data visualization does more than just make data easier to understand; it also helps communication and fosters collaboration among interested parties. When presented visually, insights can be shared with different teams, ensuring all relevant members are informed on business information. This transparency will create a data-driven culture where decisions are based on evidence, not intuition, leading to better outcomes and more collaboration.

Building AI-Driven Analytics Capabilities

SMBs that want to stay competitive in the market today must work to develop their data analysis capabilities. This process involves adopting the right technologies and developing the skills and collaborative frameworks necessary to effectively leverage these tools. When you start building these capabilities, you will likely face challenges ranging from limited budget to restricted available data. Still, with the right strategies, it is possible to create a strategy that will adjust to your company.

Personnel

To start setting up this strategy, you must take a few steps that will depend on resource availability. For example, if you have the budget, you might want to identify and hire individuals with the necessary data science, ML, and analytics skills to help you carry out the process. At the same time, this might pose a challenge, especially for those SMBs with limited budgets. To overcome this, you can look for vendors who provide the service, freelancer platforms with professionals who offer sporadic services, or even an individual who does not have as much experience but shows aptitude and determination. Another solution is to partner with universities to hire students as temporary interns so you do not have to commit to full-time hi res.

Teamwork and Collaboration

Working as a team and fostering employee collaboration is essential to successful data analytics implementation. While the data analyst will have extensive knowledge of how to conduct the study, they might not have a comprehensive view of the business with all the necessary information. At the same time, your other employees might not be proficient in data science, but they know and understand the company's inner workings. Joining these two knowledge areas together will enable you to create a powerful combination of technical and business expertise to benefit your business. Doing so will ensure that your analytics initiatives are aligned with the strategic objective and are practical and applicable for everyday use.

Training

Your strategy should also consider the training aspects of the process. Looking for programs that upskill employees and yourself is essential, helping all users become proficient in AI techniques. This could include online courses, workshops, or certifications that benefit the company. If the resources are limited, you should consider having an individual attend the training and cascade the knowledge to the other team members. By carrying out this upskilling process, you will create an internal talent pool that understands the business and analytics tools, closing the gap between data analysis and business needs.

Establishing Partnerships

External partnerships can also be extremely beneficial when you plan on integrating AI analytics. You can contact external vendors to gain access to specialized knowledge and tools that might otherwise be out of reach or too complex to implement. Partnering with specialized AI analytics companies might offer you a better cost–benefit option since it will prevent you from needing to develop the solution in-house. Additionally, with these, you might be able to scale operations as needed and obtain the necessary expertise and support if there are any technical issues.

Infrastructure

Lastly, it is essential not to exclude the need for a strong data infrastructure supporting AI-driven analytics. You should have parameters to collect, a location to store, and procedures to manage the data to make it accessible and useful for the analysis process. You must focus on data quality, integration, and governance to ensure the data used is consistent, clean, and usable. Investing in the right tools and platforms that facilitate data management and analysis enables the organization to maximize its AI-driven capabilities, allowing you to turn data into actionable insights for business s uccess.

As we move on to the final section of this chapter, you will explore the benefits of using data analysis capabilities to perform real-time analytics and aid in decision-making. These might be the greatest advantages of using data to drive your strategy. Knowing how to leverage these AI tools to aid you through these processes will give you an incredible benefit and allow you to get ahead of competitors in the market.

Real-Time Analytics and Decision-Making

In the past, SMBs often had difficulty analyzing data to make real-time responses. The reasons for this varied and included common issues such as budget limitations to collect necessary data, lack of tech capabilities, and even the lack of human resources to carry out the task. This led to delays in responding to market or operational environment changes. However, with AI-driven real-time analytics, the SMB landscape is seeing a revolution, where data can be processed and analyzed in real time, providing immediate insights and enabling on-time decision-making. Having this capability is essential in the fast-paced business landscape, and being able to react promptly to market changes and new information might be the difference to achieving success.

Within the SMB universe, real-time analytics can help in various areas. A retail business, for example, can use real-time analytics to track sales and performance throughout the day, adjusting pricing or promotions on the fly to maximize revenue. Similarly, a logistics company can monitor the status of its fleet in real time, rerouting deliveries to avoid delays caused b y traffic or disruptions. A food chain or restaurant can monitor the success of a new dish by analyzing customer reviews and understanding whether it should stay on the menu.

The same process can happen for negative impacts on the company, as real-time analytics allows a business to take action before there are negative consequences or reputational damage to the brand. In a world where information is constantly added to social media and can go "viral," being able to take action and produce a satisfactory response is crucial to avoid propagating a negative image that will affect sales. This means that it is also an essential tool for risk management and crisis response.

Other advantages include using real-time data, allowing risk and issue detection before they escalate, such as signs of a security breach, equipment failure, or supply chain disruptions. By responding immediately to these threats, businesses can mitigate risks, minimize damage, and maintain continuity. This application will help the business save money, optimize results, and trigger solutions that enhance operations.

By having immediate access to up-to-the-minute data, SMBs can make decisions that optimize their operations, improve customer satisfaction, and reduce costs. Its ability to identify and capitalize on opportunities and trends can bring significant advantages to businesses, allowing them to adjust their stock according to demand, launch targeted marketing campaigns, and "surf the wave" of trending products and events.

In another scenario, financial services firms might use real-time analytics to monitor market conditions and adjust investment strategies as new data becomes available. This ability to act on opportunities as they arise can lead to increased profitability and a stronger market position. You will see this capability as we explore the benefits of AI in financial management in Chapter 10.

However, before we get there, we must explore the application of AI to help you manage productivity. Although this has been briefly explored in other chapters, it is essential to know that adopting AI can help with other business areas that are not necessarily applicable to BPA or marketing. In the following chapter, you will understand the different ways you can use AI to help you enhance productivity, which can range from helping you manage schedules to optimizing workflows. As you will see, these solutions will allow you to save time and work on making your business grow and succeed. Read on to learn more!

Chapter Nine

Enhancing Productivity With AI

P roductivity is a cornerstone of business success, especially for SMBs. In an industry where most business owners self-manage most of the operations without support staff as well as undertake different roles and tasks, it is essential to learn how to be more productive. Small businesses are often operating with limited resources and tight margins, and when you can enhance productivity, you will do more with less—maximizing output, minimizing waste, and ensuring that every business aspect operates as efficiently as possible. Businesses that fail to optimize productivity, which does not necessarily mean implementing BPA, risk falling behind as they struggle to keep up with more efficient and fast competitors.

For an SMB, maintaining a high production level is not just about survival; it's about creating a foundation for sustainable growth and long-term success. This is when AI comes into play and can offer an excellent solution to streamline operations. By leveraging these tools, employees can focus on higher-value activities and optimize their work schedule. This will boost productivity and improve job satisfaction, reducing idle time and allowing them to engage in more meaningful and impactful work.

Beyond efficiency gains, AI can also reduce costs and drive growth by enabling your business to operate more intelligently and strategically. From data analysis capacities we have seen in the previous chapter to BPA implementations explored before that, and even marketing and sales strategies seen in Chapter 6, it is essential to understand the benefits of choosing the right solution and leveraging them to obtain optimal results. In this chapter, you will explore how SMB can harness the power of AI beyond what you have seen so far, allowing you to reduce costs and unlock new opportunities that may even lead to a better and healthier work–life balance.

Tools for Productivity Enhancement

Today's AI market has several tools—paid and free—that will help you optimize productivity. The most widely known are those referred to as chatbots, which have an NLP capacity where the user can "talk" to the computer. These include ChatGPT, Gemini, Claude, and Microsoft Copilot. Generally speaking, these tools are the go-to for most users because they have no cost and provide an easy and friendly interface. However, other options on the market can be used, sometimes at a budget-friendly cost, that will allow you to achieve the same and even better results.

Implementing these AI tools does not necessarily require large budgets or technical expertise, making them easily accessible to SMBs. Many AI solutions, for example, are cloud-based, so you do not need anything other than a computer to access them. They are also most often offered by third-party providers, offering flexible, scalable options that can be tailored to the business's specific needs. Finally, there are also the benefits that implementing these AI tools will generate for the business, such as time-saving, error reduction, and enhanced decision-making, as you have seen in previous chapters.

When a business implements AI tools to enhance productivity, it usually leads to a rapid ROI, making it the ideal choice for optimizing tasks and activities. Due to the vast number of tools on the market, ChatGPT will be used as a short example. This is not only because it is by far the most popular AI tool used in the market but also due to its free availability, ease of use, and new enhancements proposed with the new ChatGPT-4o version released in early 2024.

For a quick overview of the tool for those unfamiliar with it, today's free version of the AI chatbot provides access to the internet, a vast database to search for information, and the ability to upload documents. Additionally, several GPTs (as previously mentioned) have been created with a specialized approach, such as marketing, financial, HR, social media, and other tools that can be leveraged to assist in different business areas. Due to this versatility, it is possible to leverage its capabilities in almost all industries. However, it will not be as specific and targeted as dedicated tools built for a specialized task.

If you are just starting your AI journey, the best way to familiarize yourself with AI's capacity and start understanding its advantages is to log into one of these chatbots and see what it can do. Doing so will allow you to gain greater insight into what it can do and imagine the power targeted applications will have. Although ChatGPT was mentioned, when exploring tools to enhance your productivity, you should explore all the possibilities available in the market. This means exploring, researching, and understanding your business needs and the best way to achieve your objective.

We will explore this further in Chapter 11 as we build the roadmap to your AI implementation. Still, don't forget that sometimes, a more comprehensive solution targeted directly at your industry comes at a cost and has more advantages than several free tools. Productivity can be boosted in different ways, and it is all a matter of having the necessary information to make the best decision. If you want to optimize sending messages and create content, then ChatGPT and other chatbots will suffice. However, if you are looking to optimize machine performance, then you will likely need to find a specific program for this purpose.

Finding the right tool is not always easy. You will need to do internet searches, look for recommendations and tips, build a list, and start narrowing down the options. On the positive side, several online articles discuss these options and offer the best use cases for each industry, including ratings and user reviews. Finally, you should always remember that the technology landscape is constantly changing, and new AI tools are popping up at an amazing rate. If you do not find the best solution today, you might find it tomorrow. The key is to have patience and test until you find the one that best suits your needs for productivity enhancement.

Optimizing Workflows With AI

SMBs that want to maximize efficiency and reduce operational costs must optimize their production workflows and consider using AI. Implementing the technology will allow you to analyze processes, identify inefficiencies, and recommend targeted improvements, enabling you to optimize team performance. When AI is leveraged for these tasks, overall productivity is enhanced, leading to smoother operations and faster turnaround times.

This is only possible due to its real-time analysis of data. When the business process is uploaded into these tools, it will consider all the information and identify improvement possibilities by monitoring business operations. With the patterns it can identify, the tool can suggest areas where inefficiencies and bottlenecks might be present and propose solutions to optimize the process. For example, if your SMB is in ecommerce, you can use the AI system to analyze the time it takes for orders to be processed and identify the specific steps where delays occur. By pinpointing these bottlenecks, you can take targeted action to address the issues and address them with the proposed solutions.

Making a connection between this optimization and what we have seen in the previous chapter, consider the impact that predictive analysis can have on workflow optimization. By using historical data, AI can forecast potential disruptions or delays in a workflow before they occur. This could mean a lack of staff or product when there is more demand or even anticipating a machine breakdown due to worked hours. Forecasting these issues allows you to take preventive measures, avoid costly downtime, and ensure the business continues working smoothly. As a result, you will ensure that demands are met on time, that the business continues to work seamlessly, and that customer satisfaction and loyalty are maintained.

Still connected to its analytical capacity, it is possible to use AI to recommend improvements to the existing workflow to ensure productivity is enhanced. This does not mean that the present flow of your SMB has issues but that it can be improved to be even better. ML algorithms can analyze the effectiveness of different processes and adjustments over time, learning which changes lead to the best outcomes. Due to its continuous learning capacity, the program will refine the recommendations as the actions are taken, ensuring the workflow is continuously optimized and aligned with the current business needs. This means that you can use the tool to take action on the issues happening *now* and adjust the existing processes for better results and optimization in the future.

Another significant impact AI can produce on workflow optimization is its ability to integrate and synchronize different business areas. This purpose can be helpful for both SMBs that have you operating as a one-person show and need to have an overview of all business areas or for those that have employees who work in different places and the information is not shared. With AI tools, it is possible to close these gaps by centralizing the information and creating a unified view of operations, ensuring all parts of the business are aligned and working together toward a common goal.

However, it is not only to address present bottlenecks and optimize processes that you can leverage the power of AI tools. It can also help SMBs design new business flows from the ground up, designing an efficient process from the beginning of the operation. For example, when launching a new product or service and being provided with all the relevant data, AI can simulate different workflow scenarios to determine the most efficient way to produce and bring the product to the market. This capability will allow your SMB to innovate more rapidly and confidently, as you will know the process is working efficiently from the beginning.

It is also important to remember that workflow issues might not only be limited to your processes but also include the tasks employees need to carry out. AI can also help you understand if there are bottlenecks in employee activities, excess demand in a particular process that could benefit from BPA implementation, or even unnecessary tasks that can be discarded from the workflow. By doing this, you and your employees can focus on the tasks that bring the business value and growth and improve time management and efficiency, which will be soon explored in this chapter.

Lastly, it is essential to remember that leveraging AI to analyze your workflow data and propose improvements will likely optimize your turnaround time and create a competitive advantage over competitors. Regardless of the area in which it is applied, from processing customer orders, shortening product development cycles, or speeding supply chain operations, this will enable you to respond faster to market demands and seize new opportunities. This agility is important and can be the difference between having your company be among the leaders or being left behind.

As businesses in the market continue to face strong competition and the challenges of limited resources, it is essential to use all the existing tools to ensure they have the necessary tools to promote growth. Enhancing and optimizing workflow will be possible when you receive targeted analysis to best streamline tasks and operations. At the same time, the communication environment in the business leads to greater cooperation between employees. This is exactly what we will explore next: the power of AI to help your SBM develop efficient communication that will resonate with all relevant stakeholders.

Enhancing Collaboration and Communication

Despite the increase in electronic communication, with emails, instant messaging, and other internal communications, after the COVID-19 pandemic, companies were forced to find alternative ways to optimize communication and collaboration for employees. While large companies had the budget and the resources to ensure this implementation was done faster and that the necessary tools were adopted, this was not the case for SMBs, most of which struggled to find the best options to carry out these tasks without significantly impacting their operation. After the pandemic, the rise of remote and geographically dispersed teams made traditional communication methods less effective.

AI plays an essential role by transforming how teams interact, share knowledge, and work together, regardless of their time zone. These tools enhance productivity, making it easier for employees to connect and collaborate. They foster innovation by breaking down communication barriers and encouraging idea exchange across the company. From challenges ranging from needing to automatically translate a conversation to virtual environments and settings that allow employees to meet with avatars, different options allow companies to implement AI for better productivity results.

AI-powered collaboration tools, such as smart chatbots and virtual assistants, streamline communication by automating routine tasks and managing information flow. For instance, it is possible to use AI to automate meeting scheduling by analyzing participant's calendars and finding the most suitable time slots, eliminating the back-and-forth emails that often delay the process. These tools can also filter and prioritize communications, highlighting important messages and reducing the clutter of less relevant messages. Implementing these solutions allows employees to focus on the most relevant tasks, enhancing their productivity and reducing time wasted on administrative duties.

One of the most significant benefits of AI in collaboration is how it facilitates real-time communication across different time zones and locations. AI-powered translations and captions can provide the message in the necessary language so all participants can understand each other and foster collaboration in multilingual teams. Furthermore, these tools can transcribe and summarize meetings, ensuring all team members are kept in the loop, regardless of when or where they work. This capability is particularly valuable for SMBs with global operations, those that work with international partners, and even those with clients based worldwide; with AI, collaboration efforts are not hindered by communication.

As you have seen, AI can transcribe and summarize meetings to be sent to others, but the reach it can have for communications in SMB goes beyond these. As you have already learned, AI-driven knowledge management systems can automatically organize and categorize information. This will make it easier for employees to find the information they need and suggest relevant documents, reports, or contacts based on the query or task, reducing the time spent searching for information and preventing knowledge from being lost among all the business files. As a result, you will see your project timelines speed up and the quality of the produced work be significantly enhanced.

Lastly, AI-powered collaboration tools can analyze communication patterns and suggest improvements to enhance team dynamics. For example, AI can identify individuals within the company who frequently collaborate on successful projects and suggest they work together on future initiatives. This will allow you to measure personal KPIs and development, ensuring you can measure team and individual performance. It can also recognize when certain team members are disengaged or left out of important discussions, prompting managers and even you to take corrective action. By providing these insights, AI helps ensure efficient, inclusive, and effective collaboration, leading to better team performance and more innovative outcomes. This is exactly the next issue we will explore.

Improving Time Management and Efficiency

Effective time management and efficiency are critical for the success of SMBs. In these companies, employees and you, the owner, will usually manage multiple tasks and responsibilities simultaneously, making prioritizing tasks essential. This will enable you to manage time effectively, allowing the team to meet goals and deadlines. Together with BPA, this will allow us to work smarter, not harder, leading to improved performance.

As we explored in the previous section, one of the key ways AI enhances time management is by analyzing employee work patterns. AI tools can track time spent on different tasks throughout the day, providing insights into how employees allocate their time and identifying areas where inefficiencies may exist. Suppose an employee spends a significant portion of their day responding to emails, attending meetings, or answering the phone. In that case, AI can highlight this as a potential time to be better used and suggest better strategies to manage these activities. When you understand these patterns, employees can make informed decisions about how to structure their workday, focusing their efforts on tasks that drive value for the business.

Additionally, by pinpointing where the delays or inefficiencies occur, such as waiting for approvals, redundant steps in a process, or tasks that are consistently taking longer than expected, AI can help you resolve potential bottlenecks and process inefficiencies. Imagine your SMB has a project that is constantly delayed due to a lack of approval or tardiness in obtaining it. By using AI, you can obtain a recommendation on how to streamline the workflow or identify another person to whom to delegate the authority. Once these issues are addressed, you can ensure that processes work more smoothly and that the project is completed on time, increasing customer satisfaction and your business's efficiency.

Another aspect that can be explored with AI tools is the ability to help individuals all across the business to prioritize their tasks more effectively. AI-powered tools can analyze the urgency and importance of various tasks, providing recommendations on which should be tackled first to maximize productivity. It may suggest prioritizing tasks with tight deadlines critical to business operations or requiring input from several team members. By helping everyone focus on the most impactful tasks, AI ensures they spend their time on activities that contribute the most to the business, reducing the chances of drowning in less important work.

If you own an SMB with employees who work in shifts, AI can help you plan their workload, manage schedules, and forecast requests. For example, when you identify a peak period for the business, you can prompt the AI tool to help you define who and when each employee should work. In this case, there will be no more spending countless hours trying to figure out the best strategy to suit everyone's needs and requests. Once you add all the employees' available times, preferences, exceptions, and considerations, you will obtain a ready-to-use schedule to implement for the desired period. This process will allow employees to avoid the stress of last-minute rushes and you from having the stress of finding the necessary personnel to assist you when unforeseen events happen.

Lastly, when considering the impact of AI on SMBs, it is undeniable that its implementation will help all members achieve a better work–life balance. When employees can manage time more effectively, it reduces the chances of overworking and burnout, reducing the overhead and medical time off. Preventing these will help avoid looking for replacements and retraining staff, which take up a lot of time and, ultimately, money.

Employees who feel in control of their time and can complete their tasks are more likely to experience work satisfaction and maintain a positive outlook on the job and the company. This will benefit them individually, the group will be more motivated, and you, as the owner, will have more satisfied employees.

When discussing the work–life balance, however, the focus should not only be on employees but also yourself. How often have you missed important events or stayed late as the owner or manager to ensure that things got done on time or that problems were solved? Many business owners do not have a healthy work–life balance due to work constraints. Research shows that "only 48% of small business owners reported having a perfect or good work–life balance, compared to 61% of respondents last year [2023], and more than half (57%) reported being somewhat or extremely stressed" (*Truist Survey Shows Small Business Owners*, 2024).

SMB owners take much of the business's responsibility, especially because they want to ensure everything is right. This means you carry out all planning, research, funding, hiring, and operational tasks when necessary. All these tasks lead to less time with loved ones, and to engage in pleasurable tasks, they might want to participate in off-work time. With AI, you can organize your schedule, find your best routine, and understand the tasks you can delegate to others. Ultimately, you will be able to use AI as your assistant to help you take care of simpler tasks and administrative manners. At the same time, you can focus on making the business grow and enjoy a more balanced lifestyle.

Precautions for Ensuring Data Security and Privacy

As your SBM adopts AI-driven tools to enhance productivity, the importance of ensuring data security and privacy cannot be overstated. While there are incredible benefits to implementing AI into company operations, it also introduces new challenges and risks related to how sensitive information is handled. It is crucial to ensure that data remains protected to protect the business and customer information while complying with the law and maintaining trust.

Although we will explore more about the ethical use of AI and the challenges that come with its implementation in Chapter 14, a brief overview will allow you to explore some of the main focus points. Let's explore some of the main issues to consider when implementing these initiatives to ensure you are not faced with reputation and even legal challenges.

- **Managing sensitive information:** The vast amount of data that AI systems require to work effectively may include sensitive information such as financial records, customer details, and proprietary information. If this data is not properly secured or the tool's legal compliance is not verified, it becomes vulnerable to breaches and unauthorized access, leading to financial losses and reputation damage.

- **Data collection:** It is important to be mindful of the privacy regulations that govern how data can be collected, stored, and used. For example, laws such as the GDPR in Europe impose strict requirements on businesses to protect personal data and provide individuals control of their information. Noncompliance with these requirements can result in fines and other legal consequences.

- **Cybersecurity risks:** As AI programs become more integrated into business operations, they can become targets of cyberattacks, such as hacking, phishing, or malware. SMBs should adopt a cybersecurity protocol that will proactively manage these threats, including employee training, thus preventing human error that could lead to security breaches.

- **Ethical use of AI:** With time, it is only natural that AI systems will become more powerful and that machines will get better at "learning" the outputs and results we expect. While this is an advantage for many, it also brings up the type of data used to train these machines, which can propagate bias and misinformation. Therefore, when implementing these systems, companies should ensure that the tool is designed to respect ethical standards and rights and that the data is collected legally and ethically.

If you are considering implementing these AI-driven systems into your SMB, you should consider implementing a data governance strategy outlining how data is managed through its lifecycle. The policy should include policies for data retention, deletion, and archiving. It is also beneficial to use AI tools, which can monitor compliance, detect anomalies related to cyber threats, and enforce data policies.

While increasing productivity is crucial to all companies, adequate steps must be taken to ensure AI is implemented correctly. However, data security and privacy issues are only one part of the equation in this process; other challenges and obstacles must also be considered when using AI-driven tools. In this chapter's last section, we will explore these and how to mitigate and overcome risks.

The Challenges of Using AI to Optimize Production and Tasks

From employee resistance to system compatibility that will allow production optimization, some challenges must not be overlooked when considering integrating AI-driven systems to carry out tasks. From resistance to putting these systems to use to the other extreme of blindly trusting the programs' output and everything in between, you must be aware of all the risks and obstacles that can be presented during the process, let's take a look at four that will complement what you have seen in Chapter 7.

- **Employee resistance:** The introduction of AI tools can often be met with resistance from employees, who may fear job displacement or are uncertain about working with new technologies. This resistance can slow down the adoption process and reduce the effectiveness of using AI to enhance productivity. To address this, you should focus on transparent communication, emphasizing that AI is meant to augment and not replace human roles. Training and involving employees in the transition process can also help ease concerns and foster a collaborative environment.

- **Lack of human overview:** While AI systems are powerful and can be an incredible aid, this can lead to the other extreme of overreliance on the tools, sometimes at the expense of human judgment. Without adequate human oversight, there is a risk that AI tools might make decisions that lack context or fail to consider nuanced factors in production and task management that can only be identified by humans. Yes, these machines are powerful, but they do not consider many elements usually involved in human relationships. To mitigate this, you must maintain a balance where humans are still involved in key decision-making processes, ensuring AI recommendations are critically assessed and aligned with business objectives.

- **Limited technology knowledge:** A common challenge SMBs face is the lack of expertise in in-house AI and related technologies. This knowledge gap can hinder the effective implementation and maintenance of these tools. It is also possible that you might struggle to understand how to best use AI tools and, during the decision-making process, mistakenly select the inappropriate tools, leading to wasted time and resources. It is important to find reliable vendors and seek external support from AI consultants, invest in researching the best options for business and staff train-ing programs, or choose AI solutions that are designed to be user-friendly and require minimal technical expertise.

- **Dependency on AI tools:** When implementing AI tools, it is es-sential to remember they are still machines and that, as such, they can fail. As businesses rely more on these tools to optimize their tasks, they risk becoming too dependent on these technologies. This dependency can lead to vulnerabilities, such as difficulties in operating when the systems fail or challenges in adapting to new situations that the AI was not trained for. To mitigate this risk, it is crucial to maintain a degree of alternative processes in place to handle disruptions.

As you complete this overview on improving efficiency and production with AI tools, you should remember that while these programs can opti-mize tasks and production processes, maintaining a balance with human input is essential. Overreliance on AI can lead to overly rigid decisions or a lack of creativity, especially in a dynamic environment where flexibility is key. Therefore, when implementing AI into your business, you should ensure that it complements the existing human skills and not replace them, allowing for a partnership where AI handles routine or data-intense tasks while humans focus on strategic, creative, and complex decision-making activities.

So far, you have explored the different areas in your SMB where AI can be adopted to optimize your operations. However, you might have noticed that we are still missing one crucial if not the most important, part of the process: finances. After all, businesses exist to generate money, which makes it crucial to understand how it is also possible to leverage AI technologies into the process. As you prepare to explore this final chapter on applications, before we look at your AI implementation roadmap, let's explore how the technology can be leveraged to help you with financial management, from budgeting to preventing fraud. Let's continue and take a look!

Chapter Ten

Transforming Financial Management and Accounting

In this final chapter exploring business applications, we will look into *the* most important aspect of your business: finances! Despite how much you like what you are doing or the products or services you sell, ultimately, there is a bottom line to its purpose: generating income and allowing you to have more money in the bank. Regardless of how you use these resources, they are why your business keeps going, thus making it a crucial element to explore.

For SMBs, where resources are often limited, the ability to optimize financial operations and predict future trends can significantly improve profitability and growth. By leveraging AI tools, decisions can be made that improve financial health and ensure long-term sustainability.

This chapter will explore how AI programs can revolutionize financial management and accounting by providing powerful capabilities for financial planning, forecasting, budget optimization, and tax filing. You will be empowered with the necessary practical knowledge to harness the technology to manage your finances more effectively, reduce costs, and seize new opportunities, allowing you to achieve your business goals and, what is important, more money in the bank. If you are ready to explore AI's benefits to financial management, you are in the right place. Read on to discover what to do and how to do it!

AI in Financial Management

As financial operations become increasingly complex, with different payment methods and transaction possibilities, it is essential to be familiarized with how these can benefit your business. One of the advantages of leveraging AI for these purposes is its ability to automate routine tasks that will prevent mistakes from occurring and provide deeper insights into your financial health. When these AI-driven solutions are adopted, you can streamline financial processes and make more informed decisions regarding areas that might need special attention like reducing excess spending and costs, or visualize areas that perform beyond expectations.

Some of the areas that AI can help you with include

- bookkeeping

- invoice processing

- expense tracking

- categorizing expenses

- reconciling expenses

- monitoring transactions

- reconciling bank statements

- generating financial reports

- budgeting

- resource allocation

By implementing AI within these processes, you can reduce the likelihood of errors and speed up the process. Additionally, these AI tools can identify patterns and trends that may not be immediately apparent to human analysis, allowing you to gain deeper insights into cash flow, profitability, and financial performance, allowing more accurate forecasting and better financial planning. One example is the implementation of AI to predict revenue based on historical data and market trends, parts of which you have already seen in Chapter 8 and will be discussed further in this chapter.

Another advantage of using AI technology is its ability to provide personalized financial advice tailored to your business's unique needs. Once you input all the relevant data and compare it to industry benchmarks, you can obtain recommendations on optimizing budgets, reducing expenses, and improving profitability. This level of personalized insight, once only available to large companies with the resources to work and invest in these tools, is now accessible to SMBs, leveling the playing field and empowering small businesses to compete effectively.

Finally, you can extract more than traditional reports and forecasting by leveraging these tools. AI can improve the accuracy and reliability of financial insights by accounting for the rapid changes in the market and business environment. As a user, all you will need to do is input the relevant data, and some tools will automatically generate financial reports and forecasts along with recommendations on the decision-making process and how to manage these confidently.

Throughout this chapter, you will explore specific applications for these tools and techniques, allowing you to optimize financial operations and focus on the future. As you read each of them, remember the data privacy and security elements, especially since this is one of the most sensitive business-protected areas. Ensure that the tools you are looking at or considering for your business protect the data and that it will not be used to train the machine's algorithms. With this said, shall we take a look?

Automating Routine Accounting Tasks

Much like automating administrative tasks, AI tools can be a game-changer for your SMB if you apply them to accounting tasks. Traditionally, tasks like data entry, invoice processing, reconciliation, and journal entry are time-consuming and prone to human error. AI automation addresses these challenges by streamlining these processes, enhancing efficiency, and reducing the possibility of mistakes.

Considering data entry, for example, is one of the most impactful applications where AI can offer change. Not only is this process tedious and repetitive, but it is also highly susceptible to errors. Implementing AI tools to handle these tasks includes using programs that can extract data from documents such as invoices, receipts, and bank statements and input it into the appropriate fields in accounting software. With technology such as optical character recognition in association with AI's power, it is possible to interpret and read information from scanned documents, eliminating the need for manual data entry and reducing mistakes.

Now, suppose you look at the other tasks, such as reconciliation, invoice processing, and journal entry. In that case, they all follow the same principle: Highly manual tasks are prone to error if the individual caring for them is not careful. By implementing AI, all these time-consuming tasks that require meticulous detail can be streamlined and made more accurate when AI systems are implemented to carry them out. With this, you will be able to close books faster, reduce discrepancies, and allow those responsible for the financial department to focus on other analyses and tasks that aggregate value to the business.

While all these tools and applications prove to be critical advantages that AI can provide, it is always good to remember that these processes *must* have human input and supervision to ensure the program is not making any mistakes. This includes correctly interpreting numbers, identifying the correct categories under which to file, and ensuring the invoice values are correct, for example. Taking the necessary precautions and assigning a human to oversee these tasks can reduce the chances of incorrect mistakes and oversight of essential information.

Today, several tools will help SMBs automate their accounting and financial management, significantly decreasing the costs spent with accountants and the time used to organize documents. As you will see in the next section, some of these tools come with the additional benefit that they can help you automatically identify and categorize expenses and quickly file your taxes. This can be the ideal option for SMBs operating with limited time and resources to help ensure you have the correct credits and deductions and file taxes on time with the fewest headaches possible.

Tax Management and Filing

Keeping up with tax obligations, regardless of whether these are the dates you need to file, the credits you can discount, or the deductions you can, might be quite a task for the SMB. With continuously changing legislation and documents, knowing what you can and cannot do is essential to ensure you have all the necessary information to retain the largest value when it comes time to pay the IRS. For SMBs, adopting AI tools can be quite beneficial, as some tools enable them to manage these tasks independently, with minimum interference from an accountant, or that will only require an accountant to overview the information. Most of the time, these programs are embedded in accounting software, but this is not true for all cas es.

By uploading all the relevant information to the tool, it is possible to identify the potential tax deductions and liabilities the business will have based on current earnings and expenses. By having this information in real time, it is time to meet tax obligations without straining the business's finances. These insights will also allow you to make better strategic decisions like timing purchases or investing to optimize your tax position.

For those SMBs that operate beyond state and even national borders, these programs can help understand the complex tax scenarios that involve multiple jurisdictions or specific industry regulations. Tax compliance can be particularly challenging when operating beyond local borders because of the different tax codes and filing requirements. If this is your case, adopting AI software can help you comply with the necessary obligations and automatically adjust calculations based on its requirements. Today, you will find programs specifically designed for companies with this versatile activity, allowing the business to easily manage sales tax, value-added tax, and other region-specific taxes.

If you are worried about a potential IRS audit, you should know that these programs also help you manage these cases. While, as usual, all the processes will need human oversight, AI can help you prepare for an audit by maintaining organized, accurate, and readily accessible records. Some of these tools come with the additional benefit of allowing the user to simulate audit scenarios by reviewing financial data for discrepancies or red flags that could lead to an audit. It is also important to mention that many of these tools come with specialized assurance and consultants who can help with the right documentation for a fee.

Lastly, you should consider implementing these tools to help you with future tax returns. AI's ML capabilities can help you file the current year's taxes by analyzing what you have declared in the past. It will be able to analyze the deductions and credits that were previously applied and use the same patterns for this filing. This continuous improvement process allows your business to be more effective when the time comes to file and allows you to take full advantage of the legal tax benefits your company can use to ensure more money is in the bank at the end of the process.

Financial Reporting and Analysis

When an entrepreneur wants to identify the health of their business, the first thing they do is analyze its financial performance. Therefore, it is essential to have programs that will generate reliable and accurate financial reports to help make strategic decisions and guide the business toward its next steps. With its ability to analyze real-time data and generate reports, implementing AI tools into these businesses will allow you to go beyond the traditional analysis and look at areas that were left unexplored.

Businesses that upload all their relevant financial information into the tools will be able to have a comprehensive view of all business processes and understand the areas in which there are high costs and optimal performance. Additionally, this ability to compile information from different sources, which was previously time-consuming, is easily made, allowing the relevant data to always be updated. Since it will be pulling the essential information from the other databases in real time, the reports can be generated 24/7, allowing trends and patterns to be identified at the first signal of a positive or a negative event.

At the same time, this analytical capability will help you spot outliers and inconsistencies where the patterns are not clearly evident. Suppose your business has a sudden spike in expenses or an unexpected dip in revenue. While you might not be able to determine the cause, the AI tool can indicate an underlying issue that has to be addressed and was not immediately evident to you with the available information and reports. By flagging these anomalies, it is possible to investigate better, find the root cause, and take corrective action before the issue becomes critical, allowing better risk management and strategic decision-making.

Another advantage that cannot be forgotten is monitoring KPIs regarding financial performance. Although Chapter 13 will explore more on establishing these indicators, you should know there are financial tools that will allow the users to set targets and will constantly update the information to identify if these are being met. With this feature, you will make it easier to observe the business's performance and draw conclusions with a glance at the visual data the tool provides. In this case, if needed, you can generate a report to analyze a specific area or drill down the reports to get more accurate details on the reasons for the performance.

AI's data analysis capabilities make it essential for businesses that want accurate and on-time reporting. However, it is not only for financial analysis that these tools can be used optimally. Just as we have seen in previous chapters, they can also be used to make forecasts, in this case, financial forecasts and modeling, to help you determine the next steps to take regarding your operation. When historical data is used, and different scenarios are presented, you will be able to identify possibilities, recommendations, and solutions to help you plan and take action to ensure growth.

Predictive Financial Modeling and Forecasting

Since we looked into AI's capability to generate financial reports and analyze present data, we should take a step further and analyze how it can also aid in predictive financial modeling and forecasting. As you know, one of the best abilities of technology is to analyze historical data and incorporate external factors to see how the model behaves. With the tools available on the market today, you can do this with your business's financial data and add these factors to the model to see how they will affect your business so that you can anticipate any potential future issues. Imagine if these options were available when the COVID-19 pandemic struck in early 2020. This would have meant that businesses, especially SMBs that suffered the hardest impact, would be able to identify how it would affect them and take action beforehand.

Apart from analyzing extreme situations such as the pandemic, these models can also project revenue and potential losses by evaluating past sales data, customer behavior, and market conditions to predict future revenue streams. Unlike traditional methods, which may rely on simple averages or manual adjustments, AI algorithms can process and identify complex patterns influencing revenue outcomes. One example of this is the ability of ML models to detect seasonality effects, customer preferences, and economic shifts, allowing you to adjust your sales strategy accordingly. This precision can help you make the best pricing, marketing, and inventory decisions to ensure minimal loss and maximum yields.

By using these tools, other advantages that SMBs will benefit from include

- cash flow forecasting

- risk management

- forecasting worst-case scenarios

- anticipating contingency plans

- predict financial disruptions

When you leverage these capabilities, you will no longer have to wonder *what if* for certain situations but can be certain of how different factors will influence your business. You might use these models to simulate the financial impact of launching a new product, entering a new market, or facing a sudden increase in costs or difficulty with suppliers. These will provide insights into potential risks and opportunities, helping you prepare for the next steps for your business and increasing the chances of achieving your financial goals.

It is always good to remember that while these tools can accurately predict and forecast situations, they are constantly changing. Therefore, it is essential to continuously improve the model by adding data and new situations. This will allow the algorithm to continue learning and become more accurate with time. If the software you use comes from a vendor, remember to ask about update frequency and how often the model is fine-tuned to match the current market trends. Many tools will have limited usage or a cutoff date, which is the maximum date on which the tools were trained, and this can significantly impact the outputs and projections made for the business.

Finally, don't forget about the golden rule: Always evaluate AI output with human eyes and critical thinking. Even in these cases, by "knowing" how the market behaves, there might always be an external event or situation that was not considered, leading you to have incorrect reports and analysis. Use your own analytical capacity and experience to identify if there are any issues with the report provided by the tool or if it can be prompted to consider other situations it has not evaluated. This will ensure you have the best and most accurate information to work with, bringing you more accuracy and reliability.

Budget and Planning Processes

When a business is starting, knowing where to allocate the money that will be invested is essential to ensure long-term survival and the best way to obtain positive results. Depending on the activity your business will perform in the industry it will work with, more or fewer investments will need to be made. To ensure that you have the best forecast and plan for the business's strategy, it is essential to create a budget to identify how much you can spend in each area correctly. These might include investing in

- hardware and software

- licenses and permits

- machinery and equipment

- raw materials

- space rental and renovations

- hiring employees

- preparing an emergency fund

Those building their business from scratch might have an established value they can work with. On the other hand, businesses already operating will have to adjust this budget according to the available resources and might have to forego some of them initially. Regardless of your situation, AI tools can help you prepare this budget and estimate the costs you will have during a certain period to ensure you have all the necessary numbers. Still, implementing these AI solutions will depend on whether you are starting or already running a business. While these will each require different approaches, all will require data: from internal or external sources.

Let's look at the first situation. If you are building a business from the bottom, you must first have an overview of all the costs you will have. For those doing this for the first time, having a budget will be essential to request financing, such as building a business plan. In this case, you will need to understand all the costs it will take to launch the business and have it operating until a profit starts to be made. If you need a general idea of these costs, AI can help you by using market data to establish an average of these values and a plan. You might want to ask the tool what your idea is and ask it to provide you with a list of things you need to do and how much they cost according to the location.

At the same time, if you have the necessary cost proposals for different business areas, you can use the tool to compare the data you were given and ask it to analyze to see the best options for your available money. AI can help you prioritize and help you find the necessary areas where costs can be cut or saved for a later date. This decision support system will help you evaluate multiple options and suggest the best course of action for the strategy you have determined over the established period. This will help you organize the startup process and even put it in a business plan you can use to present to others, showing you have a real take on the best strategies and that you will be using the money wisely and rationally.

Some of the comparisons the tool can make and give you insight on include

- the characteristics of the equipment you need to buy

- renting a renovated area compared to one you need to renovate

- analyze the pros and cons of each investment decision you want to make

- characteristics of employees you will hire

- the positive aspects of the region in which you want to operate in

A similar way to operate can be used by businesses that are already working and need to prepare a budget to structure their finances. In this case, AI tools can be used to analyze the business data, as well as the best places to allocate the money for the next period. When you analyze all the data that has been generated related to the business, it will help you target the areas that need attention and, usually, more budget. This will help you determine the best ways to allocate your money and prioritize investments.

Some examples of this application of the technology include

- identifying the need to restructure services or products

- investing in new materials

- finding new suppliers

- allocating more money to marketing

- buying new machinery and equipment

These are only some examples where AI can analyze your business performance and propose enhancements and budget allocations to ensure your business thrives and grows. For instance, AI might recommend reallocating resources to higher-performing areas or suggest cost-saving measures in underperforming segments. These will help you optimize how the money is used and make it easier to achieve the company's financial goals and, ultimately, maintain its financial health and stress-free.

When you incorporate AI into business financial planning, it is possible to create more accurate, flexible, and resilient budgets to support your strategic objectives. At the same time, it will bring you another advantage that helps you run the business: efficient cash flow management. As we move on to the following section, you will understand how all the financial strategies we have seen so far will allow your business to have a healthy cash flow, enabling you to meet your financial obligations and invest in growth opportunities.

Efficient Cash Flow Management

When all your financial data is integrated into AI-powered systems, it will be easier to predict cash inflows and outflows more accurately. While traditional cash flow relies on manual calculations and the analysis of several documents, AI helps optimize this process and makes it less time and energy-consuming. As usual, implementing the technology will also make the result more reliable since errors are less likely. These models can predict when cash will come in from customers and when payments will need to be made to suppliers and creditors, allowing you to organize and make your financial management more efficient.

AI can also help identify bottlenecks in the cash conversion cycle, which is how a business turns its investments in inventory and other resources into cash. For SMBs, bottlenecks such as slow inventory turnover or delayed customer payments can significantly impact their cash flow. AI will analyze the components that make up this cycle and pinpoint the areas where cash is being tied up unnecessarily. One of the instances in which this can be applied is identifying that a particular product line has a slow turnover rate, suggesting that you should adjust your inventory strategy. This cash acceleration conversion cycle will allow you to free up more cash for other uses.

Another advantageous result that implementing AI will bring is improving liquidity by analyzing cash flow patterns. The analysis of this liquidity will show you where it is possible to take action to improve financial results, such as renegotiating payment terms with suppliers, offering discounts for early customer payments, or adjusting credit policies to encourage faster payment. As your business's specific financial dynamics are considered, the suggested solutions and strategies will be tailored to the business's needs and unique circumstances. The consequence of this is the ability to have a more stable cash flow and see a reduction in the reliance on external financing, which is often costly and difficult to obtain.

Finally, it is essential to mention once again AI's capabilities to monitor in real time how the business's cash flow is being managed and when to take immediate action. Some tools allow you to set up alerts when attention is needed and integrate your financial health by compiling the business results with your bank statements. Suppose a significant payment is due and incoming cash is insufficient. In that case, the AI system can prompt the business to take corrective action, such as delaying nonessential expenditures or drawing on a line of credit. Actions like this will allow you to promptly make the necessary adjustments to the cash flow and minimize disruptions to the business's operations.

Detecting Fraud and Financial Crimes

Banks and financial institutions have been using AI to detect fraud and financial crimes for a long time. When you are going to carry out a purchase, and it is blocked until your card is verified, the bank's system checks if the expense "fits" into the patterns of spending they have for you. If it does not, you might receive communication from your bank asking to authorize or deny the operation. The same happens in large ecommerce platforms, where banks have embedded an additional security feature for the user to validate the account or card to ensure the owner is making the purchase.

For banks and institutions with the resources to implement this technology, it can translate into significant savings and reduce the risk of fraud. However, this technology has only recently been made available to SMBs, which were initially exposed to criminal action that could lead to disastrous financial and reputational damages. This is possible, as you might guess, with the implementation of AI tools that operate on a smaller scale but have the same capability to detect patterns, trends, and anomalies in the transactions being carried out.

Before these tools were implemented, the only resource available was relying on manual and rule-based checks that could be used with much less precision if a fraudulent action occurred. As these events got more sophisticated and evolved with the evolution of technology, both banks and businesses had to develop strategies to ensure the lowest risk and the optional way to develop the programs and make them more affordable. This was possible with the spread of AI technology that analyzes, among other things, the behavior of customers and vendors to identify deviations from the norm. These deviations, which might frequently go unnoticed by the human eye, are rarely missed by machines.

These AI tools for SMBs can

- analyze transaction frequency and amount

- identify suspicious patterns and anomalies

- flag instances of financial crimes

- recognize signs of fraud

- minimize the occurrence of false positives

- analyze customer behavior against market trends

- alert the system on suspicious activity

It is also important to mention that these fraud-detection tools can be integrated into existing security and financial systems to provide a more comprehensive defense against fraud. You can implement these alongside payment gateways, accounting software, and customer relationship systems to cross-check and flag inconsistencies. Doing so will give you a more comprehensive approach to fraud detection, where data from multiple sources is analyzed collectively to uncover complex fraud schemes that might involve different parts of the business. Overall, a unified defense system will give your SMB the tools to protect itself against modern financial crimes.

When researching and selecting these systems, you should check the update frequency and security measures. Cybercrime constantly evolves, sometimes faster than the new technologies developed to protect financial systems. The tool must comply with regulatory standards and provide the essential security features that will protect the business data while sharing the necessary elements to ensure no fraud occurs. Therefore, you should ensure that the tool you select is a reliable option for the business to work with, that it comes from a trustworthy vendor, and that the industry validates it for the purpose.

Since compliance and regulatory issues were mentioned in this section, we will continue to explore AI's capabilities, but now in these fields. In a globalized world where SMBs can operate beyond borders, it is essential to have the right information to perform follow-ups on regulatory and compliance matters where they operate. Read on to the final section of this chapter and understand how AI can help your business ensure that it is prepared and abiding by the current laws, avoiding fines, penalties, and legal action.

Compliance and Regulatory Reporting

The internet has changed how we work and businesses operate. Today, a company that operates in the US can easily sell to any other company worldwide and have, for example, a third of its suppliers abroad. Failure to comply with the requirements can lead to disastrous consequences in this increasingly complex landscape of laws and regulations. However, meeting these obligations is not always easy, especially if you operate across different territories and need to gather and validate data, adjust processes, and adhere to accounting standards and regulations.

How can a company with limited financial and human resources comply with all the necessary regulations to ensure it remains compliant? This is a hard question since there are very few current AI tools that can help solve this matter. Companies that need to address different areas and regions will often face challenges when this need arises since no tool (up to this date) has all the necessary features to ensure reliable and complete information is given. These tools will usually have a specific approach, such as

- regional information only

- limited to national standards

- lack of regular updates

- difficulty in compiling the necessary information

- specific to certain industries

- lack of specification

As you can see, there are currently many challenges, meaning you will usually need to use a patchwork system to ensure you have all the necessary information. One of the most complicated aspects of regulatory reporting is the time and effort required to gather the necessary information. While you will need to use different tools to conduct the research, you can create a connection between them so that all the information is readily available in one place, making it easier to access. AI will simplify this process by automating the data collection and integrating data from multiple sources, ensuring all relevant information is captured accurately and in real time, reducing the burden on you and your employees.

Once data is collected, you can use the compiled database and upload it to the different relevant tools to check the accuracy and completeness of the data for each area you need to report to. Regulatory bodies often require that financial data be presented in specific formats and adhere to certain standards. While the tool may not be able to provide all the answers, it will help you ensure the criteria are met by identifying discrepancies or missing information that could trigger compliance issues. If any are identified, you can address them and generate a report according to the standards, which you can present to the authorities.

This process will also keep the documentation organized, ensuring your disclosure is consistent and reflects the latest regulations. You will also be able to keep track of changes, identify needs for adjustments, and generate narrative reports that explain the results or any other issues that might be required. The automation process will save time and ensure your disclosures are consistent, comprehensive, aligned to expectations, and delivered promptly.

By organizing all your information and adding it to a program or more, you can achieve optimal financial management for your SMB. Even if this was not the priority you identified, it must be considered a priority due to finances' importance to business operations and health. Putting this and all the other priorities in place will help you make your SMB more efficient, productive, and competitive.

All the information you have gained so far will be essential for the next part of the book, where you will explore the more practical part of AI implementation. Starting with Chapter 11, you will find actionable steps to help you start implementing AI in your SMB. You will be given examples of assessments, case studies, and checklists to help you prepare for this change that will happen. As you move forward, remember to look into your business and focus on the areas that need attention. For these, it is advisable to have something to take notes on to brainstorm and jot ideas as they come to you. As you can see, implementing AI is great for business and requires dedication and commitment.

Chapter Eleven

Developing Your SMB's AI Implementation Roadmap

This chapter is designed to help you assess your SMB's preparedness for AI implementation. Understanding where your business stands in this process is crucial and will allow you to identify strengths, address potential gaps, and strategically plan your AI journey. By carrying out a thorough readiness assessment, you can better position the company to take advantage of the opportunities that implementation presents within different business areas.

The primary goal of this chapter is to empower you to leverage AI's transformative power effectively. Knowing your starting point is key, whether you are looking to innovate within your industry, boost operational efficiency, or sharpen your competitive edge. As you read each element in this chapter, remember that this should be done using business eyes and that each step can help you prepare for the process. Throughout the chapter, you will find a test and a checklist to help you prepare and understand if you are ready for this change to take place, allowing you to seize the best opportunities for your business.

Assessing AI Readiness

The first step to start implementing AI into your business is to identify if your SMB is ready to adopt these tools. This process involves a comprehensive evaluation of its capabilities, resources, and data infrastructure to determine if the technology can be successfully integrated into its operations. This process comprises five steps and allows you to move on to the following part of the development. Here are the questions you should ask for each step:

- *Do I have the necessary equipment to support AI implementation?*

- *Do I have the necessary data capability to input into AI?*

- *Do I have a clear objective of the areas AI can enhance?*

- *What resources do I have to invest in AI implementation?*

- *What are my business goals that will be fulfilled by implementing AI?*

- *How can AI be integrated into my strategy?*

- *Are my employees ready to engage in training, or are there resources available to train them?*

- *What business areas could benefit from AI implementation?*

- *How much AI knowledge do I have, and what do I need to learn?*

- *Have I researched enough to understand the best applications for AI in my business?*

As you can see, most of these questions address the business's internal capabilities. This includes assessing your team's skills and expertise. Using AI requires a certain level of technical know-how, from understanding data science and ML to managing AI-driven processes. You should identify workforce needs and skills gaps that might hinder the implementation. This might involve hiring new talent, upskilling existing employees, or seeking external support to fill these gaps.

In addition to internal capabilities, you will need to consider the resources available for the adoption. AI implementation can be costly since it will require technology, infrastructure, and ongoing maintenance investment. It's important to evaluate if the business has and will have the financial resources to support and keep these initiatives going. Therefore, you should prepare a budget that includes hardware, software, data storage, and integration costs with existing systems. You must have a detailed list of all the resource requirements to plan for sustainable AI adoption without overstretching your business's capabilities.

You will also need to address any additional technical gaps, such as data requirements, that might need to be filled in for the process, especially regarding data. This can potentially include assessing its current availability and state: Is the data well organized, accurate, and comprehensive? Is it readily accessible to be uploaded to the AI tools? What is the quality of the data available? Do you have enough data to use and evaluate the business's different areas?

Lastly, you will need to understand how external factors will affect AI use in the business. You must conduct a strategic review of the operations and address the challenges and opportunities the implementation will bring. Ensure you explore areas such as optimizing customer service, enhancing decision-making, implementing BPA, and all the other processes you have seen in this book. When you can identify the problems AI can solve, you will be able to better identify opportunities and ensure the AI strategy and initiative are aligned with the business strategy.

As you explore and identify the opportunities and potential that AI can bring, you should remember to understand what that means for the business and how it will impact stakeholders. AI adoption is not just about implementing new technology; it's about integrating it into the details of the business, which requires careful planning and readiness to embrace change. Let's move on to the next section and take a small test to help you identify if you and your business are ready for AI adoption.

Are You AI-Ready?

To help you understand if you are ready to implement AI into your business, here is a test with 15 questions to help you identify your stage. This will allow you to see if any additional steps must be taken before change can occur.

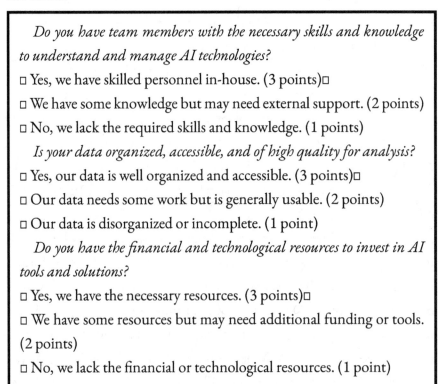

Do you have team members with the necessary skills and knowledge to understand and manage AI technologies?

☐ Yes, we have skilled personnel in-house. (3 points)☐

☐ We have some knowledge but may need external support. (2 points)

☐ No, we lack the required skills and knowledge. (1 points)

Is your data organized, accessible, and of high quality for analysis?

☐ Yes, our data is well organized and accessible. (3 points)☐

☐ Our data needs some work but is generally usable. (2 points)

☐ Our data is disorganized or incomplete. (1 point)

Do you have the financial and technological resources to invest in AI tools and solutions?

☐ Yes, we have the necessary resources. (3 points)☐

☐ We have some resources but may need additional funding or tools. (2 points)

☐ No, we lack the financial or technological resources. (1 point)

Is there strong leadership support and commitment to adopting AI in your organization?

□ Yes, leadership is fully committed. (3 points)□

□ Leadership is supportive but not fully committed. (2 points)

□ Leadership is hesitant or opposed. (1 point)

Have you clearly defined the business objectives you want to achieve with AI?

□ Yes, we have clear and measurable objectives. (3 points)□

□ Our objectives are somewhat defined but need refinement. (2 points)

□ No, we have not defined our AI objectives. (1 point)

Have you identified specific use cases where AI can add value to your business?

□ Yes, we have identified multiple relevant use cases. (3 points)□

□ We have identified some use cases but need more clarity. (2 points)

□ No, we have not yet identified AI use cases. (1 point)

How compatible are your current workflows and systems with AI technologies?

□ Highly compatible with minimal adjustments needed. (3 points)

□ Some compatibility but requires significant adjustments. (2 points)

□ Incompatible, with major overhauls needed. (1 point)

Are your data security and privacy measures robust enough to handle AI-driven processes?

□ Yes, we have strong data security and privacy protocols. (3 points)□

□ We have some security measures that need improvement. (2 points)

□ No, our data security is inadequate. (1 point)

Is your organization ready for the changes AI will bring, including potential shifts in roles and responsibilities?

□ Yes, we are fully prepared for the changes. (3 points)□

□ We are somewhat prepared but anticipate some challenges. (2 points)

☐ No, we are not ready for significant changes. (1 point)

Do you have a plan for training employees to use AI tools and adapt to new processes?

☐ Yes, we have a comprehensive training plan. (3 points)☐

☐ We have some training plans but need to develop them further. (2 points)

☐ No, we do not have a training plan. (1 point)

Have you conducted or planned a pilot or proof of concept (POC) for your AI initiatives?

☐ Yes, we have successfully conducted a pilot/POC. (3 points)☐

☐ We are planning a pilot/POC but haven't started yet. (2 points)

☐ No, we have not considered a pilot/POC. (1 point)

Are you confident that your AI solution can scale across your organization?

☐ Yes, we are confident in our ability to scale. (3 points)☐

☐ We are somewhat confident but have concerns. (2 points)

☐ No, we are not confident in scaling. (1 point)

Do you have mechanisms in place for gathering feedback and iterating on AI implementations?

☐ Yes, we have strong feedback and iteration processes. (3 points)☐

☐ We have some processes that need improvement. (2 points)

☐ No, we do not have feedback or iteration mechanisms. (1 point)

Are you prepared to ensure your AI initiatives comply with relevant regulations and standards?

☐ Yes, we are fully prepared for compliance. (3 points)☐

☐ We are aware of regulations but need to strengthen compliance. (2 points)

☐ No, we are not prepared for regulatory compliance. (1 point)

Are you committed to continuous improvement and staying up-to-date with AI advancements?

□ Yes, we are committed to continuous learning and improvement. (3 points)□

□ We are somewhat committed but may struggle with ongoing efforts. (2 points)

□ No, we do not have a plan for continuous improvement. (1 point)

Scoring and Readiness Key

1. **41–45 Points: AI-Ready** – Your SMB is well prepared to adopt AI technologies. You have strong internal capabilities, clear objectives, and the resources needed to implement AI effectively. Start developing your roadmap for full-scale AI implementation.

2. **31–40 Points: Near Ready** – You are close to being AI-ready, but some areas need improvement. Before proceeding, focus on refining your objectives, enhancing employee training, and addressing gaps in resources or capabilities.

3. **15–30 Points: Preparation Needed** – You have some foundational elements, but significant work is needed before you're ready for AI adoption. Concentrate on building internal skills, securing leadership support, and developing a clear strategy for AI implementation. Before considering AI initiatives, you should also focus on strengthening your internal capabilities, understanding the potential benefits of AI, and developing a robust plan.

Matching AI Objectives and Use Cases

Once you have assessed your business's AI readiness, the first step you will need to take is to align your AI objectives with specific use cases that can drive value to the business. This involves defining clear, measurable goals for the initiatives and identifying where AI can make the most impact. The business areas in which you decide to create objectives for the implementation should be strategic and aligned with the short- and long-term goals you established.

To define these objectives, you should use a SMART approach, where these are **s**pecific, **m**easurable, **a**chievable, **r**elevant, and **t**imely. Once the objectives are set, the next step is identifying specific use cases where AI can be applied to achieve these goals. Use cases should be chosen based on their potential to deliver significant value, ease of implementation, and alignment with your strategic priorities. Here are some examples of this application:

- Reduce customer service response time by 30% within 6 months by using AI-powered chatbots.

- Improve demand forecasting accuracy by 20% within a year with predictive analysis.

- Streamlining invoice issuance by 50% within 1 month by using AI financial automation tools.

- Optimizing the time it takes to manufacture a product by 15% by implementing BPA within the next 9 months.

- Increase the website traffic by 40% by creating targeted marketing strategies within the following 3 months.

During this process, it is important to prioritize use cases based on their feasibility and expected impact. You should consider starting with the tasks that will be easier to automate or have AI integrated into and have a greater likelihood of success. Early wins can bring momentum and demonstrate the value of AI to the rest of the business and its stakeholders, making it easier to justify further investments.

At the same time, you should not overlook the potential of AI to drive innovation in less obvious business areas. While in some cases, such as process automation or customer service enhancement are common, AI can also be leveraged in more creative ways to develop new products, optimize pricing strategies, or enhance employee training programs. The more you open up to the applications of AI use, the more unique opportunities you will have to differentiate the business from its competitors.

As you establish objectives, remember that they should always be aligned with the business's long-term strategy and vision. AI implementation should not be seen as a standalone initiative but as an integral part of the broader strategy. Consider that the investment you will make now must impact how your business will operate in the future; while some of the solutions might seem more fit for the short term, consider how this will build the foundation for the long term. This strategic alignment will help you focus on achieving meaningful outcomes instead of getting distracted by AI trends that do not deliver real value.

Selecting AI Tools and Platforms

Now that you have identified AI objectives and their most relevant use cases, it is time to select the tools and platforms you will use. This decision will influence the success of AI implementation, impacting everything from cost efficiency to adoption ease. To make the right choice, you must carefully evaluate 10 key factors that will make implementation easier. These are

- **Cost and budget:** The cost of the tool you will implement must be within the budget you have established. You need to find the best alternatives that will provide the business with the best cost–benefit balance to help you optimize your tasks but do not extrapolate the established limit. There are several tool options in the market, most with a wide variety of plans and subscriptions, allowing you to select the one that best fits your business needs.

- **Technical requirements:** You must evaluate the tool's technical requirements to see if you have the necessary infrastructure to support it. This is closely related to the budget you have since if you have not allocated a budget to update equipment or software, you must find a tool that fits the business's existing capabilities. As you research the different options, remember to ask if there are any specific technical capabilities you must have to ensure they can be easily integrated into the business.

- **Scalability:** Although we will explore this in the following chapter when you find an AI tool to implement in your business, you must consider whether it has the necessary scalable capacity. The tool you select should be able to support business growth and increase the amount of data. Ideally, the best tools will provide you with a plan, allowing you to select the range of data and resources you will use. For example, you can choose a tool that covers different business areas but decide to implement it in one business area or process at a time to see how the employees respond. With time, you will pay for the additional services and scale its use.

- **Integration capacities:** If you already have software you commonly use for business tasks, ensure that the AI software you select can be integrated into it. The AI solution you choose should complement the programs you already use and pay for, not render them useless. You should ensure one program can read the information from the other to generate meaningful insights into your business processes.

- **Vendor support and documentation:** As you have seen, having the appropriate vendor support and documentation to support the AI tool's use is essential. This means robust customer service that is easy to reach, possibly at a low or zero cost, and easy to read and follow documentation. Another feature the vendor should offer is training services for employees and yourself to ensure the tool is appropriately used and leveraged to the best of its capacity.

- **Updates and features:** The AI tool you select should have the necessary features you need for the business. With the variety of tools on the market today, you can conduct a comprehensive search for a tool with all the characteristics you need. At the same time, it is essential to check with the vendor if there are regular updates to the tool to align with the most recent market developments and technology. Remember to check if the tool has a cutoff date for the training data and how frequently this is updated for more accuracy and reliability.

- **Accessibility and user-friendliness:** When selecting a tool, you should ensure that it is user-friendly and has an easy-to-use interface that all employees can understand. There is no use in implementing a tool that others do not know how to use or that you will need to manage yourself. The selected tool should be accessible and understandable by those who use it daily.

- **Reliability and accuracy:** The tool you select must be reliable and accurate. If you are going to make strategic business decisions and use its output to determine the next steps to take regarding the business, it should be reliable and accurate to ensure that no missteps happen. You should test the tool extensively to ensure that it brings you reliable and accurate information that adds value to the business and generates usable insights.

- **Data management capacity:** Similar to what we have seen in scalability, the AI tool you select should have an extensive data management capacity. This means it will not slow down when you put in the information, and you can continue uploading data as the business grows. The AI software should have the necessary processing and storage capacity to take care of all the data you need and continue to work reliably. Check if the data is stored in the cloud or other places to ensure data safety and privacy.

- **Reporting and output features:** The last resources you must look at are how the reports are generated and the outputs produced. These must be relevant to the business and bring you added value. There is no use in having a tool that will not bring you the information you need and the necessary reports. When you look at the output it produces, it must be a comprehensive view of the process you want to examine and use. Ask the vendor to create sample reports so you can know what you can extract from the system and ensure they will be useful to you.

Once you have analyzed all the above elements, you should create a shortlist of the tools you will research more on and test to see how they perform with the business activities. This will allow you to move to the following step of the process: developing POCs to test how they would integrate into your business.

Developing Proofs of Concept

Before committing to a full-scale AI implementation, developing POCs to validate AI use case cases and demonstrate their potential value is essential. These POCs serve as a critical testing ground where the business can assess the feasibility, effectiveness, and ROI. By starting with a POC and implementing the solution on a smaller scale, you can identify potential challenges, refine the approach, and build confidence in the AI solution before investing more money and resources.

The primary purpose of a POC is to provide a clear and tangible demonstration of how AI can address a specific business challenge or opportunity. It will allow you to test the AI tool or platform in a controlled environment, using real data and relevant scenarios for the business. This helps ensure the AI solution performs as expected and delivers measurable benefits. Suppose you are considering an AI tool to improve customer service. You should then use a POC to deploy a chatbot for a small set of customer inquiries to assess its impact on response times and customer satisfaction.

Designing a successful POC requires careful planning and a clear focus on the objectives. You must start by defining its scope, in other words, what specific problem or opportunity is being addressed and what a successful outcome would look like. To do this, you will need to set measurable goals, such as identifying the efficiency that was gained. Keep in mind that selecting adequate metrics is crucial to identifying the results of the POC. These should align with the business's objective and offer the clear impact the POC has produced.

Another key element to having a successful POC is using the correct data and the use case it will apply to. The data used in the POC should represent the data that will be used in the full-scale implementation, ensuring the results apply to the broader business context. The use case you want to implement should be relevant and manageable, something that, if successful, can be scaled up. An application example would be if your company works with inventory and supply. You might want to start with a POC focused on a single product line and location and, if it works, expand to other lines and products.

When executing the POC, you should ensure that it is deployed within the AI tool or platform you will need to run. You must monitor the performance and gather information on the results, seeing how the outcome affects the business area to which it was applied. During this part of the process, staying flexible and open to learning is essential since the POC might reveal unforeseen challenges and opportunities, showing you what could happen during the full-scale implementation. Use regular feedback loops to refine the solution's outputs and maximize its potential aggregated value.

Finally, once the POC is completed, you must carry out a full analysis of its results. Ask yourself the following questions:

- *Did the AI solution meet the predefined goals?*

- *What were the key learnings?*

- *How can the learnings be applied to the broader implementation?*

- *Does this solution meet my needs?*

- *Are the results satisfactory enough to justify the investment on a larger scale?*

By analyzing the outcomes, you will be able to decide whether to proceed with full-scale development, adjust the strategy, or look for other solutions. This process is essential for AI adoption since it will help you mitigate risks and build a foundation for the tool's use. By testing and refining AI solutions through POCs, your business can ensure you invest in the right technology to deliver value and align with the business objectives.

Piloting and Scaling AI Initiatives

After developing a POC, the next step is to pilot the AI tool in a controlled environment. Piloting the tool is essential because it will allow you to test the AI solution on a larger scale compared to the POC but still within a manageable and low-risk setting. This stage will enable you to collect real-world feedback, make necessary adjustments, and ensure the AI tool functions effectively for your business operations.

When piloting the initiative, select a segment of the business that represents significant use but is still small enough to allow for close monitoring adjustments. One example of this application would be to pilot the AI-driven inventory management system in one warehouse or region before rolling it out across all locations you operate. This will help minimize the disruption while providing valuable insights into how the solution will perform in the real world. It is also essential that during the pilot, you gather feedback from the relevant stakeholders, including employees, managers, and customers, to understand how the tool impacts the process.

This feedback will be essential to refining the solution and understanding if it caters to all the business's needs. You should be prepared to make adjustments based on the feedback you receive, and the vendor must be open to making the necessary changes. The goal is to fine-tune the AI solution to deliver maximum value with minimal friction. Iteration based on pilot feedback will ensure that any potential issues are addressed before the AI tool is deployed more broadly, reducing the risk of failure and increasing the chances of a smooth transition.

Once the pilot has been refined and proven successful, the next step is to scale the AI initiative across the business. This process requires careful planning to ensure the AI solution can handle the increased volume, complexity, and variability across the different business areas. It is important to maintain the lessons learned during the pilot phase and apply them to the full-scale rollout. This might involve gradually expanding the tool's usage, continuously monitoring performance, and being ready to make further adjustments if needed. As you will see in the next chapter, scaling should be done strategically, ensuring the AI solution remains aligned with the business's goals and delivers consistent results.

During the scaling phase, you must also ensure that integration with existing systems is performed smoothly. For AI to be effective, it must work seamlessly with the existing tools and processes. It is essential to prioritize the solutions that offer strong interoperability with the current data software, data management systems, and operational processes. This might involve custom integrations, and vendors must be willing and able to carry out this process to ensure compatibility or even reengineer certain workflows to ensure seamless integration. The objective is to ensure that the AI solution enhances rather than disrupts the existing operations, enabling a smooth transition and sustainable adoption.

Finally, remember that communicating and collaborating with stakeholders during this process is one of the keys to success. Ensuring everyone understands the benefits of the AI tool and is comfortable with its use is essential to achieve buy-in and maximize the tool's impact. Training and support should be ongoing, focusing on empowering employees to leverage AI to its full potential. Clear communication about the AI initiative's goals, progress, and successes can help build enthusiasm and support across the organization, promoting relevant results and full adoption.

Managing Change and Adoption

Now that the AI tool is fully integrated into your business, it is time to check if the change is positive or developing concerns and resistance among employees. Addressing these challenges head-on through effective change management strategies ensures that AI initiatives deliver their intended benefits. A few steps must be taken for this to happen, and the final step of the process is to help you ensure that the change is well accepted and adoption is complete.

The first step in managing change is clear and consistent communication about AI's benefits. Employees need to understand that changes are coming, why they are happening, and how they and the business will benefit from it. For instance, you can explain how AI can reduce repetitive tasks, allowing them to focus on more strategic and fulfilling work and helping alleviate their fears about job security. Highlighting real-world examples or case studies where AI has successfully enhanced productivity or customer satisfaction can also build trust and enthusiasm for the new technology.

A critical part of this process is providing the necessary training and ongoing support. Employees must feel confident in their ability to use the new programs effectively. This might involve hands-on training sessions, access to online resources, or even one-on-one coaching. Training should be tailored to different user groups within the business, ensuring everyone, from frontline workers to managers, understands how to leverage AI in their roles. Additionally, ongoing support from the business and the vendor will help address any issues or questions that arise after implementation-

.

Encouraging early adopters and champions within the organization can also help with the adaptation process. Identifying enthusiastic employees about new technologies and involving them early in the AI implementation process can create a positive impact. These early adopters can serve as role models, demonstrating the benefits of AI to their peers and helping encourage buy-in. Recognizing and rewarding those who embrace the new technology can reinforce positive behavior and motivate others to follow them.

Finally, it is important to approach AI implementation as a continuous process, not a one-time event. You must continuously follow the metrics and numbers to ensure there is optimal and increasing usage. You will explore this in Chapter 13, where the implementation monitoring will be explained further. Regular check-ins, updates, and opportunities for feedback can help address any new challenges. By staying engaged with employees and continuously reinforcing the value of AI, you will be able to ensure the initiative is successfully implemented and brings long-term benefits.

Your AI Assessment Checklist

If you are ready to implement AI into your SMB's processes, here is a checklist you can use. This list covers the essential steps and considerations at each phase of the AI adoption process, ensuring your business is well prepared and aligned with the established goals.

Assessing AI readiness

☐ Evaluate internal capabilities (skills, knowledge, and resources) related to AI.

☐ Review data quality and readiness for AI analysis (organization, accessibility, and accuracy).

☐ Assess financial and technological resources available for AI investment.

☐ Ensure leadership support and commitment to AI initiatives.

☐ Identify specific business challenges and opportunities that AI can address.

Matching AI objectives and use cases

☐ Define clear, measurable objectives for AI's implementation.

☐ Identify key areas of your business where AI can add the most value.

☐ Align AI objectives with overall business goals.

☐ Consult with relevant stakeholders to prioritize AI use cases.

☐ Document AI use cases and their expected outcomes.

Selecting AI tools and platforms

☐ Research available AI tools and platforms that align with your business needs.

☐ List tools that best align with needs and objectives.

◻ Evaluate AI solutions based on budget, technical requirements, and scalability.

◻ Assess ease of integration with your existing systems and workflows.

◻ Consider the availability of vendor support and training.

◻ Choose AI tools and platforms that align with your long-term strategy.

Developing POCs

◻ Identify key AI use cases for POC development.

◻ Design POCs to test the feasibility and value of AI use cases.

◻ Allocate resources and set timelines for POC development.

◻ Gather and prepare data needed for POC execution.

◻ Analyze POC results and document lessons learned.

Piloting and scaling AI initiatives

◻ Select a controlled environment or department to pilot AI initiatives.

◻ Collect feedback from pilot participants and refine the AI solution.

◻ Ensure interoperability between AI solutions and existing systems.

◻ Develop a plan for scaling successful AI initiatives across the organization.

◻ Monitor and measure the impact of AI on business processes.

Managing change and adoption

◻ Develop a change management plan to support AI adoption.

◻ Communicate the benefits of AI to all employees and stakeholders.

◻ Provide comprehensive training and support for users of AI tools.

◻ Address employee concerns and resistance to AI-driven changes.

◻ Foster a culture of innovation and continuous improvement within the organization.

Ensuring data security and privacy

☐ Review and strengthen data security protocols in preparation for AI integration.

☐ Ensure compliance with relevant data protection regulations (e. g., GDPR, CCPA).

☐ Implement measures to safeguard sensitive information during AI processing.

☐ Establish procedures for regular audits and monitoring of AI systems.

☐ Prepare a response plan for potential cybersecurity incidents involving AI.

Monitoring and continuous improvement

☐ Set up KPIs to monitor the performance of AI implementations.

☐ Regularly review AI processes and outcomes to identify areas for improvement.

☐ Stay updated on the latest AI advancements and trends.

☐ Foster ongoing collaboration between data scientists, IT, and business units.

☐ Plan for regular updates and iterations of AI tools and strategies.

Final steps

☐ Review the entire checklist and ensure all steps have been addressed.

☐ Develop a timeline for full-scale AI implementation.

☐ Allocate responsibilities for each phase of the AI adoption process.

☐ Schedule regular meetings to assess progress and adjust the implementation plan as needed.

☐ Celebrate milestones and successes to build momentum and encourage continued adoption.

Assessing and preparing for AI implementation is essential to leverage the tools for innovation and growth. As you understand the business's readiness and objectives, you will be able to select the right tools and manage change effectively. This will help you build a strong foundation for a successful adoption. With these steps in place, you are now ready to scale new solutions, which will be explored in the next chapter. You will understand how to focus on strategies to expand AI capabilities and maximize their impact across the business.

Chapter Twelve

Scaling AI Solutions

A s your business grows and develops, scaling AI solutions becomes critical to maintaining a competitive advantage and operational efficiency. In this chapter, you will explore the strategies that can be employed to effectively scale your AI initiatives, ensuring the business continues to meet the demands of a large and more complex environment. You will also understand the infrastructure considerations necessary to support expanded AI operations, such as cloud computing, data storage, and processing capabilities.

Beyond the infrastructure, AI scaling also involves identifying and hiring the right talent or building strategic partnerships. As AI becomes increasingly integrated into your business operations, the need for skilled professionals who can develop, manage, and optimize these solutions will grow. Creating and expanding partnerships with technology providers, consultants, and other businesses can provide the necessary expertise and resources to scale AI solutions successfully. These elements will allow you to expand AI capabilities with the business.

SMBs and Scaling

After you have first implemented AI tools into your business operation, scaling them is the next natural step. Scaling allows you to maximize the AI program's impact, efficiency, and value. As your business grows, this scalability ability becomes essential to meeting the increasing demands of a larger operation. Whether handling more data, supporting more users, or expanding AI applications to new business areas, scales ensure that AI continues to bring benefits without producing bottlenecks. However, this process has challenges; it requires careful planning, resource allocation, and an understanding of technology and business needs.

One of the primary reasons your SMB might need to scale AI solutions is to meet growing demand. As the business expands and the longer it operates, the greater the volume of data it generates and the complexity of the operation. AI systems that once could handle the given tasks may struggle to keep up with this increased demand if they are not scaled accordingly. This will lead to inefficiencies, slower processing times, and reduced effectiveness of something that previously worked well. As a result, you can have problems in the supply chain, increased customer complaints, and even delays in processing information. Scaling ensures the system can handle larger workloads, process data efficiently, and provide timely insights that drive decision-making.

To start the scaling process, you must follow the step-by-step process you adopted in the previous chapters. Initially, you might use AI to address specific problems or tasks, but as the business grows and develops, you will likely have the opportunity to apply AI to other areas. This previous knowledge and experience with the tool will allow you to explore these new cases and fully leverage the technology's potential across the entire organization. By following the steps you have seen, you can optimize the AI scaling process and ensure you carry out a smooth and seamless scaling process.

Apart from expanding, you might want to improve the performance presented by the tools. The program can be refined and optimized to deliver better results as it is exposed to more data and complex scenarios. This might involve enhancing ML models, increasing the speed and accuracy of data processing, or improving the user experience. By scaling your AI solution to achieve these objectives, it is possible to maintain your current performance levels and open up the possibility for continuous improvement and innovation. This, in turn, can lead to better business outcomes and a stronger competitive edge.

Finally, remember that scaling AI can help you innovate and grow. As AI becomes more deeply integrated into your business's operation, it can deliver new insights, identify trends, and even suggest new models, services, and products. However, to do this, you must ensure that the necessary infrastructure is in place and that you have the necessary talent to manage your AI technology. To address these elements, let's look at what should be considered regarding infrastructure and resources before you decide to scale AI use and integration.

Infrastructure and Resource Strategies

As you might imagine, when you want to scale your AI solution, you must ensure that the necessary infrastructure and resources are in place to support your plan. Usually, when scaling AI solutions, the demands are significant and require advanced computer power, storage, and data management capabilities. Planning and provisioning the right infrastructure is essential to maintaining AI systems' performance, reliability, and efficiency as they expand. Therefore, you must adopt strategic approaches to support this scaling while controlling costs and maximizing investment value.

Regarding infrastructure, it is essential to consider five elements to support AI scalability. They are

- **Cloud computing:** Cloud platforms such as Amazon Web Services, Microsoft Azure, and Google Cloud offer flexible and scalable resources that can be adjusted to meet your expanding needs. They will help you leverage cloud computing and avoid the high upfront costs of purchasing and maintaining hardware on-premises. These solutions will provide computing power, storage, and AI-specific tools on a pay-as-you-go basis, allowing you to scale up or down as needed. This solution is particularly important for businesses with fluctuating workloads and higher and lower demand periods.

- **Distributed computing frameworks:** Tools such as Apache Hadoop and Apache Spark enable the processing of large datasets across multiple computing nodes, increasing the speed and efficiency of data analysis. When dealing with large amounts of data, these frameworks break down the processes into smaller, manageable pieces that can be executed simultaneously. This parallel operation will be essential for your business if it deals with large amounts of data and complex ML algorithms. When you implement this solution, you will ensure that the systems can perform optimally even as the data volumes grow.

- **Storage solutions:** Since AI applications generate and process increasing amounts of data, you must ensure that you have the necessary storage capacity to handle the information. This includes raw data and the ability to store and manage AI models, datasets, and results. Cloud-based storage solutions will offer scalable and cost-effective options, allowing the business to expand its storage capabilities without investing in hardware. You can also leverage storage solutions such as data lakes and data warehouses that will provide the necessary environment to store large datasets to be queried and efficiently accessed.

- **AI-specific hardware:** To scale AI applications, you must also consider integrating AI-specific hardware, such as graphics processing units (GPUs) and Tensor Processing Units (TPUs). These are designed to accelerate the processing of complex AI tasks. Although these are hardware, they can significantly boost your AI model's performance, especially in areas such as DL and neural networks, when the data has to be processed quickly. It is important to consult a specialist to help you identify if these would benefit your business and, if they are, consider incorporating them into the infrastructure if the budget is available. You can also consult with cloud providers, who offer GPUs and TPUs on demand, making it easier to integrate the technology without a substantial upfront investment.

- **Security and compliance:** Security and compliance must remain essential as you scale up your AI integration. As you become more reliant on technology, you will become more vulnerable to cyber-security threats and data breaches. To minimize the potential issues, you should implement security measures such as encryption, access controls, and regular security audits to protect sensitive data and maintain trust with customers and stakeholders. You should also ensure that your AI infrastructure complies with the relevant standards and regulations to mitigate risks and safeguard operations.

Planning and provisioning the necessary infrastructure and resources is essential when scaling AI integration into your company. Remember that you need to consider these in your budget, as they can represent a hefty amount, especially if you are going to purchase the hardware yourself. As you may imagine, this solution also comes with the need to improve the models you are using and how they are deployed among the different business areas. To help you better understand what this will entail, read on to the following section and understand the current best practices and steps to ensure you are implementing the best possible model.

Model Development and Deployment

If you are considering scaling your AI solution, there are two paths to decide upon: The first is to use a vendor and leverage their AI program in your business. The second is to develop a proprietary model that will operate according to your business's needs and the complexity of what you do. If you decide on the first option, then you will need to see if the vendor can adjust to all your requirements, which can be harder and costlier but faster. However, if you decide on the second alternative, you will also incur a cost, but you can determine and build something exactly according to what you need. It is for those considering the section option for which this section is.

Ensuring that AI models can scale effectively requires careful consideration of the model architecture, including training techniques, hyperparameter tuning, and deployment strategies. When you follow the best practices in these areas, you can create solutions that perform well at scale and continue to deliver accurate and reliable results. They will also be easier to integrate into your business model since they will handle the complexity and intricacies of what your business does.

This process comprises five steps that must be followed to ensure the model's optimal performance and integration. Let's look at what they are.

1. Developing a Robust Model

The first step you will need to take is to define the architecture of the model that will be adopted. It will determine how the program will process the input data, make predictions, and learn new information. You need to choose a tool that can handle increasing data volumes and complexity without crashing or degrading performance. If you use a model with neural networks, for example, it can be designed in multiple layers to capture complex patterns in datasets. You should also consider incorporating modular and flexible architectures, such as those using transfer learning, allowing models to be easily adapted or extended to new tasks due to their versatility.

2. Define the Training Techniques

As datasets grow, AI training can become more intensive, complex, and time-consuming. To address this, you can implement strategies such as mini-batch training, where the model is trained on smaller subsets of data at a time, reading the load for the model and speeding up the training process. You can also adopt distributed training, which involves splitting the training workload across multiple machines, thus accelerating the learning process. When these solutions are implemented, it is easier to have greater efficiency in the training and obtain better results, even if there is a significant data increase.

3. Fine-Tune the Hyperparameters

Hyperparameters, such as the learning rate, batch size, and regularization strength, can significantly impact the performance of AI models. While these are essential to understand and correctly apply, finding the right set can be challenging, especially with your model gaining complexity. Automated hyperparameter tuning techniques can help you explore different options and combinations to identify the best settings for your business. It is also important for the developer creating the program to use techniques that have proven results in tuning these hyperparameters to ensure they are done optimally. If the hyperparameter tuning is properly performed, you will have a model that performs optimally and at scale, delivering accurate predictions even in complex scenarios.

4. Identify Best Deployment Alternatives

Regarding deployment, ensuring that the AI models can operate optimally in distributed environments is essential for scalability. Using distributed deployment means running the AI model across multiple servers or cloud instances, allowing them to handle larger workloads and deliver fast results. Some technologies, such as Docker and Kubernetes, are commonly used since they provide flexibility and scalability by packing the model and its dependencies into a portable container. This approach will simplify the deployment process and enable you to scale the model seamlessly as the demand grows, ensuring consistent performance across different environments.

5. Monitor and Maintain Model(s)

Lastly, you must consider how the model will be monitored and maintained. As these models are deployed at scale, they must be continuously monitored to ensure expected performance and adaptation to changes in the data or environment. You can implement automated monitoring tools that track model performance and metrics, such as accuracy, latency, and resource usage, in real time. It is also ideal to implement a version control for the models you are using, allowing you to manage updates and ensure the most accurate and efficient version is in use. This proactive approach to monitoring and maintenance helps your business maintain the reliability and effectiveness of the AI solution.

As you might imagine, model monitoring and maintenance are critical components when scaling an AI solution, especially when they are critical to your business. Due to this, it is essential to explore more of how this can be done and the critical elements that must be considered for optimal performance. As we move on to the next section, let's explore how you can carry out these tasks so the AI tool is continuously updated and performing as expected.

Model Monitoring and Maintenance

Once AI models are deployed at scale, it is crucial to ensure they continue to perform accurately and reliably. This involves implementing strategies for performance monitoring, detecting and managing drift, scheduling regular retention, and maintaining model versions. These are a few of the steps you will need to monitor, and although in the next chapter, we will explore how to establish KPIs for some of these, let's first understand what they are and the steps to ensure this is performed optimally.

Performance monitoring is the first step in ensuring AI models continue to deliver accurate and relevant results as the scalability is implemented. This involves real-time tracking of KPIs and ensuring the model delivers according to the expected parameters. By continuously monitoring these metrics, you can quickly identify any deviations in the performance, which might indicate underlying issues that cannot be immediately recognized. One of the best solutions is to implement automated monitoring tools and dashboards to help you keep a close eye on the model's performance and act promptly if any issues arise.

Another essential element to keep in mind is drift detection. Over time, AI models will change, and the data they will use will increase, which can lead to a change in the data the models rely on. This is called data drift, which can happen in two ways: concept drift and data drift. In the first, the relationship between input and target variables changes, and in the second, the statistical properties of the input data change. Both types of drift can negatively impact model performance if action is not promptly taken. To solve this issue, you will need to incorporate mechanisms such as statistical tests or periodic model performance monitoring to detect when it starts deviating from the expected outcomes. If the data drift is identified, you must update or retrain the model to ensure it starts performing again.

At the same time, retraining the model might not necessarily be needed only because of data drifting. Regular training schedules are vital to maintaining your model's relevance and accuracy. As new data becomes available, you must retrain the model to adjust to this new information to make new predictions more accurate. When establishing these restrainings, you should consider the speed at which new data is generated in the business, which is the main parameter to determine how frequently this should be carried out. This process can also be automated but must be followed closely by the model's developer to ensure fewer mistakes and that the results are accurate and within the expected.

As you change the model, you should always keep track of the version you use. This process will allow you to track changes made to the model, ensuring you can return to the previous version if a new update causes unexpected behaviors. This will be particularly important when multiple versions of the same model are deployed simultaneously in different environments or business areas. By having control of the model versions, you will be able to test the new models or adjustments in a controlled environment without interfering with the business operation as it happens. With this practice, you will ensure a reliable and effective model is always in place, even when it is being updated and tested.

Throughout model maintenance and updates, you should always remember to incorporate user feedback as a quality control. This feedback can also include customers and other stakeholders who can provide insight into how the model performs in real-world scenarios. Obtaining this feedback will enable you to see the process and performance with different eyes and identify areas for improvement that might not be apparent to you or by analyzing metrics alone.

These practices, along with the others you have seen, will help mitigate risks and ensure the solutions continue to deliver value as your business grows and evolves. At the same time, scaling AI use to different business areas might prove to be more challenging, especially if the data that needs to be analyzed is different. If this is the case, you will need to strategically elaborate a plan that will allow these areas to use the tool while ensuring your operation remains unaffected while benefiting from the technology's benefits. Shall we take a look at how this can be done? Read on to find out!

Scaling AI Across Business Functions

As you prepare to harness the full potential of AI in your business, extending its capabilities beyond isolated projects and interesting them into core business processes, it is always good to remember the areas in which these can be implemented. Below, you will find a short list of some of the areas we have explored in the book:

- **Customer service:** As you have seen in Chapter 5, AI can be widely implemented in customer service by using chatbots, automated responses, and answering FAQs to decrease the time on the phone and free up agents to tend to other needs.

- **Marketing and sales:** AI can help you with customer targeting, lead generation, and personalizing your marketing efforts. This will allow you to achieve more precise targeting and higher conversion rates. For more information, refer to Chapter 6.

- **Operations:** This business area can benefit from using AI to help you organize inventory, optimize supply chain operations, and streamline production. Leveraging AI in your operations can enhance business processes and save costs. Read more about the subject in Chapter 7.

- **Finances:** In this critical area explored in Chapter 10, you have seen how AI can significantly impact your financial management, from issuing invoices and managing payments to filing taxes. By applying the tool to these processes, you can gain strategic advantages and enhance decision-making.

Depending on your business structure, there are other areas in which you can integrate AI tools—it will all depend on what you want to achieve! Business areas such as human resources, training, project development, and others can all benefit from the power of AI, and your business will only gain from its implementation. The essential part is sharing information among all stakeholders, from customers to users, to ensure everyone has the necessary knowledge to collaborate and improve the processes.

Collaboration and Knowledge Sharing

As part of the escalation process, you must ensure that all the necessary information and knowledge is shared across business areas. Despite limited resources, leveraging collective expertise and fostering a collaborative environment is key to ensuring an all-around buy-in and use of newly implemented or scaled AI tools. Ideally, you should establish cross-functional teams to ensure these initiatives are properly scaled and adopted. These teams will be composed of members from different departments and will be essential to identifying and overcoming challenges in AI implementation.

Cross-functional teams will be crucial in closing the gap between technical and nontechnical team members. While you might have a team of data scientists and AI specialists to focus on developing the tools, other team members might provide them with useful insight into how these solutions can be best applied to business needs. This collaboration will ensure that AI projects are not only technically sound but also that they are aligned with your strategic objectives. Furthermore, by involving a broad range of business areas from the beginning, you can obtain more support for AI initiatives, which is crucial for success.

Simultaneously, to build these teams with employees from different business areas, documenting and sharing lessons learned, successful strategies, and any pitfalls and challenges faced along the way is essential. This knowledge exchange helps other teams avoid the same mistakes and adopt proven methodologies, accelerating the overall scaling process. It will also promote a culture of continuous improvement, where teams are encouraged to refine their approaches and contribute to the business's collective knowledge base.

Collaboration and knowledge sharing are also essential to increasing acceptance of AI solutions. When employees see that this is not just a top-down initiative but something that involves input and collaboration from across the organization, they are more likely to embrace the changes brought by AI. Creating spaces for open discussion, where employees can voice concerns and share ideas, will further foster an inclusive environment where everyone feels part of the journey.

By implementing all the steps you have seen in this chapter, you will find that scaling your AI solution will be smoother than you imagine. At the same time, you must have a comprehensive view of the company to ensure that it is ready for this scalation to avoid missteps. As you have seen in the previous chapter, the last part of this chapter brings you a checklist that will help you identify if the business is ready to scale its operations throughout different areas. Are you ready to try?

Checklist: Are You Ready to Scale AI Solutions?

Here is a 10-question checklist that will help you identify if you are ready to scale AI within your business and ensure it is prepared for the challenges and opportunities it will bring:

☐ Does your business have the technical infrastructure (hardware and software) to support the increased demands of scaling AI solutions?

☐ Is your data management system capable of handling larger datasets? Is your data cleaned, organized, and easily accessible for AI applications?

☐ Are your AI models designed for scalability? Do they allow for easy adjustments and retraining as your business and data volumes grow?

☐ Do you have the necessary AI expertise in-house or access to external experts to guide the scaling process and manage the more complex AI needs that will arise?

☐ Are there established cross-functional teams in your organization that can collaborate to ensure AI solutions align with business goals?

☐ Have you allocated sufficient budget to cover the costs of scaling AI solutions, including infrastructure upgrades, training, and ongoing maintenance?

☐ Do you have systems in place to monitor the performance of AI models at scale, including detecting drift and ensuring accuracy over time?

☐ Is a change management strategy in place to manage the transition and ensure employees are prepared and trained for the scaled AI implementation?

☐ Are your AI solutions compliant with industry regulations, and do you have mechanisms to ensure ongoing compliance as you scale?

☐ Are your AI scaling efforts closely aligned with your overall business goals, and do you have clear metrics to measure the success of your AI initiatives?

Assessment Key

- **8–10 "Yes" Answers:** Your business is well prepared to scale its AI solutions. You have the infrastructure, talent, and strategies needed to expand AI initiatives effectively.

- **5–7 "Yes" Answers:** Your business is on the right track but may need to address a few areas before scaling AI solutions. Focus on strengthening infrastructure, talent acquisition, and change management.

- **0–4 "Yes" Answers:** Your business may need to pause and re-assess its readiness for scaling AI. Before proceeding, consider developing a more robust strategy and addressing the key gaps.

For growing businesses, scaling AI solutions to improve efficiency is key to optimizing processes. All the information you have seen in this chapter will help you implement this and ensure processes are seamlessly and smoothly integrated. As you assess your readiness to scale, you can ensure your AI initiative continues to grow with your business and continuously deliver value. Now that you are prepared to scale, it is time to see how you can measure the effectiveness of your adopted solutions. In the next chapter, you will learn more about establishing indicators and metrics to evaluate performance, ensuring your investments bring the best results to the business.

Chapter Thirteen

Measuring the Impact of AI in Your SMB

B uilding on the strategies you have read about for implementing and scaling AI solutions, this chapter will focus on the crucial process of measuring AI impact in your business. As AI becomes more integrated into your business operation, understanding its true value and added benefits is essential. This involves not only determining whether the technology is delivering the expected ROI but also ensuring that it aligns with and supports your long-term objectives.

Measuring the impact of AI is important for several reasons. First, it allows you to determine if the initiative meets the intended goals. Second, by analyzing its performance, you can identify areas for improvement and make the necessary adjustments to optimize its effectiveness. Lastly, validating the initiative's success provides the necessary evidence to justify further investments in AI and ensures your business continues to evolve in a competitive market.

In this chapter, you will learn how to develop indicators and measure the effectiveness of your AI solutions. These will include creating KPIs and conducting cost–benefit analyses. By implementing what you will see there, you will be able to continuously monitor and enhance AI's impact on your business, ensuring your AI strategies contribute to sustained growth and success.

Defining Key Performance Indicators

As part of the performance evaluation, the first thing you will need to do is to define KPIs. They will serve as quantifiable metrics that reflect how well your AI strategies are performing in relation to your business objectives. These indicators help translate the abstract benefits of AI into concrete, measurable outcomes, allowing you to track progress, make data-driven decisions, and demonstrate the value your tool has for the business and its stakeholders.

Here are some of the critical KPIs you should consider implementing into your business process analysis:

- **Cost savings:** If you are using AI to automate repetitive tasks, optimize resource allocation, and reduce operational inefficiencies, measuring the impact this will have on cost reduction is key. By tracking cost savings KPIs, you can measure the tool's financial impact on your business. This KPI is important for businesses with budget constraints that may limit the ability to invest in new technologies. Demonstrating cost savings through AI can justify continued or increased investment in integrating these tools into your operation.

- **Revenue growth:** By using AI to identify new market opportunities, personalize customer experiences, and optimize pricing strategies, you can measure how this impacts your revenue growth. If you add this metric as a KPI, you can assess how effectively the tool contributes to the business's bottom line. This

KPI will be relevant, especially if you want to scale operations and expand your market presence.

- **Customer satisfaction:** Possibly one of the most important KPIs you will implement, measuring the impact of AI in customer interactions is essential to understand if they are providing benefits. AI-powered tools like chatbots, recommendation engines, and sentiment analysis can enhance customer service and increase satisfaction. Measuring this KPI through satisfaction surveys, feedback, and other tools will help you identify if the initiatives meet expectations and build brand loyalty.

- **Productivity gains:** If you use AI tools to streamline workflows, reduce manual errors, and enhance decision-making processes, you should measure if the expected outcome is being reached. These include measuring productivity and efficiency to provide insights into how AI improves business performance. This measurement might be determined to understand if you are achieving optimal productivity and efficiency rates that will allow you to maintain competitiveness and reliability.

While these are some of the KPIs you can implement in your business, it is essential to remember that each business area or industry will have unique KPIs that reflect its specific goals, challenges, and context. Therefore, it is essential to understand and assess the business's immediate needs when determining these KPIs. By carefully selecting and tracking the right performance indicators, you can ensure that your AI initiatives deliver measurable value and contribute to your business's long-term success and growth.

Metrics for AI Impact

When considering the metrics for your AI initiative, it is important they are quantitative and can provide a clear picture of its financial and operational benefits. Financial metrics are particularly critical, as they directly correlate with your business's profitability and long-term sustainability. These should be used with all the other relevant metrics for your business, especially for those areas that deliver value and target customer satisfaction.

One of the most widely used financial metrics is ROI, which measures the financial return generated by AI adoption relative to cost. Calculating the ROI will allow you to determine if your AI investments yield sufficient returns to justify continued or expanded use. If you have implemented an AI-driven automation tool that reduces manual labor costs, for example, comparing the savings with the initial investment will provide a tangible success metric.

These metrics you decide upon must be tracked over time to help you quantify the financial benefits AI has brought to the areas in which it was implemented. Some of the examples of where these metrics could be applied include

- measuring if there was a decrease in the labor costs for tasks that previously required manual data entering

- analyzing sales metrics before and after AI tools were implemented

- monitoring leads to customer conversions

- identifying if there was an increase in conversion rates on a website by using recommendation engines

- measuring supply chain management metrics such as delivery fulfillment time and speed

- monitoring transportation costs and fuel economy with optimized route implementation

- analyzing inventory levels and stock efficiency

- controlling the amount of defects in a product that had AI implemented into its production

- calculating costs saved with preventive action on machine maintenance using AI

As you have seen in the previous section, finding the right tools to measure and monitor these metrics, such as implementing dashboards and visual tools, will be important. To support open communication, these should be visible to all relevant employees so they understand the benefits of implementing AI. The visual aids should be continuously updated to reflect real-time information and allow everyone to follow business progress.

However, you should also consider adding qualitative metrics to the quantitative metrics, including customer satisfaction reviews, employee feedback, and stakeholder perceptions. While an AI system might, for instance, increase operational efficiency, it is also crucial to understand how it impacts customer experiences, employee morale, and stakeholder confidence. These will reveal whether the AI implementation is resonating with the relevant key users and how it is impacting company culture. By comparing and understanding the full impact of AI on your business, it will be possible to achieve measurable gains and foster a positive environment for all parties.

As you might imagine, to understand how the solution impacts your business, you should be able to compare and establish the ideal targets you desire to reach. This means comparing them against industry standards, competitors, and your own historical data. Benchmarking and comparing your results to these numbers will be key to understanding how you are performing in the market, and this is exactly the next element we will look at. Benchmarking will provide a snapshot of your current performance and help you set realistic goals and expectations for the following AI actions.

Benchmarking and Comparison

One of the primary benefits of benchmarking is the possibility of assessing your AI performance in the context of industry standards. By understanding how your AI tools and processes compare to those commonly accepted in your industry, you can identify gaps and areas where your business might be lagging. Let's say you have AI-driven customer service support with slower times than the industry average. This could mean you need to optimize the tool further or invest in more advanced AI technologies. However, if your AI system outperforms industry standards, this validates your strategies and could provide a competitive edge.

To carry out this analysis, you should consider evaluating what your competitors are doing and how they are performing to benchmark performance. When you compare your outcomes with your direct competitors, you can uncover insights into where you excel and where you might need to catch up. This is especially important in a highly competitive market and industries where technological advances can make or break a business.

For example, suppose a competitor is using AI to achieve higher levels of automation in their supply chain, leading to faster delivery times and lower costs. In that case, this benchmarking exercise can highlight the need for your business to enhance its capabilities in the area. This form of comparison will drive improvement and help you optimize your processes.

In addition to external benchmarks, internal benchmarking against your previous performance metrics is vital for tracking progress over time. Although we will explore this in the next section, when we look at the before-and-after analysis, you should know that using your business's historical data can help you measure the impact of AI initiatives for growth and efficiency.

If AI has led to an increase of 20% in productivity compared to the previous year, this will provide concrete evidence that AI brings value to your business. This, perhaps, might be one of the most important indicators you will use since it will enable you to tie the results up with future investments and results. Therefore, you should regularly conduct internal benchmarking to help you understand the AI journey the business is undergoing and ensure the benefits are sustained and built upon over time.

During the benchmarking process, you will also find that it is possible to identify areas that need improvement. Not only will you be able to identify examples of areas that can benefit from AI implementation, but you will also understand where the technology can play a greater role and be enhanced. When you discover that your AI performance is behind that of the industry or competitors, this will prompt you to analyze the underlying causes deeper.

This could involve reevaluating your AI tools, retraining models, or refining processes to enhance efficiency and effectiveness. As you carry out this process, you can investigate the areas where AI can be further integrated to drive continuous innovation and growth within the business.

Finally, as you carry out the benchmarking process, it is essential to remember this must lead to actionable insights. This will help you understand and also how this overview can help you make strategic decisions and operational changes. This can lead to insights such as the need to invest in new technologies, reassigning resources to underperforming areas, or adopting best practices from industry leaders.

You should always remember that the ultimate goal of the process is to improve your AI capabilities and outcomes. As you regularly benchmark AI practices, this will allow you to prepare for the future and ensure you are competitive in the present.

Before-And-After Analysis

As mentioned earlier, the ideal path is to carry out a before-and-after analysis to understand how your AI initiative is performing. This method will help you assess the true impact of the AI implementation and understand the benefits it has brought to the business. By comparing the metrics before and after implementation, you will clearly see how the technology has influenced your operations, productivity, and efficiency. This type of analysis provides concrete and tangible evidence of the value brought by AI, justifying the investment and guiding the business toward its next steps.

A five-step process must be followed to carry out the before-and-after analysis, allowing you to create a comprehensive strategy for measuring AI's effects on the business. Here is the breakdown of what must be done:

1. **Establish objectives:** Start with an accurate picture of how your business is currently operating. Evaluate the relevant KPIs you want to monitor and their importance to the business. Ensure that these KPIs are directly connected to the business objectives and strategy, as well as the reasons for implementing AI in the business.

2. **Collect the relevant data:** After establishing the objectives you want to measure, you must collect all the relevant data to understand how your business is performing today. This includes gathering data on relevant areas such as process cycle times, error rates, customer satisfaction, financial performance, and any other applicable data you will measure. The information you collect and the indicators you identify will be the baseline for the monitoring you will perform after AI implementation.

3. **Implement the AI tool:** Implement the AI tool according to the strategies in this book. Remember to document and measure the initial results and follow up as the technology is integrated into the company. You should monitor the process until it is fully used and implemented into the business's operation.

4. **Collect new data:** After the tool is fully implemented, you will need to collect the same data previously used to establish the baseline. These will provide the necessary information on how the AI tool performs in each area where it was implemented. It is essential to remember these must have the same parameters to ensure the reliability and accuracy of the comparison you will make, which is the last step.

5. **Compare metrics:** Now that you have all the information, you can evaluate and compare the metrics on how the business process has changed with the AI implementation. Ideally, these will bring positive results, but they must be evaluated closely to ensure their impact on the business. These metrics should then be communicated to stakeholders through reports and visual tools to ensure transparency and accountability.

As you complete the process, you will see that the insights gained from the analysis extend beyond confirming AI effectiveness. This approach also helps to identify unexpected outcomes or unintended consequences that might arise from AI integration. This means that while the tool might improve efficiency in one department or business area, it could create bottlenecks in the other, highlighting the need for a more comprehensive approach to the solution. This analysis will allow you to make adjustments and optimizations to ensure AI positively contributes across the business.

The last thing that should be mentioned is that this before-and-after analysis will help you communicate the success of AI implementation to stakeholders and throughout the organization. As you quantify the impact of the technology in measurable improvements, you will be able to justify future investments in other areas. This transparency will bring confidence to employees and strengthen the relationship with external partners and customers by demonstrating a commitment to leveraging cutting-edge technology to enhance business performance.

Remember that these analyses should not be carried out only once but should be continuously evaluated metrics that are constantly monitored and communicated. By iterating the process and measuring its impact on the business, you can fully understand, maximize, and leverage AI's benefits over time, leading to increased optimization and process improvements.

Iterative Improvement and Optimization

Building on the insights gained from the before-and-after analysis, you can continuously refine your strategy to ensure sustained performance enhancements. The iterative approach involves regularly revisiting AI processes, incorporating feedback, testing variations, and making data-driven adjustments. This continuous improvement cycle helps maintain its effectiveness and ensures it evolves according to business changes, needs, and market conditions.

One of the best ways to carry out the improvement processes is to use feedback loops. To do this, you must establish mechanisms and strategies to capture feedback from stakeholders and key users to gain valuable performance insight. This will give you a comprehensive view of how the AI tool is performing internally and externally in real-world scenarios; therefore, the more input you obtain, the more accurate the snapshot.

Employees can provide accounts on efficiency and usability, and customers can shed light on the impact of AI on quality and satisfaction.

These will form the foundation to identify areas that require refinement, from adjusting algorithms to enhancing user interfaces.

Another effective strategy is to conduct A/B testing, where you will compare two versions of the AI-driven process or tool. In this case, Version A can be the current implementation, and Version B is the same tool with a specific change or improvement. You can determine which approach offers the best results by running these versions simultaneously and analyzing outcomes. You can apply this throughout the different business areas and processes as the tool is implemented, allowing you to fine-tune and adjust as necessary.

These adjustments, based on insights gained from interactive processes, are crucial to maintaining the relevance and effectiveness of the AI solution. You will need to determine the areas that need to be adjusted, which may include, but not be limited to

- retraining algorithms

- evaluating the data

- fine-tuning the model

- adjusting hyperparameters

- reconfiguring workflows

- allocating resources

- finding alternative solutions

As you consider these elements, you might even need to rethink the full AI strategy, especially if the solutions are not delivering as expected. The key is to remain agile and responsive to the data, ensuring the implementation continues to align with the business objectives and adapts to any challenges or obstacles that might appear.

The iterative improvement and optimization processes will help address potential pitfalls and mitigate risks associated with AI adoption. As you implement AI solutions into your business, you may encounter unexpected situations, such as biases and integration issues with other systems. These should be considered when implementing the strategy so you are not surprised and can modify the plans accordingly. As you refine the process, you will be able to address these issues proactively and ensure that what you have integrated delivers value responsibly and ethically.

Remember that these initiatives will allow your business to enter a continuous improvement and innovation cycle. As you revisit each adopted tool, you can test new ideas, refine strategies, and search for enhancement areas, allowing you to stay ahead of the curve compared to competitors. Focusing on the feedback, testing, and adjustment cycle will ensure that AI remains a powerful tool for overall business performance.

I understand the importance of these metrics, but what are the tools and technologies I can use for these purposes? Are there any specific tools I should use for optimal performance understanding and analysis? If these are your concerns, you should not worry! As we move on to the next section, you will explore a variety of platforms and services you can use to help you monitor and measure performance based on your needs and preferences.

Tools and Technologies for Measurement

Several tools in the market can help you understand the performance data you have gathered. These tools offer a wide array of features, such as data collection, analysis, and reporting, which will give you a clear insight into the numbers you have gathered. They will help you track key metrics, identify trends, and make informed decisions based on real-time data. Here are some reliable tools you can use for this purpose and how they can help you effectively measure AI performance:

- **Analytics platforms:** Analytics platforms such as Google Analytics, Tableau, and Power BI are commonly used by businesses to analyze performance. These allow you to collect vast amounts of data, efficiently process it, and visualize the results in user-friendly dashboards. Google Analytics, for example, is used to track user interactions on websites and apps, providing valuable insight into customer behavior influenced by AI-driven recommendations or recommendation systems. Tableau and Power BI offer advanced data visualization capabilities, enabling you to create interactive reports and dashboards, making it easier to understand complex data sets and monitor outcomes in real time.

- **Performance monitoring software:** Tools such as Datadog, New Relic, and Splunk are essential to track the performance of AI systems and applications. While Datadog provides comprehensive monitoring for cloud-based applications, including AI models, New Relic focuses on performance management. Both tools will collect data across various sources and provide alerts when performance issues arise, including bottlenecks or inefficiencies. On the other hand, Splunk will aid with log management and can be used to analyze data from AI applications, providing insights into operational performance and helping diagnose and resolve issues quickly.

- **Dashboards:** Another option are interactive and customizable dashboards, such as Kibana, Grafana, and Looker. These provide powerful capabilities, allowing you to track KPIs, visualize data trends, and share insights with others. Kibana is often used with Elasticsearch, which will aid in analyzing large datasets and creating interactive dashboards that reflect AI performance, system health, and other critical metrics. Grafana is known for its flexibility and ability to integrate various data sources, which are excellent for monitoring AI performance across multiple systems. Finally, Google Cloud Looker offers a comprehensive BI platform with robust data exploration and visualization features, which is ideal for tracking the impact of AI on business processes.

- **Automated reporting tools:** If you are looking for tools to generate automated reporting, you must explore options such as Domo, Sisense, and Qlik Sense, which will help you assess impact without manual intervention. Domo offers a cloud-based platform that integrates several data sources, automates data workflows, and generates real-time reports highlighting AI-driven outcomes. Sisense is known for its data integration capabilities, allowing you to create complex reports and visualizations without extensive technical expertise. Qlik Sense is also a popular tool that provides intuitive data exploration and reporting features, enabling your business to quickly generate insights from AI-driven data and share them with stakeholders.

- **ML operations (MLOps) platforms:** Tools such as MLflow, Kubeflow, and DataRobot will help you manage the end-to-end lifecycle of ML models, including monitoring and measuring performance. MLflow is an open-source platform that allows you to track experiments, monitor model performance, and manage model deployment. Kubeflow, built with Kubernetes technology, provides a scalable solution for deploying and managing ML workflows, making it easier to monitor models in production. Lastly, DataFlow offers an automated ML platform that will help build and deploy models that it can later monitor, ensuring the product delivers consistent, accurate, and reliable results.

Regardless of the tool you select, leveraging them will help you measure the impact of the AI initiative. This will help you achieve the desired outcomes and optimize your AI strategies. These tools will also enable you to, most of the time, generate reports that will facilitate communication with stakeholders and have a significant advantage in ensuring buy-in and engagement.

Stakeholder Engagement and Communication

As you measure the impact of your AI initiative on the business, it is essential to consider stakeholder engagement and communication. You must ensure they are involved in the measurement process to enhance the accuracy and relevance of gained insights, as well as foster a sense of ownership and commitment to the AI transformation. When you bring in stakeholders early into the process, it is possible to ensure open communication and that your strategy is aligned with the business's goals and initiatives. This allows the tracked metrics to reflect what truly matters in all business aspects.

To do this, relevant organization members, such as department heads, IT teams, and senior management, must be involved in the measurement process. These individuals will usually have a deep understanding of business operations and strategic goals, allowing them to provide valuable input on which KPIs and metrics should be prioritized. For example, the finance team might focus on cost savings and ROI metrics, while the marketing team might be more interested in customer engagement and conversion rates. By incorporating perspectives from all these departments, you can develop a more comprehensive and targeted approach to measuring AI impact for meaningful understanding.

During this process, you should also remember to communicate the insights and findings to all relevant stakeholders. This transparency will help bring trust and ensure everyone is on the same page. To ensure this, you can schedule regular meetings, provide detailed reports, and use interactive dashboards to cater to all audiences. You can use the tools seen in the previous section to demonstrate how AI has affected business processes and improved the relevant KPIs. As you implement transparent communication, it will be easier to identify potential issues or areas for improvement by gathering the relevant input.

This feedback will be another crucial aspect of the process since you must understand the impact the AI tool has had on these individuals and their business areas. You can carry out feedback sessions to identify potential gaps in the measurement process, discover new opportunities, or suggest changes to improve the AI application. When you listen to what those affected by the AI solution have to say, you will find it easier to implement adjustments and make the tools more user-friendly and applicable to their work.

The collaboration across departments will bring different perspectives and expertise, which can trigger innovative solutions and better overall results. This cross-functional collaboration ensures AI initiatives are not isolated but integrated into the broader business strategy, consequently maximizing their impact. As departments collaborate to find effective uses and applications, the business benefits from actionable insights that are technically sound and coordinated, allowing better performance and outcomes.

This process should be ongoing rather than a one-time effort. As AI initiatives evolve and scale, continuous engagement helps ensure that the selected strategy follows the desired path and achieves relevant outcomes. When this happens, you will be better equipped to meet business goals and match market conditions. Be sure to implement regular updates and open communication challenges to maintain this process continuously and encourage employees to support new ideas and projects thought out for the future.

Continuous Monitoring and Evaluation

As you focus on the initial measurements and likely get excited with the first positive impacts, it is essential to continuously monitor these KPIs to ensure the AI tools are effective. Initial measurements can provide valuable insights into the implementation's success, but periodic assessment and evaluation will help maintain the accuracy and relevance of these insights over time. Therefore, you must establish regular review cycles to understand how these tools operate in real-world conditions and how they adapt and change in the business environment.

Here are a few practical actions that will allow you to perform this monitoring and ensure you have all the necessary feedback to continue creating meaningful change in the business:

- **Establishing regular review cycles:** The first and most crucial step is always to have a continuous review cycle of AI performance. You must use all the necessary tools to ensure that this analysis and measurement is made optimally, especially when evaluating predefined KPIs and metrics. These review cycles should be periodic and consistent—monthly, quarterly, bi-annually—as long as they fit the business purpose and needs. This will allow you to track progress, identify trends, and address any issues that may arise. It can also help you identify areas for improvement and potential bottlenecks that might appear. If you establish a calendar for these reviews to take place, remember to follow through so that the tools continue to deliver value and adapt to business needs.

- **Updating KPIs as needed:** Over time, the initial KPIs set for AI initiatives may need to be adjusted to reflect changes in business priorities or market conditions. This could happen if you are making changes to production, changing your strategy, or implementing a new product or service. As you make the necessary changes to remain relevant in the market, ensure that the metrics follow the same path and provide a true reflection on how AI is aiding the business in enhancing its operations. Use these opportunities to capture more nuanced aspects of how AI affects the business and obtain insights into new possibilities that can be implemented in the future.

- **Adapting measurement strategies:** Although you might have initially established a metric or measurement strategy for your KPIs, you should remember that these can be changed and adapted. These modifications will depend on the business circumstances and how the market evolves. If this happens, you might need to adjust how you measure and analyze business metrics. This could involve integrating new tools or technologies for data analysis, revising data collection processes, or employing advanced analytics techniques. The more flexible you make changes, the better your results will be. An important reminder is that if you change the measurement strategies, you must restart the KPI establishment process to ensure you are comparing the same elements.

- **Encourage feedback loops:** As you have seen in the previous section, encouraging feedback is essential to communication and improvement. Use the information obtained to identify gaps and areas for improvement in the measurement process. This opportunity should also be used to identify potential areas for future AI implementation and scaling existing programs. Use the necessary and adequate communication channels to monitor and encourage users to provide their feedback, opinions, and suggestions on the processes.

- **Consider flexibility and scalability:** AI systems must remain flexible and scalable. Implementing continuous monitoring enables you to identify when adjustments are needed to accommodate growth or changes in the business process. This can involve upgrading AI infrastructure, expanding data processing capabilities, or retraining models to handle new data types. You must ensure that your AI solution can adapt to these changes to remain relevant to your processes and offer maximum impact and value.

Ultimately, continuous monitoring and evaluation are integral to achieving long-term success with AI. As you regularly review AI performance and carry out the actions you have seen in this section, it will be possible to ensure the AI tools continue to be effective across all business areas. Remember to remain proactive to identify and address issues that will collaborate in achieving business goals and improving processes.

Despite all its incredible benefits, AI still presents challenges to those who implement the technology. These include ethical and legal challenges that have been increasingly discussed across all industries. To help you understand the potential challenges you may face and the most common issues when the technology is implemented, we will explore the ethical and legal obstacles you might face in the next chapter. As you will see, these are essential to keep in mind, as any missteps might lead to pitfalls and negative consequences, including reputational damage.

Chapter Fourteen

Navigating the Ethical and Legal Landscape

A s you integrate AI into your business operations, navigating the ethical and legal challenges associated with its adoption becomes a priority. The main reason is that AI technology has the potential to transform business processes, enhance efficiency, and drive growth, but it also raises significant concerns about privacy, fairness, transparency, and accountability. These concerns are not just theoretical; they have real-world implications that can affect a company's reputation, customer trust, and legal standing. Therefore, addressing ethical and legal issues is essential for businesses to fully leverage AI's benefits while minimizing potential risks.

Ethical challenges in AI include ensuring that AI systems are fair, transparent, and free from bias. For instance, AI algorithms used in hiring processes must be designed to avoid discriminatory outcomes, and customer-facing AI tools must respect privacy and data protection standards. Legal challenges involve compliance with a rapidly evolving regulatory landscape. Governments and regulatory bodies worldwide are increasingly scrutinizing AI technologies, and you must stay informed and compliant with these regulations to avoid legal issues with the authorities. Understanding and addressing these concerns will help build trust with customers, employees, and other stakeholders and ensure AI is used responsibly and sustainably.

In this chapter, you will explore the key ethical and legal considerations SMBs must navigate when adopting the technology. Here, you will find strategies for ensuring transparency, fairness, and accountability in AI systems, as well as how to comply with relevant regulations and standards. Knowing this before implementing the tools in the business will allow you to address these challenges, mitigate them, and position yourself as an ethical leader in your industry.

As you explore the different stages and areas you must pay attention to, you should take notes to ensure the integration you will carry out follows best practices in the market. To help illustrate the disastrous consequences these can have on a company, at the end of this chapter, you will explore some case studies in which AI did deliver the expected results. You will see that when the necessary preventive measures are not taken, the negative impact can be overwhelming. However, before we look into what *not* to do, let's start by understanding what responsible AI is and how you can adopt the practice in your business.

Responsible AI

Integrating the guiding principles of responsible AI is essential to ensure these tools are used ethically and transparently. When we talk about *responsible AI*, this refers to the development, deployment, and use of AI systems where societal values and ethical standards are considered. Critical principles that must be addressed include fairness, transparency, accountability, privacy, and bias mitigation. As you consider these principles in the initiatives, it will be possible to avoid potential pitfalls.

Responsible AI stands on five essential pillars to ensure a robust implementation. Although we will explore more of each in the coming sections, you should know they are broken down into the following:

- **Fairness:** Customer service, where biased algorithms can lead to discriminatory outcomes. To implement fairness, you must carefully audit AI models to identify and mitigate any biases in the training data, algorithms, and outputs. Techniques such as algorithm fairness testing and diverse data sampling can help reduce the issue, leading to more equitable outcomes for all stakeholders.

- **Bias mitigation:** Must be an ongoing practice with constant vigilance. Even with the best intentions, AI systems can still produce biased outcomes due to flaws in the data or algorithms used. You must implement regular monitoring and evaluation processes to detect and correct biases as they arise. Implementable solutions include retraining AI models with more datasets, refining algorithms, or adjusting decision-making processes to reduce bias.

- **Transparency:** Involves making AI systems understandable and explainable to all interested parties. This means providing clear information on how AI decisions are made and ensuring that these processes are not "black boxes" that no one understands. Transparency is essential for building trust, particularly in customer-facing AI applications. Therefore, you should work to develop and implement explainable AI techniques to provide the necessary insights into how your AI models work, why certain decisions are made, and how those decisions can be challenged or verified.

- **Accountability:** Refers to ensuring there is clear ownership and responsibility for AI systems and their outcomes. As a business owner, you must establish governance structures that define who is responsible for AI-related decisions and who will be held accountable if something goes wrong. This includes creating clear protocols for addressing errors, biases, or unintended consequences. This accountability also includes ensuring AI systems comply with legal and regulatory requirements as AI regulations evolve globally.

- **Privacy and security:** This means that AI systems must respect user privacy and comply with data protection regulations, such as GDPR in Europe or the CCPA in the US. Implement strong data governance practices, secure personal data, and be transparent about data usage and storage practices. Protecting privacy helps avoid legal repercussions and strengthens customer trust and loyalty.

With a comprehensive overview of these file pillars, we will now explore more of them in detail, allowing you to better understand how each applies to your business and the preventive and proactive measures you can take. Once again, as you read, remember that these must be tailored to your business needs and the process in which AI will be implemented. This will allow you to scale operations in the future, and best practices will be implemented and considered for the new systems.

Addressing AI Bias: Ensuring Fairness and Equity in AI Systems

The issue of bias in AI has become a significant concern. It can arise from various sources, including biased training data, flawed algorithmic design, or human biases inadvertently embedded into AI models. Addressing bias is essential to ensure that AI-driven decisions are fair and equitable and do not disadvantage certain groups.

One of the most publicized examples of AI bias occurred with Amazon's AI recruitment tool, which was found to favor male candidates over female ones. The tool was trained on resumes submitted over a 10-year period, reflecting how the tech industry is male-dominated. As a result, the algorithm learned to favor resumes that contained predominantly male-associated terms and penalized resumes with words like "women," leading to biased hiring decisions.

To mitigate bias in AI decision-making, you can employ various techniques. Some of these include

- data preprocessing for the careful selection and preparation of training data to ensure it is representative and free from harmful biases

- applying fairness-aware algorithms designed to minimize bias during the model training process

- algorithmic transparency used to better understand how and why certain decisions are made and identify potential sources of bias

- ongoing monitoring and evaluation to continuously monitor AI performance and detect any emerging biases

You can add to your strategy by conducting regular audits and performance reviews to help identify biased outcomes and take corrective actions. This might involve setting up a feedback loop or working with groups to discuss potential issues.

Another positive action to take is to look at real-world examples of how to address AI bias. For instance, a small ecommerce company might use AI to recommend products to customers. If the system disproportionately suggests products based on biased assumptions about gender or race, it could exclude certain customer segments. To address this, you could implement fairness-aware algorithms and regularly audit its recommendation system to ensure all customers receive fair and relevant suggestions.

Reducing bias in AI systems is a constant task that must be continuously monitored. This will allow your business to promote fairness in decision-making processes and build trust with customers and stakeholders. However, you must consider that you must not only prevent these issues but also understand and explain why they are happening. For this, we have the next three pillars: transparency, explainability, and accountability.

Transparency, Explainability, and Accountability: Building Trust in AI Systems

The need for transparency and explainability in AI systems has become a critical concern as AI becomes integrated into business processes. *Transparency* refers to the openness and accessibility of information about how these systems operate. At the same time, *explainability* involves clearly articulating the decision-making process in a way that stakeholders can understand. Together, these concepts are essential for building trust in AI technologies, especially where AI-driven decisions impact individuals, businesses, and society.

When AI systems make decisions that affect people's lives, such as credit scoring, hiring, or customer service, it is important that these decisions can be explained in simple terms. This helps to demystify AI and enables stakeholders to understand how and why certain decisions were made. This will allow you to foster a culture of trust and openness, both essential for successfully adopting AI technologies.

Transparency and explainability also play a key role in ensuring that all stakeholders use AI systems responsibly. When the inner workings of AI systems are transparent, it is easier to identify and address potential biases, errors, or unintended consequences. This will allow you to refine the AI model and ensure the system aligns with ethical standards, market best practices, and business objectives. For example, if an AI system's decisions are questioned, you must have a clear and explainable rationale to respond effectively and take corrective actions if necessary.

This level of accountability is crucial for maintaining the integrity and fairness of AI systems and extends beyond just understanding how AI decisions are made. It also involves assigning responsibility for those decisions: Decisions are shared responsibility among AI developers, providers, users, and regulators. This includes implementing safeguards against bias, ensuring data privacy, and providing tools for transparency and explainability.

Developers must document the decision-making processes of AI systems and make this information available to users and regulators. Users must also be prepared to justify the use of AI in decision-making and take responsibility for those decisions' outcomes. This means being vigilant in monitoring AI systems for performance and fairness and being willing to intervene when AI-generated outcomes raise concerns.

Regulators, as we will see further along in this chapter, play a critical role in establishing frameworks that enforce accountability and ensure that AI systems are used ethically and legally. These regulation bodies are increasingly focused on creating guidelines and regulations that mandate transparency, explainability, and accountability in AI systems, including setting standards for how AI decisions should be documented.

One of the main concerns for these regulators, and one that should also concern your business, is how customer data is protected and kept private. Regulatory authorities constantly scrutinize companies to ensure data is only used when explicitly authorized. The last pillar we will explore is the importance of securing customer data when using AI applications.

Data Privacy and Security: Safeguarding Customer Data in AI

Data privacy and security are critical concerns, especially when AI systems process sensitive personal information. The increasing use of AI raises the stakes for ensuring that data is handled in a way that preserves customer trust and complies with legal standards. To achieve this, your business must implement reliable data protection strategies, including ensuring its confidentiality, integrity, and availability.

One of the most effective strategies for protecting customer data is using privacy-preserving techniques such as *differential privacy* and *federated learning*. These allow AI models to learn from data without directly accessing it. Differential privacy adds noise to the data, ensuring that individuals cannot be traced back to specific users. At the same time, federated learning allows AI models to be trained across decentralized devices without transferring the raw data to a central location or server. These approaches help maintain customer data privacy, reducing the risk of breaches and unauthorized access.

In addition to implementing privacy-preserving techniques, you must also ensure the confidentiality of the data. This means protecting data from unauthorized access and ensuring that it is only accessible to those who have legitimate reasons to use it. Encryption is a key tool for this purpose, as it secures data at rest and in transit. Consider adopting strong encryption protocols and ensure sensitive data is stored in encrypted formats. You can also add access controls to limit who can access different data types, reducing the risk of insider threats and data leaks.

Data integrity is another critical aspect of data privacy and security. The data must be accurate and free from tampering for AI systems to work correctly. You can ensure this integrity by implementing validation techniques, conducting regular audits, and using measures such as digital signatures to verify that data has not been altered and that it is available when necessary for authorized purposes and uses.

This data must be accessible when needed for AI operations, so it is important to implement measures to protect against data loss. This can happen for several reasons, such as cyberattacks, system failures, or natural disasters. Program your systems and data to be regularly updated, establish disaster recovery plans and use redundancy to help ensure data remains available despite unexpected events.

Finally, all these processes must ensure compliance with data protection regulations and standards when using AI. Regulations such as the GDPR and CCPA impose requirements on how businesses collect, process, and store personal data. Stay informed about relevant regulations and ensure that your AI systems are designed to comply with these laws. To better understand the legal frameworks, regulations, and compliance issues you must abide by, let's move to the next section and see the essential elements to consider.

Legal Frameworks and Regulations

Understanding and adhering to the relevant legal frameworks and regulations is critical when planning to implement an AI tool. The legal landscape governing AI is complex and evolving, including data protection laws and industry-specific and specific regulations. These are designed to protect individual rights, ensure the responsible use of AI, and prevent harm. As mentioned, the GDPR, the CCPA, and emerging AI-specific regulations like the European Union's (EU's) AI Act are essential to understand to ensure your business can operate and leverage these tools to the maximum.

One of the most significant legal frameworks impacting AI adoption is the GDPR, which applies to businesses operating in or serving customers in the EU. The GDPR imposes strict rules on collecting, processing, and storing personal data, with a particular emphasis on obtaining explicit consent from individuals before using their data, such as approving cookies when navigating a website.

Suppose your AI systems rely on personal data, such as customer analytics or personalized marketing. In that case, you must ensure that the data is collected lawfully and that individuals' rights to access, rectify, and erase their data are respected. Noncompliance with GDPR can result in severe fines, making it crucial for businesses to implement robust data protection practices when using AI tools.

Similarly, the CCPA provides data privacy protections for California residents, giving them the right to know what personal information is being collected, the right to opt out of the sale of their data, and the right to request the deletion of their data. Businesses that use AI for customer insights, targeted advertising, or any other data-driven application must comply with CCPA requirements. This includes being transparent about data collection practices, providing clear-out mechanisms, and ensuring third-party AI vendors adhere to CCPA standards.

Industry-specific regulations also play a crucial role in governing the use of AI. For example, the U.S. Health Insurance Portability and Accountability Act (HIPAA) establishes the standards to protect sensitive patient health information. If your business operates in the healthcare sector and uses AI for patient diagnosis, treatment recommendations, or healthcare sector analytics, you must ensure your AI systems comply with HIPAA's privacy and security rules. This involves implementing stringent data encryption, access controls, and audit trails to protect patient data from unauthorized access or breaches.

In addition to local and industry-specific regulations, others aim to regulate the development of AI-specific frameworks. The EU's AI Act, effective in 2024, is one such regulation that established a comprehensive legal framework for AI technologies. The AI Act categorizes AI applications based on their risk levels—ranging from minimal to unacceptable risk—and imposes varying requirements accordingly. The Act mandates rigorous risk assessments, transparency, and accountability measures for high-risk AI systems, such as those used in critical infrastructure, healthcare, and law enforcement. Those using AI in such contexts will need to carefully assess the risk level of their AI applications and ensure compliance with the AI Act's provisions once it is enacted (*EU AI Act*, 2024).

It's essential to use resources like the International Association of Privacy Professionals to further understand and act according to the complex legal landscape surrounding AI adoption. The association offers a global tracker of data privacy and AI legislation, which helps you stay informed about the regulations you must adhere to across different regions. This resource is invaluable for businesses looking to ensure that their AI initiatives comply with evolving legal requirements.

You should have a proactive approach to compliance to prevent breaking these regulations of the AI tool you are implementing or developing. Some of the items that will help adhere to the regulations include

- conducting regular audits of AI systems to ensure they align with legal requirements

- providing training for employees on data protection and AI ethics

- implementing governance frameworks that promote accountability and transparency in AI use

- staying informed about emerging regulations and engaging with legal experts

- integrating legal considerations into the AI adoption process and strategy.

As the regulatory landscape evolves, you must remain vigilant and proactive, understanding and adhering to relevant laws to mitigate risks and reduce your liability exposure. To help you navigate these challenges and anticipate the actions you can take to prevent issues, let's look at the strategies you can implement for risk management and liability reduction.

Risk Management and Liability

AI systems offer significant advantages in terms of efficiency, productivity, and innovation but also introduce new types of risks that you must be prepared to manage business-wise. These range from operational disruptions and data security breaches to ethical concerns and potential legal liabilities. A proactive approach to assessing and mitigating these risks is essential to ensure that the benefits of AI adoption are fully realized without exposing the business to undue harm.

One of the key aspects of AI-related risk management involves identifying potential risks early in the adoption process. This includes understanding the risks associated with implementing AI tools and technologies. During the strategy and implementation process, you should conduct thorough risk assessments that evaluate the likelihood and the sensitivity of the data being processed and how critical the decisions are being made. The earlier you can identify the associated risks, the faster you can act.

The mitigation strategy for AI-related risks usually involves a combination of technical, procedural, and organizational measures, such as

- **Technical:** Implementing security protocols, such as encryption, access controls, and continuous monitoring to protect AI systems from cyber threats and data breaches.

- **Procedural:** Establishing clear guidelines for the use of AI, conducting regular audits of AI systems, and creating contingency plans for responding to AI-related incidents.

- **Organizational:** Creating a culture of risk awareness and ethical responsibility, including training employees on the potential risks associated with AI and how to manage them.

As you take each of these steps, consider the role of governance in risk management and establish committees or working groups to oversee AI initiatives. This will help you ensure that risks are being properly managed. When you can embed risk management into the organization's processes and activities, you will create a more resilient and responsible AI adoption strategy, decreasing the possibility of having to deal with liabilities related to these newly implemented programs.

After the implementation process, it is natural that AI systems take on more decision-making responsibilities, which may lead to questions about who is liable when things go wrong. The answer to this question is important, and you should be able to address it when necessary immediately. Liability for AI-related harm or errors can be complex, often involving multiple parties, including AI developers, providers, and users. Therefore, before adopting an AI solution, you must carefully consider it, especially when these decisions harm customers, employees, or other stakeholders. As you develop your risk mitigation strategy, it is essential to establish clear accountability guidelines and understand the legal frameworks in your specific industry and jurisdiction.

To mitigate liability risks, ensure you have adequate legal protections in place, including negotiating clear contractual terms with AI vendors that outline the responsibilities and liabilities of each party and obtaining appropriate insurance coverage for AI-related risks. You must also stay informed about evolving legal standards and regulations related to AI, as these will influence liability considerations over time.

If necessary, hire a specialized legal counsel to ensure you comply with all required regulations and practice legal challenges, and ensure it is prepared when facing AI-related liability. As you continue to read, the following section will help explore the role of ethical frameworks and guidelines in AI adoption, providing insight into how the ethical and legal challenges of AI use.

Ethical AI Governance

Ethical AI governance provides the foundation for managing the ethical risks and challenges associated with AI. It will work to promote transparency, fairness, and accountability. As a business owner, creating and implementing governance frameworks helps mitigate potential ethical issues and fosters trust among customers, employees, and other stakeholders. This governance must be built considering five essential elements, which complement each other and will lead to a robust approach.

Here are the five core elements of ethical AI governance and how they should be used and implemented within your organization:

- **Clear policies and procedures:** These policies should outline AI development and use principles. For example, a policy might stipulate that all AI systems must be designed to avoid biases and regularly audited to ensure they operate as intended. You should establish accomplishable procedures to continuously monitor AI systems, address any ethical concerns that arise, and take corrective action when necessary.

- **Oversight mechanisms:** Oversight mechanisms will help enforce ethical AI governance. This might include the creation of an AI ethics committee or a dedicated governance board responsible for overseeing AI initiatives. These bodies will then be tasked with reviewing AI projects, assessing their ethical implications, and ensuring compliance with the established policies. They will also play a role in addressing ethical dilemmas or conflicts that arise during AI deployment.

- **Ethical decision-making processes:** These processes involve evaluating the potential ethical risks and benefits of AI initiatives before they are implemented. Ethical risk assessment, for instance, can help SMBs identify potential ethical issues and evaluate the potential impact on various stakeholders. This proactive approach helps ensure that AI technologies are designed, built, deployed, and implemented responsibly.

- **Stakeholder engagement:** Engaging stakeholders in the decision-making process can provide valuable insights and help AI systems meet the needs and expectations of those affected by them. This can take many forms, including consultations, focus groups, or surveys. These should be integrated into all phases of your project development.

- **Impact assessments:** These assessments evaluate the broader ethical implications of AI systems, including their potential social, economic, and environmental impacts. Doing this will allow you to identify potential risks and unintended consequences, thus allowing you to take preventive measures before AI systems are widely deployed, safeguarding against ethical breaches and enhancing the project's long-term sustainability and success.

As you might imagine, ethical AI governance is essential for businesses looking to leverage AI responsibly. Use strategy development to incorporate the tasks seen in this section to create a solid foundation for responsible AI use. These will all culminate in the last and most essential element that needs to be explored concerning AI use: obtaining user consent and building trust that will ultimately make or break the AI implementation process.

User Consent and Trust

User consent and trust can make or break the successful deployment of AI technologies. As these systems interact and handle sensitive data, it is crucial to ensure users understand how their data is being used and are comfortable with AI processes. Building and maintaining trust through transparent communication and obtaining informed user consent upholds ethical status standards and allows the user to be aware of how their information will be used.

The primary aspect of establishing user trust is transparency. The business must clearly explain to users when and how AI is being employed, whether for personalizing customer experiences, automating customer service, or analyzing user behavior. This transparency helps demystify AI, allowing users to understand the benefits and limitations of the technology. Suppose your business uses AI to recommend products based on previous purchases. This should then be openly communicated to customers, explaining how their data is being utilized to enhance their shopping experience.

They will then have to explicitly consent for this data to be used. Consent should not be a one-time checkbox but a continuous, informed process where users are made aware of how their data is collected, processed, and stored and can opt in or out at any point. Users must be given clear and accessible information about data practices, ensuring that consent is obtained in a manner that respects their autonomy and privacy.

One example of how this is applied in the market is through cookie acceptance and management policies. These ensure users have control over which cookies are used, how their data is tracked, and the purposes for which it is utilized. However, beyond obtaining consent, maintaining user trust requires ongoing transparency regarding data practices and potential risks associated with AI use. Users and customers should be informed about how their data is protected, who has access to it, and what measures are in place to safeguard their privacy.

Building trust also involves being responsive to user concerns and feedback. Early in the process, you should establish mechanisms for users to voice their concerns or ask questions about AI systems used in the business. Options for these mechanisms include customer support channels dedicated to AI-related inquiries or feedback loops we have already explored that allow users to report issues and suggest improvements. This two-way communication reinforces the idea that AI adoption is a partnership between the business and its users, built on mutual respect and understanding.

Lastly, you must remember that trust in AI systems is closely tied to the business's broader ethical practices. Users are more likely to trust businesses that commit to ethical AI use. This involves adhering to legal requirements and going beyond compliance to ensure that AI is used in ways that benefit society and respect individual rights. Therefore, when considering AI tool implementation, this might also mean adopting ethical AI principles, participating in industry-wide discussions on AI ethics, or publicly sharing your ethical commitments and how they are implemented.

When the appropriate measures are taken to ensure ethical and legal compliance of AI tools within the business, you will be able to operate with the safety that you are doing all that is needed. However, when these elements are overlooked or taken for granted, they can have disastrous consequences. This chapter's final section will illustrate how AI implementation can lead to business disasters when the appropriate measures are not taken.

Ethical Dilemmas and Case Studies

Let's examine real-world case studies in which AI adoption presented complex ethical dilemmas. These examples provide insights into the challenges of implementing AI ethically and the decision-making process that organizations must navigate to avoid negative outcomes.

Air Canada

Air Canada implemented AI-driven chatbots to enhance customer service, but the deployment raised concerns when customers reported that the bots struggled with nuanced customer queries, leading to dissatisfaction. The company then faced the ethical challenge of balancing automation with quality service. The decision-making process involved weighing the efficiency gains against the potential harm to customer experience. Air Canada had to reassess the deployment and improve the AI's capabilities to handle more complex interactions while ensuring that customers still had access to human support when needed (Leo, 2024).

ChatGPT in the Courtroom

Rapid advancements in large language models like OpenAI's ChatGPT sparked widespread interest in generative AI across industries. By 2023, businesses were exploring how AI could revolutionize various aspects of work, including legal research. However, a case involving attorney Steven A. Schwartz demonstrated the technology's current limitations, particularly in high-stakes environments like courtrooms.

The lawyer used ChatGPT to research legal precedents for a lawsuit against Colombian airline Avianca. However, the AI-generated brief he submitted contained references to at least six nonexistent cases. These cases included fabricated names, docket numbers, and citations, leading U.S. District Judge P. Kevin Castel to punish Schwartz and his colleague, Peter LoDuca, who signed the brief as Schwart's lawyer of record. Schwartz admitted to the court that he was unaware that ChatGPT could produce false information and failed to verify the AI-generated sources, resulting in a $5,000 fine and underscoring the critical need for rigorous verification of AI outputs, especially in legal contexts (Olavsrud, 2024).

COVID-19 Miscount by Public Health England

In 2020, Public Health England (PHE) faced a significant issue when implementing an AI-driven system to manage COVID-19 test data. The system automatically converted positive test results into CSV files, which were then transferred into a Microsoft Excel spreadsheet. However, Excel has limitations regarding how much data it can handle per worksheet, specifically a maximum of 1,048,576 rows. Once these limits were exceeded, the additional data from the CSV files was not included in the spreadsheet, leading to the omission of thousands of positive COVID-19 test results.

This oversight had serious ethical implications. By underreporting COVID-19 cases, the PHE compromised the accuracy of public health data and potentially hindered contact tracing efforts. This raised significant concerns about the reliability of AI handling critical tasks, especially when those systems are not fully understood or properly managed by the organizations that deploy them (Hassel, 2023).

Tesla

Tesla's Autopilot system has been at the center of several ethical controversies, particularly regarding the system's safety and the transparency of Tesla's communication about its capabilities. There have been multiple incidents where drivers overrelied on the Autopilot system, leading to fatal accidents in 2021. These cases raise ethical questions about the balance between innovation and safety, as well as the responsibility of companies to clearly communicate the limitations of their AI systems. Tesla's ongoing development of Autopilot features and its handling of these incidents provide a crucial lesson in the ethical considerations of deploying AI in environments where human lives are at stake (Hassel, 2023).

Other Misuses and Challenges

Numerous other cases highlight the ethical challenges of AI, such as the misuse of AI in surveillance technologies that can infringe on privacy rights or in social media algorithms that can increase the spread of misinformation. To name a few, the controversy surrounding facial recognition technology used by law enforcement agencies and the ethical concerns related to privacy, consent, and potential misuse; social media platforms like Facebook have faced criticism for their AI algorithms, which have been shown to prioritize engagement over accuracy, and individuals creating deepfake videos to spread misinformation.

Since we have started looking at some case studies on how AI has negatively impacted some companies, it is time to look at the other side, when AI positively impacted businesses. As you move on to the next chapter, be ready to explore 20+ cases of successful AI implementation in companies of all sizes. Maybe one of the solutions you will see is ideal for you!

Chapter Fifteen

Case Studies and Success Stories

A I is rapidly transforming the business landscape, offering valuable opportunities for companies of all sizes. Regardless of your resources, you can leverage AI tools and strategies to streamline operations, enhance customer experiences, and drive growth.

This chapter explores how different AI capabilities can be implemented across various business areas and the potential results you can expect. Here's a glimpse into the transformative power of AI based on relevant statistics (*AI Statistics for Small Business, 2024*):

- The AI market size is projected to reach $641.30 billion by 2028, highlighting the rapid adoption of this technology across industries.

- Marketing leaders cite AI as the most significant factor influencing customer interactions, indicating its power to personalize and improve customer experiences.

- Ecommerce companies report significant success with AI, with 51% leveraging it to deliver a seamless shopping experience.

- Almost 30% of small businesses have already adopted AI into their operations and tasks, and 41% are developing an AI strategy for the future.

- Small business owners claim that technology helps them succeed, and almost 1,500 CEOs of SMBs claim AI significantly impacts their business.

These statistics clearly show that AI is not just for large corporations. Small and medium-sized businesses can also harness its power to achieve significant competitive advantages. In the upcoming study cases, you will have the chance to explore situations and implementations that showcase how AI is used in various business areas. These will be reported along with the results these companies have achieved when available.

Airbnb

The property rental platform has successfully used the power of AI to revolutionize its business operations. AI has allowed Airbnb to enhance its matching process, connecting suitable guests with appropriate hosts. This has significantly improved the user experience, ensuring that both guests and hosts optimize their pricing strategies and receive fair compensation for their listings. The technology is also used to assess guest trustworthiness, contributing to a safer and more secure environment for all users (Tiernan, 2023).

Amazon

Amazon has been one of the pioneers in implementing AI into its processes, allowing the company to optimize its processes well before others. The company uses AI recommendation systems to provide relevant products customers might be interested in purchasing according to the items in their cart, developed Alexa, the AI-powered voice assistant integrated into other Amazon platforms, and integrated AI to manage inventory and warehousing. The company undoubtedly has one of the most significant integrations into its operations and products, especially if other products, such as Amazon Prime, Amazon Music, and Kindle Direct Publishing, are considered.

Finally, the company was also responsible for developing and launching the first business without employees, where all customer interactions would be monitored by cameras using image recognition. Using this software, Amazon claimed that customers could enter the store, get the needed product, and walk out, and the bill would be credited to their accounts. While this seemed too good to be true, recent reports claim that this is not exactly how the company operates.

While they do not have employees physically in stores, there are hundreds of employees in a room analyzing video footage of what customers are doing. This has impacted the company's reputation in the eyes of some customers due to the false claims. However, the fact is that the company continues to be a reference point in AI implementation in online business segments.

BACA Systems

This company focuses on the global stone industry and has doubled sales productivity by implementing AI into its production system. The technology was leveraged to generate summaries of sales opportunities, suggest personalized interactions, and write customized emails to customers and leads. Due to its characteristic of managing several small accounts instead of a few large ones, AI could optimize its processes and increase personalization despite the number of emails and phone calls received (*Democratizing Innovation*, 2024).

BeeHero

The startup started using technology to maximize crop yields by using ML algorithms and sensors in commercial beehives. By mapping commercial beekeepers worldwide, the company uses AI to measure pollination quality and help ensure quality. They use this available data to optimize pollination and increase crop yields during the blooming season. With this pollination quality tracked in real time, it was possible to increase crop yields by 30% for different products by creating targeted and specific data on what was needed for their purpose (Manning, 2019).

Blue River

Blue River adopted computer vision AI in agriculture to identify and target the plants in crop fields to increase production yields. By analyzing each plant, the company aimed to reduce the use of herbicides and minimize production costs. The AI program can identify weeds and crops, select which plants the herbicides will be applied to, and consequently reduce the costs for product purchase and improve sustainability (*AI for Business*, n.d.).

Compass

Compass, a real estate technology company, has integrated AI into its platform to offer home buyers and sellers personalized recommendations. The ML platform analyzes listings and suggests properties that align with buyers' preferences. This has increased customer engagement and satisfaction (*AI for Business*, n.d.)

Cocoa & Chia

Cocoa & Chia, an Australian health food company, faced the challenge of providing top-notch customer service with a limited team. To address this, they implemented an AI-powered chatbot, which proved to be a game-changer. Within 6 months, the chatbot handled over 20,000 customer conversations and resolved 87% of inquiries without human intervention (Blackett, 2024). This not only improved customer satisfaction but also freed up staff to focus on more complex issues. The chatbot also provides 24/7 support at a fraction of the cost of hiring additional staff.

Creative Minds

The marketing agency was looking to show a differential in the market to increase its client base. Clients were looking for innovative solutions, and the agency's methods needed to be updated. It implemented AI to transform how campaigns were created and used the tool to analyze online information in real time. By leveraging AI for one client, it was able to get an increase of 40% in engagement rates and a 30% increase in subscriptions in 3 months. The results with other clients showed that using AI helped streamline operations, obtain relevant insights into data, allow creative teams to focus on strategy and ideas, and increase customer satisfaction and growth demand (Luxora, 2024).

Domino's Pizza

Domino's, a major global pizza chain, is actively integrating AI to streamline its operations and enhance the customer experience. One key area of focus is developing an AI assistant for store managers. This AI assistant would handle inventory management, product ordering, and staff scheduling tasks. By automating these time-consuming tasks, store managers can focus on more strategic initiatives and ensure smoother day-to-day operations. The company is also exploring how AI can personalize the customer experience, such as AI providing targeted promotions or optimizing interfaces (*Case Study: How Domino's Leverages*, 2023).

Ennube

To help its sales team based in Ecuador, which does not speak native English, this American company based in California leveraged AI to improve communication. The company could streamline email writing, proofreading, and correction using AI tools to ensure optimal and mistake-free communication with clients. This helped decrease the time dedicated to writing correct emails and allowed employees to focus on other business areas, representing an increase of 5,600% in emails sent and a 50% increase in sales time (*Democratizing Innovation*, 2024).

GetTransfer

GetTransfer, a ride-sharing service that matches passengers in airports with rides, has successfully leveraged AI to optimize operations and enhance customer experience. AI has streamlined various processes, from driver bidding systems to email categorization and software testing, saving time and costs. By developing its own AI solutions, GetTransfer has gained a competitive edge. Its AI-powered tools optimize driver pricing and help clients find suitable rides, improving overall customer satisfaction (Lewis, 2024).

Google

Google has seamlessly integrated AI into various products to enhance user experience. Products like Search, Maps, Pixel, Photos, YouTube, Assistant, Gmail, and Ads leverage AI to optimize functionalities. A prime example is Google Search, which utilizes AI to understand the context of a user's query and deliver highly relevant results. For instance, when a user searches for "restaurants near me," AI helps determine the user's location and suggests nearby dining options. Another application leveraging AI technology is Google Translate, which employs AI for language translation. By using its language knowledge, the program can accurately translate text between over 100 languages (Burr, 2023).

H&M

Launched in 2021, H&M's Creator Studio focuses on offering a holistic solution for bespoke clothing printing and fulfillment. The integration of AI shows the brand's commitment to innovation and creates a more sustainable and cost-effective approach to personalized fashion. The Creator Studio platform utilizes AI to generate unique, artist-quality designs based on text input from users. The tool empowers anyone, from artists to consumers, to design their own clothing, democratizing the design process and making it accessible to a wider audience (Wightman-Stone, 2023).

Healx

This pharmaceutical company leverages AI to identify drugs that can treat rare diseases based on existing drugs in the market. This allows the company to find solutions that will help treat patients and increase the success rate of treatment. The company's proprietary platform integrates scientific data on existing drugs, published medical journals, disease targets, compounds, and other relevant information to predict through ML algorithms what additional purposes existing drugs can be used for. The company has already found an alternative use for an existing drug to treat a rare medical condition. It plans to expand its study cases to over 50 diseases by the end of 2025 (Gray, 2022).

Hilton

The hotel chain has introduced Connie, an AI-powered concierge service. Connie uses ML to understand guest preferences and offer personalized recommendations for local attractions, restaurants, and events; Connie's ability to process natural language queries and offer timely assistance has significantly enhanced guest satisfaction and made their stays more enjoyable (*AI for Business*, n.d.).

IBM

The tech giant takes a problem-solving approach to AI. Its solutions, built on a foundation of ML, NLP, and other advanced techniques, are designed to tackle real-world business challenges. For instance, IBM's AI can automate tedious tasks like data entry and report generation, freeing up human employees to focus on more strategic work. In the healthcare industry, IBM Watson assists doctors with diagnostics and treatment plans by analyzing vast amounts of medical data.

Similarly, in finance, AI can identify patterns in financial markets to help with risk management and investment decisions. These are just a few examples of how IBM's AI solutions are being implemented across various industries to improve efficiency, optimize processes, and gain valuable insights from data (*Artificial Intelligence (AI) Solutions*, 2024).

John Deere

John Deere is harnessing AI and ML to revolutionize farming practices. These technologies enable farmers to optimize resource allocation, increase crop yields, and reduce waste. In its precision farming solutions, the program analyzes data from sensors and satellites to provide farmers with insights into soil conditions, crop health, and weather patterns. This allows farmers to make data-driven decisions regarding resource allocation, such as fertilizer application and irrigation. Additionally, the company's AI-powered autonomous equipment is transforming the way farming is done. Self-driving tractors and combines can operate around the clock, reducing labor costs and increasing productivity.

KLM

One of the most successful examples of AI implementation is the chatbot Blueboat, which the Dutch airline KLM implemented. The chatbot was integrated into the company's webpage, allowing customers to manage their air tickets. It also sends confirmation, provides flight updates, and answers customer queries. The AI program has enabled the company to respond to over 2 million messages sent by more than 500,000 customers without needing to be physically present 24/7 but constantly present online (*10 Inspiring Artificial Intelligence Success*, 2020). This has increased customer satisfaction, boosted sales, and optimized customer service operations.

The company has also launched an AI initiative to reduce food waste. By leveraging the technology and ML algorithms, the company can predict the number of customers who have booked a flight and will board them, allowing the company to prepare the exact amount of meals for the service. According to KLM (2024), "The AI model prediction starts 17 days before departure and continues until 20 minutes before the flight departs." This allowed the company to waste 63% less food than operations in which AI is not Implemented.

Mastercard

The credit card operator is leveraging generative AI to increase its security measures and safeguard both consumers and the entire payment network.

This approach uses AI's ability to learn and adapt, allowing the system to stay ahead of evolving fraud tactics. Initial results are promising, with Mastercard reporting fraud-detection rate increases averaging 20%, with some instances experiencing an incredible 300% improvement (*Mastercard Supercharges Consumer Protection*, 2024). This leap in protection stems from AI's ability to analyze vast amounts of transaction data, identifying subtle patterns and anomalies that might slip through traditional fraud-detection methods. This translates to a safer payment environment for consumers and financial institutions alike.

Meta

Meta Platforms Inc., formerly known as Facebook Inc., is actively integrating generative AI into its platforms. One key area of focus is creating AI personas that can assist users in various ways. This could lead to AI-powered chatbots on platforms like WhatsApp and Messenger, providing enhanced customer service and personalized interactions.

Additionally, Meta has developed its image generation technology, which can create more diverse images compared to traditional generators. This has implications for synthetic data generation, which can be used to train other ML algorithms. The company is also exploring the integration of generative AI into its metaverse platform, Horizons. By leveraging AI, the company aims to simplify the process of creating virtual environments, making them more accessible to a wider audience (Marr, 2023).

NASA

AI is pivotal in NASA's Mars rover missions, enhancing data analysis capabilities and enabling groundbreaking scientific discoveries. By leveraging AI algorithms, scientists can process vast amounts of data collected by the rovers, identifying patterns and anomalies that would be difficult or impossible for humans to detect.

One significant application of AI in Mars rover missions is image analysis. AI-powered algorithms quickly and accurately analyze images captured by the rovers, identifying features such as rocks, minerals, and potential signs of past or present life. For example, AI was instrumental in helping scientists identify organic molecules in Martian rocks, providing valuable clues about the planet's habitability.

Another area where AI is making a significant impact is in autonomous navigation. By equipping rovers with advanced AI systems, scientists can enable them to navigate challenging terrain and avoid obstacles without constant human intervention. This autonomy allows rovers to explore a wider range of environments and collect data from areas inaccessible to human-controlled rovers *(Here's How AI Is Changing NASA's*, 2024).

Netflix

When introducing its streaming service recommendations, Netflix revolutionized how the general public perceived AI. By leveraging a robust ML algorithm, the platform can learn user preferences and recommend content they want to watch. In this case, reinforcement learning will be an added benefit since the user can rate the content they have watched, teaching the algorithm more about the content they like and what should not be recommended. Today, the company's algorithm is known as one of the most powerful in the market, allowing users to select from a wide range of programs tailored to their interests with little to no mistakes.

Nike

Nike, a leader and trailblazer in sportswear, is harnessing AI to transform its industry. AI-powered design tools analyze data to create personalized products, while recommendation engines guide customers toward ideal choices. Behind the scenes, AI optimizes supply chain management, ensuring efficient operations and faster delivery. With AI, the company offers unparalleled customer experience, achieving increased customer satisfaction rates and brand loyalty (Matthews, 2024).

OnDeck

OnDeck, a financial services company, was challenged to process numerous small business loan applications manually. It implemented robotic process automation (RPA) to automate the application process, including document verification and credit checks. AI was integrated to enhance decision-making by analyzing borrower risk profiles and suggesting optimal loan terms. This combined approach led to a significant reduction in processing time, improved customer satisfaction, and a 20% increase in loan approvals without additional staff (Panwar, 2024).

Patrón Tequila

Patrón Tequila uses AI to innovate in the cocktail world. In 2023, to celebrate National Margarita Day, it announced the launch of AI-powered tools to generate unique recipes. The tool allowed users to personalize their margaritas by specifying flavors, ingredients, and desired alcohol content, catering to the growing trend of customized experiences. The company leveraged AI's ability to analyze data and identify patterns to analyze customer preferences and associate them with existing recipes, generating new flavor combinations and pushing the boundaries of the classic margarita (Deyo, 2023).

PayPal

PayPal employs data analytics to combat online fraud, a growing concern with rising costs. By analyzing vast amounts of data, PayPal's systems can identify suspicious patterns and flag potential fraudulent activity, reducing financial losses for both PayPal and its users. Overall, data analytics is a crucial element in PayPal's fraud management strategy. By leveraging this powerful tool, PayPal protects its financial interests and customers' trust, creating a secure and reliable platform for online transactions.

This process also benefits customer experience. By leveraging AI, PayPal can focus on identifying fraudulent activity rather than blocking legitimate transactions, ensuring a smooth and secure experience for its users. This is done by analyzing user data to distinguish between typical spending patterns and activities that might be indicative of fraud (*A Guide To Leveraging Data Analytics*, 2024)

PhoenixFire Designs

At PhoenixFire Designs, a design and consulting company, AI is a catalyst, generating first drafts that require human refinement and editing. Significant efficiency gains were achieved through prompt engineering, emphasizing how questions are phrased, which dramatically impacts AI-generated results. By using tools like ChatGPT and Google Gemini, the company has minimized AI costs and avoided external collaborations (Lewis, 2024).

Pinterest

Pinterest integrates AI to personalize the user experience and optimize content discovery. One core function of Pinterest's AI is understanding user intent and preferences based on past activity. This allows for highly curated recommendations and suggestions for new pins related to their interests.

For example, if a user frequently saves pins on home décor ideas, the AI engine will identify this trend and suggest similar content, such as DIY projects, furniture recommendations, or even recipes for baking treats for a housewarming party. This intelligent filtering system not only simplifies the search process for users but also helps them discover inspiring content that aligns with their tastes.

AI also plays a role in optimizing creators' content. By analyzing user behavior and engagement, Pinterest's AI can identify popular trends and styles within specific categories. This empowers creators to tailor their content to resonate better with their audiences, maximizing their reach and engagement on the platform (K. Ahl, 2023).

Pilot

The bookkeeping firm Pilot faced the challenge of inefficient manual processes. They implemented AI-powered automation in tasks like expense categorization, account reconciliation, and financial report generation to address this. By doing so, Pilot increased its efficiency and scaled its operations. This allowed it to onboard clients faster, reduce errors, and provide more comprehensive financial insights (Blackett, 2024).

Salesforce

Salesforce Einstein is a comprehensive suite of AI tools the company uses to enhance business operations. It offers a variety of functionalities, including NLP, ML, and predictive analytics. Within these tools are several branches such as Einstein Analytics, which uses AI to analyze data from various sources and generate valuable insights for decision-making; Einstein Language, which understands customer sentiment and intent, enabling personalized responses; Einstein Vision, which analyzes visual data to identify objects and patterns, and Einstein Discovery, which uncovers trends and insights to drive sales. Additionally, Salesforce Datorama provides a unified view of marketing data for data-driven decision-making (Chaunhan, 202 4).

Sephora

Sephora has harnessed AI to revolutionize the customer experience. Their AI-powered virtual try-on feature allows customers to experiment with makeup looks without physical application. AI also analyzes customer data to recommend personalized products. These AI-driven innovations have not only enhanced the customer experience but have also fueled significant growth. Sephora's ecommerce net sales have increased by an impressive four times over six years, which is clear evidence of the transformative power of AI in the beauty and retail industries (Parsani, 2024).

Something Sweet

This family-owned frozen cookie dough company has implemented AI to aid it with marketing, social media, and content development. AI was adopted for inventory and financial management in logistics, especially to scale ingredients, aiming to eliminate waste and enhance resource efficiency. Finally, AI has been used to create videos to answer frequent customer questions on its website. AI has allowed the company to expand its reach and optimize operations (Crenshaw, 2024).

Spotify

Spotify leveraged AI to create a personalized and engaging user experience with Spotify Wrapped, an annual feature that gives users a personalized summary of their listening habits. Powered by AI, Spotify Wrapped curates insights based on user data, creating a highly shareable and visually appealing experience. This feature has boosted user engagement and served as a powerful marketing tool, generating organic promotion and fostering a sense of community.

The success of Spotify Wrapped can be attributed to its strategic use of data personalization, gamification, and social sharing. By making Wrapped highly shareable, Spotify taps into users' desire to showcase their music preferences, leading to widespread promotion across social platforms. This strategy has solidified Wrapped as one of Spotify's most effective marketing tools, demonstrating the power of AI in creating compelling user experiences (Meliana, 2024).

Thread

Thread, a UK-based online fashion service, is revolutionizing the way people shop. By combining the expertise of human stylists with the power of AI, Thread creates personalized clothing recommendations tailored to each customer's unique preferences. Its AI algorithms analyze style, size, and feedback to curate a selection of clothing that perfectly suits the customer (*David vs. Goliath: How AI Is Helping Small Businesses*, n.d.).

Trendy Threads

The local retailer constantly faced stockouts and overstocked items, affecting profit margins and customer satisfaction. The business adopted AI to manage its inventory, which allowed it to forecast demand. The business data used ML to analyze seasonal demands, historical data checks, and other events affecting sales patterns. The result was a reduction in the stockout frequency and an increase in in-stock items, allowing popular products to be in stock when needed, translating to a 20% rise in sales (Luxora, 2024). An additional benefit of the solution was to have more liquidity to make new investments and allocate resources to other business areas.

Turbulent Hydro

Turbulent Hydro, a Belgium-based renewable energy company, faced the challenge of optimizing its micro-hydro turbines. To address this, it implemented AI and RPA solutions. AI monitored and predicted water flow levels, while RPA automated data collection and analysis. This system also automated turbine adjustments based on environmental conditions. The results were impressive, with a 15% increase in energy output and reduced maintenance costs. This allowed engineers to focus on innovation (Panwar, 2024).

Uber

The ride-sharing company has pioneered leveraging AI to optimize its operations. One of its most notable innovations has been the use of dynamic pricing. Uber's AI algorithms adjust fares to balance rider availability and driver income by analyzing real factors such as demand, supply, and traffic conditions. This dynamic pricing model has helped Uber maintain a sustainable business model and contributed to efficient resource allocation within the transportation industry.

UPS

The company has incorporated AI tools to help optimize its routes. For this, it created a specific tool called ORION (which stands for On-Road Integrated Optimization and Navigation) to analyze large amounts of data regarding weather, traffic, road closures, and other patterns affecting delivery times. Using the AI tool to optimize the delivery routes, the company achieved a more cost-effective and efficient delivery system that reduces miles driven and delivery times (*AI for Business*, n.d.).

Walmart

Walmart, a leader in retail technology, embraced generative AI to enhance its operations and deliver exceptional customer experiences. The applications range from improving the shopping experience to automating internal processes. For customers, Walmart has introduced AI-powered features like voice shopping and text-to-shop, making reordering items and finding products easier. An online AI shopping assistant also helps customers discover relevant products and plan events.

Behind the scenes, Walmart's AI-powered conversational assistant, Ask Sam, assists in-store associates with finding products and looking up information. Walmart has also leveraged AI to automate supplier negotiations, achieving cost savings and improved terms. Moreover, the company encourages employees to explore and suggest ways to utilize AI daily, fostering creativity and innovation (Marr, 2024).

The case studies presented in this chapter offer insights into how AI can be leveraged across various business areas to drive performance and growth. AI can transform small businesses from enhancing customer experiences to optimizing present and future operations. As we arrive at this book's next and final chapter, you will explore how to future-proof your SMB by identifying and embracing AI opportunities. Read on to understand how you can position your business for long-term success in the digital age by keeping your eye open for the latest AI advancements.

Chapter Sixteen

Future-Proofing Your SMB

Emerging AI Trends and Strategies

F uture-proofing has become essential in a fast-changing business landscape where businesses want to remain competitive. When speaking about AI, future-proofing means you are preparing your business to adapt to new technologies, market shifts, and customer expectations. Therefore, SMBs must anticipate and embrace technological advancements to stay ahead in an increasingly digital world.

As the technology evolves, new capabilities and applications that can transform the business will certainly appear. Businesses that want to remain relevant must be able to keep up with these trends and innovations and leverage these opportunities to enhance decision-making, optimize processes, and deliver better customer experiences. Using the currently available tools is no longer enough; you must start forecasting and strategizing for what the future will bring.

But how can this be done? What are the best ways to future-proof my business and ensure that my business is not technologically outdated? This is exactly what we will explore in this last chapter: why you should future-proof your business and strategy and how to ensure it remains agile and responsive to future challenges and opportunities. You will explore strategies for building a robust AI infrastructure that can scale with your business. As you prepare your business for the future, you must be ready to capitalize on the next wave of advancements that seem to come more often than ever.

Current State of AI Adoption in SMBs

The adoption of AI among SMBs has constantly increased as more companies recognize its potential to drive growth, efficiency, and innovation. However, despite all the optimism that exists in the market regarding the opportunities the technology can bring, there is also a sense of caution about their impact. Many SMBs are eager to start implementing AI but face significant challenges ranging from limited resources, such as budget and technical expertise, to the complexity of integrating these into their existing systems. Nonetheless, as you have seen in the previous chapter, several success stories demonstrate its potential.

Here is a list of the top obstacles faced by these businesses:

- initial cost of implementation and deployment

- difficulty finding the right professionals

- lack of infrastructure

- difficulties in integrating with existing systems

- resistance to change

- perceived complexity

- lack of expertise in selecting tools

- absence of organizational structure

- job displacement

- fear of failure

There are several alternatives to overcome these barriers, but the first must come from you. As the business owner, you should be the first to take the step and start considering its implementation into the business. To all other challenges, there are solutions: For lack of infrastructure, there are cloud-based services; for lack of expertise can be solved by finding the right partners; budget constraints can be solved by implementing ready-to-use solutions; and perceived complexity is addressed with education and information.

As you debate whether or not to adopt AI, it is clear that while challenges exist, they are not impossible. Essentially, there are alternatives to all challenges except for those that have to do with your beliefs, availability, and disposition to start the process. Rest assured that with the right strategies, resources, and mindset, it *is* possible to overcome these barriers to fully integrate AI into your operations. This on its own will help future-proof your business, as you will be positioned to thrive in an increasingly digital market. The following sections will explain how and show you that by using specific tools and strategies, you can effectively adopt and scale AI, ensuring long-term success, sustainability, and competitiveness.

Emerging Technologies

As you have seen throughout this book, AI technology is revolutionizing various sectors, which has deep implications for companies of all sizes, especially SMBs. To ensure that you stay apprised of the most promising future technologies, here is a short list of the trends you should keep an eye out for and how they might affect your business:

- **Edge AI:** Unlike centralized AI models that depend on a centralized cloud computing structure, edge AI processes data locally on devices such as sensors or cameras. For restaurants, for example, this means obtaining real-time analysis directly at the point of sale. You can observe customer behavior to optimize menu recommendations or predict peak hours for staffing adjustments. In ecommerce, it will help you monitor and track stock levels in real time and predict when reorders are needed.

- **Federated learning:** This term was previously used in Chapter 14, and now it is time to explore some more on what it means. The federated learning approach allows multiple devices to train an AI model collaboratively without sharing sensitive data. This will allow your business to improve personalization while maintaining data privacy. This can help online retailers develop more accurate customer segmentation models by aggregating insights from different sources while keeping individual customer information secure. As a result, you can carry out more targeted campaigns and enhance customer experiences without compromising privacy.

- **Conversational AI:** This AI format is what you might imagine: the voice assistants we have on phones and other applications. In the future, these will likely become more sophisticated and able to identify natural language more accurately, including voice tones to establish a sentiment. For restaurants, this might mean streamlining, handling reservations, answering customer queries, and managing orders through voice interfaces. This will bring more inclusivity into the market, allowing different audiences to leverage these services, improving customer satisfaction, and freeing human resources for more complex tasks.

- **AI-driven automation:** As you have seen several times throughout this book, the best and most promising AI application is performing repetitive and time-consuming tasks more efficiently than humans. Today, larger companies are already investing in these enhancements to improve their productivity, and soon, this will also be more feasible for SMBs to apply to all business areas. This means using AI-driven automation to manage inventory, forecast demand, handle supply chain logistics, and, parallel to this, reduce overhead costs and minimize human error.

- **Enhancement of existing tools:** As technology evolves, the tools that already exist will become more powerful and effective. Chat-GPT, which previously only offered internet access to subscribers, today offers limited online research to free users. Video and image creators that previously showed evidence that use synthetic information can now produce content that is so seamless and similar to reality that many get confused. The same can be said for all tools constantly being enhanced and presented on the market. In the future, it is not only about what is *new* but learning what is available now to use in the future with its enhancements.

Integrating these technologies into your business operations can level the playing field with larger competitors. For example, a small restaurant chain using edge AI for inventory management and predictive analysis can operate more efficiently and offer a more personalized dining experience, similar to what larger chains with substantial resources can do. Similarly, a small online store using conventional AI for customer service can provide a high-quality shopping experience comparable to major ecommerce platforms.

With these advancements in AI, the landscape is likely to change. They will lead to enhanced operational efficiency, better customer service and engagement, and new growth opportunities. As you study, learn, and research these alternatives, you will be able to consider and elaborate different strategies that will benefit your SMB and help you stay ahead of the competition. This, in fact, is exactly what we will see next.

Staying Ahead

To stay ahead of the competition and ensure your strategy to adopt and implement AI is effective for the future, here are 10 essential steps you must take:

1. **Develop a clear AI strategy:** Establish a clear strategy aligned with the objectives you want to reach. Identify specific areas where AI can add value and where it will bring you benefits. A well-defined strategy will help prioritize projects, efficiently allocate resources, and set measurable objectives to evaluate success. As time passes, do not be afraid to redesign the strategy to adjust to current market conditions and emerging trends. The strategy can be modified as long as you remain true to the goals you want the business to achieve.

2. **Invest in AI training and talent:** Invest in training for existing employees to bridge the skills gap and ensure they are well versed in the latest AI advancements. Hire or consult with AI experts who can provide valuable insights and guidance during the development and implementation phases. Your team must have a solid understanding of AI to ensure the tool is optimally leveraged for business operations and the best results are achieved.

3. **Start small and scale gradually:** Start with small, manageable projects that can provide valuable insight and build confidence. Implement pilot projects to test the desired AI solution on a smaller scale and assess their effectiveness before fully committing. Make all the necessary adjustments during the testing phase, in-

cluding those regarding the data that will be required, the integrations that will be done, and the business areas to which it will be applied.

4. **Leverage partnerships and AI solution providers:** Collaborate with AI solution providers and technology partners. Many AI vendors offer tailored solutions, providing tools and platforms to address specific needs. Engage in industry-specific partnerships to stay informed about the latest AI trends and best practices relevant to the sector.

5. **Stay updated with AI developments:** Stay informed about the latest trends, research, and updates in AI. Read industry publications and participate in conferences, webinars, and online courses. Engage with AI communities and forums to obtain insights and learn from other businesses' experiences and innovations.

6. **Measure, monitor, and optimize performance:** Continuously monitor AI systems' performance and impact against predefined objectives. Conduct regular reviews and updates to ensure the technologies are still effective and aligned with business needs.

7. **Prioritize data quality and security:** Ensure the business is using high-quality, accurate, and relevant data. Invest in data management practices, including data cleaning, validation, and integration. Additionally, protect sensitive information and comply with privacy and regulations. Create a data governance framework to help ensure compliance.

8. **Foster a culture of innovation:** Promote an environment for experimenting with new technologies and ideas. Create cross-functional teams with members from different departments

to ensure diversity. Recognize and reward innovative efforts that contribute to the company's technological advancement.

9. **Develop change management strategies:** Develop and communicate a change management plan that addresses potential challenges and outlines steps for adaptation. Provide clear communication, training, and support for employees to support the implementation process and motivate buy-in.

10. **Monitor industry trends and competitor strategies:** Analyze competitors' AI initiatives to differentiate them and identify potential threats. Engage with industry analysts to obtain a broader understanding of emerging AI technologies and market dynamics.

Implement these steps to seize opportunities and ensure your AI implementation is sustainable in the long run. This comprehensive approach will help ensure that your business successfully adopts AI and continues to thrive in a dynamic technological landscape.

Long-Term AI Strategy

When you develop a long-term strategy for your SMB, you take the first step to ensure sustainable growth and a competitive advantage. Similar to creating the initial AI strategy you read about in previous chapters, this process requires planning, alignment with business objectives, and commitment to continuous improvement. Although most of the steps for this process have a repeated theme, you will see they have a different approach when the matter at hand is thinking about the future.

Engage in the following action to future-proof your business and ensure long-term success for AI implementation and scalation in existing programs:

- Align AI strategy with business goals, define your strategic objectives, and identify how AI can support them. Ensure these projects are directly tied to the desired outcome, allowing you to maximize ROI and drive meaningful growth.

- Invest in scalable AI infrastructure that can grow with the business. Select AI platforms and tools that can handle increasing data volumes and evolving analytical needs. This will ensure your current AI system continues to deliver insights and support business operations without requiring frequent overhauls or significant additional investments.

- Promote learning and access to information by staying updated with the latest technological advancements and investing in training. This will help ensure that knowledge and skills remain accurate and effective over time.

- Focus on data governance and ethics by implementing policies that ensure data quality, security, and privacy. Doing so will build customer trust and avoid potential legal and ethical issues that could impact your long-term success.

- Continuously measure and evaluate AI impact to make informed decisions. Set clear metrics and KPIs to monitor AI system performance and their contributions to business objectives and performance.

- Build strategic partnerships and collaborations with technology providers, industry experts, and research institutions. These will provide access to cutting-edge technologies, specialized expertise, and industry insights.

Establishing a long-term AI strategy will vary according to your business goals, but when you adopt the necessary steps, you can create a sustainable plan to help ensure your business is prepared for future change and market fluctuations. Once this is done, the following step is to evaluate how fast the business can adjust to changing conditions and make the necessary adjustments.

Agility and Adaptability

To consider Agile and adaptable practices, it is foundational to embrace a culture of change within your business. Encourage an environment where change is viewed as an opportunity rather than a threat. Open communication is key—create spaces where your team feels comfortable sharing new ideas and discussing potential innovations. Regular brainstorming sessions can help the team stay ahead and ensure you are always ready to adapt and innovate.

One solution is implementing Agile methodologies, which can significantly transform how your business operates. Agile practices, like iterative development and regular feedback loops, allow you to refine your products and services in real time based on what your customers need. For example, if you are running an ecommerce business, using Agile sprints to test and improve website features ensures a quick response to customer feedback, keeping their experience at high levels and increasing customer satisfaction.

As you embrace agility, it is essential to establish processes that enable rapid iteration. This means creating systems where experimentation is encouraged, but risks are minimized. This could mean piloting new products or services with a select group of customers to gather feedback and make the necessary adjustments before a scale launch. This will allow you to fine-tune your offerings and position your business to respond swiftly to market demands.

During this process, there will likely be failures and lessons to be learned, especially if you are starting. Learning from these is essential to the journey, where adaptability will make a difference. Instead of seeing setbacks as failures, you should view them as opportunities for growth. Analyze what went wrong, understand why, and apply those lessons to future initiatives. Doing so will allow you to turn mistakes into valuable insights and help you make better business decisions.

These strategies create a cohesive approach to making your business more agile and adaptable. This will allow you to prepare and shape your business for the future while remaining resilient, innovative, and ready to seize new opportunities. With these changes, you will be exposed to risks and challenges you must deal with. Understanding the best way to do this is what we will explore next, especially considering the resilience you must develop to overcome these obstacles.

Risk Management and Resilience

Managing and mitigating present and future risks associated with AI technology implementation is crucial for building a resilient business that can thrive and avoid obstacles in different areas. These include system incompatibility, data quality problems, and software reliability concerns. To efficiently manage these risks, you must focus on factors like scalability, reliability, and support, such as beginning by piloting AI tools on a smaller scale and ensuring they integrate smoothly with your existing systems.

Another issue that must be considered is the cyberattack threats these solutions might make your business vulnerable to, opening it to new vulnerabilities and making it a data for data breaches and attacks. Integrating AI into your operation requires you to implement strong cybersecurity protocols and educate employees on security best practices. It is widely accepted that when dealing with technology, the best approach is to be proactive, where the company will invest to prevent issues rather than spend to fix them.

Ensuring regulatory compliance is also key. Adherence to data protection and privacy regulations like the GDPR or CCPA is mandatory. Work closely with legal and compliance experts to understand and implement the necessary requirements. Regular audits and updates to your data handling practices will help avoid legal issues.

It is also important to prepare for potential market disruptions that these technologies can bring. Stay informed about market trends and be agile in your response to help face these changes. Develop contingency plans and conduct scenario analyses to prepare your business for these events. Being ready to adjust product offerings and marketing strategies to stay competitive must be a priority within the developed strategy.

Finally, develop a solid risk management framework to manage the complexities of AI adoption and scalation. This framework should include processes for risk assessment, mitigation strategies, and response plans tailored to various types of risks. Regularly review and update this framework to ensure you are prepared for new challenges. Stimulate a culture of resilience within the business, where employees are encouraged to learn from setbacks and adapt to new challenges to further strengthen the business's ability to manage risks effectively.

Future-Proofing Talent and Capabilities

Future-proofing your business also includes cultivating the skills, expertise, and partnerships that will allow it to thrive. Developing these capabilities requires a strategic approach that balances investment in training, smart hiring practices, and leveraging external partnerships—all while keeping costs in mind. While some business owners might believe this is hard to do, you are about to see that with the correct planning, this is not only feasible but can bring your business significant advantages. To understand how to attract and retain talent effectively, read on and see strategies for what can be done.

The first and most cost-effective way to build AI capabilities is through training and upskilling your existing workforce. Rather than bringing in new hires, consider the potential within your current team. Identify employees eager to learn and upskill, cultivating AI-savvy talent without the high external recruitment costs. You can transform your workforce by implementing comprehensive training programs, such as forma sessions, online courses, and hands-on workshops tailored to the specific AI technologies relevant to your business. By investing in your existing employees, you retain valuable staff and increase a motivating and people-centric culture of continuous learning.

If you need to expand your team to adjust to new needs, adopting a cost-effective hiring strategy will be necessary, especially if you have limited resources. To achieve this, rather than searching for high-cost experts, focus on bringing in individuals with foundational skills in AI who demonstrate strong potential and a willingness to grow with your business. For example, hiring a recent graduate with a solid background in data science who is eager to apply and expand their skills in your industry can be a more affordable and scalable option than recruiting senior-level AI specialists. Look for candidates who are not only technically skilled but also align with your business's values and industry focus,

As mentioned several times throughout the book, you can also leverage collaboration with technology providers as an alternative to augment your AI capabilities without incurring excessive costs. Partnering with AI vendors will allow you access to advanced tools, resources, and technical support that would be expensive to develop internally. For example, a logistics company might collaborate with an AI vendor specializing in route optimization to enhance efficiency without significant in-house development. These partnerships allow you to implement cutting-edge solutions while managing costs effectively, especially if you negotiate favorable terms with those vendors who want to expand their market presence.

Engaging with academic institutions and research centers can also strengthen your AI capabilities. These partnerships will provide access to recent research and offer cost-effective ways to access emerging talent and expertise. Collaborating with universities on joint projects or offering internships allows you to benefit from fresh ideas and new approaches at a fraction of the cost of traditional hiring. For instance, a heal-tech startup might work with a local university's AI research lab to codevelop innovative healthcare solutions, providing a cost-effective way to stay at the forefront of technological advances. Such collaborations also build relationships with emerging talent, potentially leading to future hires already familiar with your business and its characteristics.

You can also collaborate with startups to access valuable resources and expertise to support your AI efforts without significant financial investment. This collaboration will offer a fresh perspective and access to how more recent solutions can be adapted to your business. By leveraging these newer companies, you gain access to a broader ecosystem of innovation, helping your business stay agile and responsive to new opportunities.

Finally, remember to keep an active network and participate in events relevant to your business's industry. Engaging with these networks provides opportunities for knowledge sharing and networking with peers, which can be a rich source of low- or no-cost learning and innovation. This will also help you identify what is up-and-coming for AI applications and uses in the market. With these interactions and insights, you will be able to keep up to speed, remain competitive, and find opportunities to develop new products leveraging the technology.

Although each business has its own needs, having a strategic approach that balances investment in your current workforce and leveraging external partnerships can benefit your company. These will help you build a strong foundation of AI expertise, enhance your ability to leverage the technology, and position your business within industry leaders and competitors—all while managing costs and maximizing ROI.

But how can this be done? What steps must I take to ensure that my business is prepared for any events or circumstances the future might bring? This answer you will see in the final two sections of this chapter, where you will learn how to create a roadmap to help increase chances of success and a checklist to guide you through the process. Are you ready to see and take this final step?

Creating a Future-Proofing Roadmap

To ensure your business remains competitive and adaptable, you must create a comprehensive roadmap for future-proofing your AI initiatives. Based on the information you have seen in this chapter, the following guide will help you refine, optimize, and prepare your AI operations for long-term success:

1. **Evaluate current AI initiatives:** Start by thoroughly assessing the performance of your existing AI tools. Identify what is working well, where improvements are needed, and which goals have been met. This step will give you a clear understanding of the strengths and weaknesses of your current AI deployments, setting the stage for future enhancements.

2. **Align AI initiatives with business goals:** Ensure your AI initiatives are aligned with the business's broader goals, and consider how AI can help achieve them. Give thought to how AI contributes to your long-term strategy, ensuring that every investment supports your overall goals and takes you one step closer to achieving the desired objective.

3. **Identify future needs:** Identify the AI capabilities and features

your business will need to anticipate future challenges and opportunities. These could include advanced analytics, improved automation, or enhanced customer interaction tools. Planning for the AI tools and technologies your business might need in the future will keep your business ahead of the curve.

4. **Prioritize AI enhancements:** Once future needs are identified, prioritize the AI enhancements that will significantly impact your business. Focus on initiatives that drive growth, improve efficiency, or offer a competitive edge. This strategy will help you allocate resources and ensure critical upgrades are implemented first.

5. **Plan technology upgrades:** Develop a clear plan for upgrading your AI technologies. It should include detailed timelines for implementation, budget considerations and constraints, and a phased approach. Creating a formal document will help minimize disruption, which, in turn, should be communicated across all business areas.

6. **Enhance data management practices:** Ensure your data is accurate, well organized, and accessible. Implement advanced data governance practices to maintain data quality and security. Ensure that your data is as free as possible of bias and comprehensive enough to provide usable and actionable output.

7. **Invest in employee training:** Offer ongoing training and development to prepare your team for evolving AI technologies. Equip employees with the skills to use AI tools effectively and understand their impact on business operations.

8. **Stimulate a culture of innovation:** Encourage a culture of innovation within the business and among stakeholders. Promote

openness to change and experimentation with new technologies. Motivate employees to adopt an innovative mindset, making them more likely to embrace AI advancements and find creative ways to apply them to your business.

9. **Implement necessary measures:** As implementation takes place, ensure all the necessary preventive and reactive cybersecurity measures are in place. Protect your systems and data from potential threats by implementing advanced security protocols, conducting regular audits, and training employees on best practices. Additionally, remember to have a contingency plan to follow and react to any system intrusions.

10. **Continuously monitor and adapt:** Establish ongoing monitoring processes to track AI initiative performance against established KPIs. Stay informed about industry trends and advancements. You must be ready to adjust the business strategy if needed.

By following these 10 steps, you can future-proof your AI operations. This roadmap will ensure your business is well prepared for tomorrow's opportunities and challenges. As a final aid, read on to find a checklist that will help you organize and determine the steps that must be taken so this roadmap can be successfully fulfilled.

Are You Prepared for the Future?

To effectively future-proof your AI initiatives, use the following checklist to guide your preparations and ensure you cover all the essential areas and tasks. The list you will see will help you evaluate your current AI operations, plan for improvements, and build a resilient and adaptable AI strategy.

Goal alignment and strategy

☐ Have you clearly defined your long-term AI goals and objectives and ensured they align with your business strategy?

☐ Are your AI initiatives prioritized based on their potential impact and feasibility?

Technology and infrastructure

☐ Have you assessed the performance of your existing AI tools and identified areas for improvement?

☐ Are you planning and budgeting for necessary technology upgrades and new AI integrations?

Resource allocation

☐ Have you allocated sufficient resources for current and future AI projects, including budget, personnel, and technology?

☐ Do you have a resource plan that addresses immediate and long-term needs?

Training and upskilling

☐ Have you implemented training programs to upskill your employees in AI technologies and best practices?

☐ Are there ongoing opportunities for professional development and learning related to AI?

Strategic hiring

☐ Have you identified key AI skills and expertise needed for your business and planned for strategic hiring to fill these gaps?

☐ Are you recruiting candidates with experience in relevant AI technologies and your industry?

Risk management

☐ Have you developed a comprehensive risk management framework to address technology risks, cybersecurity threats, and compliance issues related to AI?

☐ Are there contingency plans for potential disruptions and challenges associated with AI implementation?

Data governance and security

☐ Have you established data governance policies to ensure the quality, security, and privacy of data used in AI systems?

☐ Are you regularly conducting security audits and updating your data protection measures?

Monitoring and evaluation

☐ Do you have metrics and KPIs in place to regularly monitor the performance of your AI systems and initiatives?

☐ Are you conducting periodic reviews to assess progress and make adjustments as needed?

Collaboration and partnerships

☐ Have you explored partnerships with technology providers, academic institutions, and research centers to enhance your AI capabilities?

☐ Are you actively participating in industry networks and collaborating with startups to stay informed about new technologies and trends?

Culture and adaptability

☐ Have you fostered a culture within your organization that embraces change and encourages continuous learning and innovation?

☐ Are employees encouraged to share knowledge and collaborate on AI projects to drive collective improvement?

Change management

☐ Have you developed a change management plan to support the integration of AI technologies and address potential employee resistance?

☐ Are you providing clear communication and training to help employees adapt to new AI-driven processes and tools?

Strategic planning

☐ Are you prepared to adjust your AI strategies based on emerging trends and evolving market conditions?

□ Have you created a phased implementation plan for your AI initiatives, including specific milestones and deliverables for each phase?

Compliance and legal considerations

□ Are you staying updated with regulatory requirements related to data protection and privacy, ensuring compliance in your AI operations?

□ Do you have legal and compliance experts involved in reviewing and implementing AI-related policies and practices?

Performance metrics

□ Are you tracking the ROI and effectiveness of your AI initiatives, including their impact on business objectives and operational efficiency?

□ Have you set up reporting mechanisms to evaluate and communicate the results of AI projects to stakeholders?

Continuous improvement

□ Are you regularly evaluating and updating your AI initiatives to incorporate new advancements and enhancements?

□ Do you have a process for learning from failures and applying lessons to future AI projects?

As you address these questions, you can ensure that your AI initiatives are well prepared to adapt to future changes, mitigate risks, and achieve success. By implementing all you have seen in this book, you will be ready and prepared for whatever changes and new technologies appear in the market. As we move on to the conclusion, let's revisit what you have learned and prepare for the next steps that will revolutionize your business!

Conclusion

A s you read this book, you discovered a comprehensive guide to transforming your SMB through effective AI integration. You learned to
harness AI technologies to optimize operations and tasks, drive efficiency,
and ensure long-term success. However, this was not only about adopting
new technology; it was about revolutionizing how you work and setting
up your business for the future, and adaptability is key.

Apart from the different ways you can incorporate AI into your business, you also learned how to set clear and achievable goals for the initiatives
that will take place so they are aligned with the business's objectives. You
saw how to assess and refine your existing AI tools, leverage them for
optimal results in different business areas, create a structured roadmap
to the present and the future, and ensure your strategy is aligned with
practical and forward-thinking. This approach will allow you to focus on
high-impact projects, allocate resources wisely, and stay ahead of advancements and innovations.

Another key element you were able to explore was the importance of
building your team's AI capacities. You should remember that investing
in training and upskilling is essential to keep your employees updated and
that these should be considered in association with hiring the right talent.
Empowering employees with the skills they need to use AI will allow you
to achieve your goals faster and more efficiently, bringing positive overall

results to the business. This will foster a culture of continuous improvement and innovation, setting up the team and the company for success.

As you read, some checklists were made available and can be used to evaluate and enhance your AI initiatives. By addressing the key areas for each implementation you will carry out, you can ensure that goals are aligned, resources are optimally allocated, training and collaboration initiatives take place, and the business can grow sustainably. Use these whenever you need to start a new project and remember to iterate; this is a crucial part of the process that will allow you to achieve better results over time and ensure AI programs are optimized for current and future needs.

With all the strategies, instructions, and processes in the book, you will certainly have new insights to implement the best plan. Now, it is time to take action. Use what you learned to transform your operations and business processes. Automate tasks to streamline processes by leveraging the power of AI to enhance your business. With the tools you have read about, it will be possible to make impactful changes, drive innovation, and build a more resilient organization that can support market changes and the advancement of technology.

If you found this book helpful in using AI to transform your business, you are encouraged to leave a review and share your thoughts. Your feedback will help other SMB owners like yourself discover how AI can enhance their operations. Spread the word to peers and colleagues, and together, let's empower more businesses to harness the power of AI for greater success and innovation.

Equipped with the knowledge that will lead to transformation, it is now your turn to take action, lead change, and revolutionize your operations for a future of unstoppable success! See you in the next book, and good luck on your journey!

References

Aggarwal, R. (2024, August 2). 10 ways to acquire high-quality leads using AI lead generation tools. *Improvado*. https://improvado.io/blog/ai-lead-generation-tools-best-practices

AI for business - 30 case studies that led to competitive advantage. (2023, March 6). Digital Transformation Skills. https://digitaltransformationskills.com/ai-for-business/

AI statistics for small business in 2024. (2024, July 15). ColorWhistle. https://colorwhistle.com/artificial-intelligence-statistics-for-small-business/

Anyoha, R. (2017, August 28). *The history of artificial intelligence*. Science in the News, Harvard University. https://sitn.hms.harvard.edu/flash/2017/history-artificial-intelligence/

Artificial intelligence (AI) solutions. (2024). IBM. https://www.ibm.com/artificial-intelligence

Ayushjoshi599. (2024, May 17). *Types of artificial intelligence*. Geeks-

forGeeks. https://www.geeksforgeeks.org/machi
ne-learning-types-of-artificial-intelligence/

Bell, E. (2024, March 20). *How small
businesses can use AI tools*. Investope-
dia. https://www.investopedia.com/how-small-b
usinesses-can-use-ai-tools-8609366

Blackett, P. (2024, April 18). *AI unleashed:
How small businesses are scaling to new heights
(case studies)*. LinkedIn.
https://www.linkedin.com/pulse/ai-unleashed-ho
w-small-businesses-scaling-new-heights-philip
-blackett-qcnne

Burr, J. (2023, January 19). 9 ways we use AI
in our products. *Google*. https://blog.google/t
echnology/ai/9-ways-we-use-ai-in-our-products/

Chauhan, D. (2024, January 31). How does
Salesforce use AI for business growth?
TechForce Services.
https://www.techforceservices.com/blog/how-doe
s-salesforce-use-artificial-intelligence

Chui, M., Manyika, J., & Miremadi, M.
(2015, December 14). *How many of your daily
tasks could be automated?* Harvard Business
Review. https://hbr.org/2015/12/how-many-of-y
our-daily-tasks-could-be-automated

Crenshaw, J. (2024, May 2). *AI's big impact
on small business*. US Chamber.
https://www.uschamber.com/technology/enhancing
-entrepreneurship-ais-big-impact-on-small-busi
ness

David vs Goliath: How AI is helping small businesses outperform larger ones. (2023, May 12). Wildwood Digital. https://wildwooddigital.co.uk/small-business-ai/

Democratizing innovation: Why some SMBs are outshining enterprises in AI implementation. (2024, April 29). Salesforce. https://www.salesforce.com/news/stories/small-business-ai-success/

Deyo, J. (2032, February 21). *Patrón Tequila serves AI-generated cocktails for National Margarita Day.* Marketing Dive. https://www.marketingdive.com/news/patro-tequila-ai-generated-cocktails-margarita-day/643098/

Doble, N. (2024, April 10). *How to implement business process automation in small businesses. Beez Labs.* https://www.beezlabs.com/resources/blogs/how-to-implement-business-process-%20automation-in-small-businesses

Dreamhunter, J. (2024, April 16). 8 ways you can use AI for small business. *GoDaddy Blog.* https://www.godaddy.com/resources/skills/how-to-use-ai-for-small-business

EU AI Act: First regulation on artificial intelligence. (2023, June 8). European Parliament. https://www.europarl.europa.eu/topics/en/article/20230601STO93804/eu-ai-act-first-regulation-on-artificial-intelligence

General Data Protection Regulation (GDPR). (2018). Intersoft Consulting. https://gdpr-info.eu/

Global AI Legislation Tracker. (n.d.). International Association of Privacy Professionals. https://iapp.org/resources/article/global-ai-legislation-tracker/

Gray, C. (2022, February 2). *Healx: Innovating drug discovery with AI and data*. AI Magazine. https://aimagazine.com/ai-applications/healx-innovating-drug-discovery-with-ai-and-data

Guide to data cleaning: Definition, benefits, components, and how to clean your data. (2022). Tableau. https://www.tableau.com/learn/articles/what-is-data-cleaning

A guide to leveraging data analytics in fraud management. (2024, January 15). PayPal. https://www.paypal.com/us/brc/article/data-analytics-fraud-management

Hassel, K. (2023, August 24). AI gone wrong: Failed experiments & tools. *PIA VPN Blog*. https://www.privateinternetaccess.com/blog/ai-gone-wrong/

Here's how AI is changing NASA's Mars Rover science. (2024, July 16). NASA. https://www.nasa.gov/missions/mars-2020-perseverance-rover/heres-how-ai-is-changing-nasas-mars-rover-science/

Hicks, I. C. (2024, April 24). *How AI tools revolutionized customer service: Real case studies from thriving small businesses.*

Autonomi. https://getautonomi.com/how-ai-tools-revolutio nized-customer-service-real-case-studies-from -thriving-small-businesses/

History of artificial intelligence. (n.d.). JavaTpoint. https://www.javatpoint.com/histor y-of-artificial-intelligence

How DNB automated 20% of all customer service traffic with a "chat-first" strategy. (2024, February 22). Boost.ai. https://boost.ai/case -studies/ai-chatbot-banking/

How Domino's leverages AI for streamlined operations. (2023, October 7). AIX: AI Expert Network. https://aiexpert.network/case-study-how-domino s-leverages-ai-for-streamlined-operations/

Hyken, S. (2024, April 14). The personalized customer experience: Consumers want you to know them. *Forbes.* https://www.forbes.com/sites/shephyken/2024/04 /14/the-personalized-customer-%20experience-cu stomers-want-you-to-know-them/

Jain, D. (2023, May 6). *Data preprocessing in data mining.* GeeksforGeeks. https://www.geeksf orgeeks.org/data-preprocessing-in-data-mining/

Lacerte, R. (2024, August 12). The SMB dilemma: How to build AI that SMBs actually need. *Forbes.* https://www.forbes.com/councils/forbesbusiness council/2024/03/14/the-smb-dilemma-how-to-buil d-ai-that-smbs-actually-need/

Lewis, G. (2024, February 23). *How four small businesses are getting a bang for their AI buck*. Raconteur. https://www.raconteur.net/technology/four-ai-case-studies

Loe, M. (2024, February 21). *Oh, Air Canada! Airline pays out after AI accident*. TechHQ. https://techhq.com/2024/02/air-canada-refund-for-customer-who-used-chatbot/

Luther, D. (2024, May 26). *10 best practices to automate business processes*. Oracle NetSuite. https://www.netsuite.com/portal/resource/articles/business-strategy/automate-business-%20processes.shtml

Luxora, R. (2024, August 21). *Inspiring small business AI success stories*. Medium. https://medium.com/@RaphaelLuxora/inspiring-small-business-ai-success-stories-c3306aa45c76

Manning, L. (2019, November). *Startup spotlight: BeeHero is using tech to make pollination-as-a-service a bit sweeter for farmers and bees*. AgFunderNews. https://agfundernews.com/startup-spotlight-beehero-is-using-tech-to-make-pollination-as-a-service-a-bit-sweeter-for-farmers-and-bees

Marr, B. (2023, May 2). 5 amazing ways Meta (Facebook) is using generative AI. *Forbes*. https://www.forbes.com/sites/bernardmarr/2023/05/02/5-amazing-ways-how-meta-facebook-is-using-generative-ai/

Marr, B. (2024, July 2). The amazing ways Walmart is using generative AI. *Forbes*. https://www.forbes.com/sites/bernardmarr/2024/02/15/the-amazing-ways-walmart-is-using-generative-ai/?sh=5113c8faa2f9

Mastercard supercharges consumer protection with gen AI. (2024, February 1). Mastercard. https://www.mastercard.com/news/press/2024/february/mastercard-supercharges-consumer-protection-with-gen-ai/

Mathews, A. (2024, July 3). *How Nike is using AI to transform product design, customer experience, and operational efficiency.* AIM Research. https://aimresearch.co/uncategorized/how-nike-is-using-ai-to-transform-product-design-customer-experience-and-operational-efficiency

Meliana, P. (2024, July 2). *AI marketing tools: Real-world success and case studies.* ContentGrip. https://www.contentgrip.com/ai-marketing-tools-case-studies-success-stories/

Naveen Joshi. (2022, April 14). 7 types of artificial intelligence. *Forbes*. https://www.forbes.com/sites/cognitiveworld/2019/06/19/7-types-of-artificial-intelligence/

Northumbria Healthcare NHS Foundation Trust adopts the responsible AI philosophy with Azure machine learning. (2022, May 24). Microsoft Customers Stories. https://customers.microsoft.com/en-us/story/1501250636823351323-northumbria-healthcare-nhs-f

oundation-trust-health-provider-azure-machine
-learning

Olavsrud, T. (2024, April 17). *10 famous AI
disasters*. CIO. https://www.cio.com/article/1
90888/5-famous-analytics-and-ai-disasters.html

Panwar, Y. (2024, August 21). *Case studies:
How small and medium businesses are thriving
with AI and RPA*. LinkedIn.
https://www.linkedin.com/pulse/case-studies-ho
w-small-medium-businesses-thriving-ai-rpa-yash
-panwar-3qksc

Parsani, P. (2024, February 23). *Beauty and
the bot: How Sephora reimagined customer
experience with AI*. cut-the-saas.com.
https://www.cut-the-saas.com/ai/beauty-and-the
-bot-how-sephora-reimagined-customer-experienc
e-with-ai

*Report reveals how AI will transform the
SMB landscape*. (2024, June 18). SME Hori-
zon. https://www.smehorizon.com/report-reveal
s-how-ai-will-transform-the-smb-landscape/

*The role of AI and machine learning in sales
in 2024*. (2024, January 22). Zendesk. https:/
/www.zendesk.com/sell/features/ai-for-sales/

Sinha, P., Shastri, A., & Lorimer, S. E. (2023,
March 31). *How generative AI will change sales*.
Harvard Business Review. https://hbr.org/2023
/03/how-generative-ai-will-change-sales

State of California Department of Justice.
(2024, March 13). *California Consumer Privacy*

Act (CCPA). State of California. https://oag.
ca.gov/privacy/ccpa

Tiernan, K. (2023, August 28).
*Airbnb uses artificial intelli-
gence to transform their business.*
BDO. https://www.bdo.com/insights/digital/air
bnb-artificial-intelligence-transform-business

*Truist survey shows small business owners
focused on short-term challenges at the expense
of long-term planning.* (2024, March 1). Trusit.
https://www.prnewswire.com/news-releases/truis
t-survey-shows-small-business-owners-focused-o
n-short-term-challenges-at-the-expense-of-long
-term-planning-302132814.html

Types of artificial intelligence. (2011). JavaTpoint. https://www.javatpoint.com/types-of
-artificial-intelligence

*Unleash the power of business process automa-
tion: A complete guide [2023].* (2024, August
14). Kissflow. https://kissflow.com/workflow/
bpm/business-process-automation/

What is Microsoft's approach to AI? (2023).
Microsoft. https://news.microsoft.com/source/
features/ai/microsoft-approach-to-ai/

Wightman-Stone, D. (2023, October 25). *H&M
Group integrates AI for first time with custom
clothing creation tool.* FashionUnited.
https://fashionunited.uk/news/fashion/h-m-grou
p-integrates-ai-for-first-time-with-custom-clo
thing-creation-tool/2023102572238

www.ingramcontent.com/pod-product-compliance
Lightning Source LLC
La Vergne TN
LVHW022335060326
832902LV00022B/4054